Litigation Library

# CIVIL COSTS

AUSTRALIA
Law Book Co.
Sydney

CANADA and USA
Carswell
Toronto

HONG KONG
Sweet and Maxwell Asia

NEW ZEALAND
Brookers
Wellington

SINGAPORE and MALAYSIA
Sweet & Maxwell Asia
Singapore and Kuala Lumpur

LITIGATION LIBRARY

# CIVIL COSTS

*Second Edition*

SUPPLEMENT 2

*By*

**Peter T. Hurst, LL.B., M.Phil. (LOND)**
*Senior Costs Judge*
*of the Supreme Court Costs Office*

LONDON
SWEET & MAXWELL
2002

Published in 2002 by
Sweet & Maxwell Ltd of
100 Avenue Road, London NW3 3PF
(http://www.sweetandmaxwell.co.uk)
Phototypeset by Wyvern 21, Bristol
Printed and bound in Great Britain by
MPG Books Ltd, Bodmin, Cornwall

No natural forests were destroyed to make this product;
only natural timber was used and replanted

A CIP catalogue record for this book is available from the
British Library

**Main work ISBN** 0421 654201
**Supplement ISBN** 0421 79030X

# HOW TO USE THIS SUPPLEMENT

This is the Second Supplement to the Second Edition of Civil Costs, and has been compiled according to the structure of the main volume.

**Supplementary Materials to the Appendix** has been included at p. 65 *et seq*.

At the beginning of each chapter of this Supplement there is a mini table of contents displaying the headings within each chapter of the main work. Where a heading in this table of contents has been marked by the symbol ■, there is relevant information included in this Supplement to which you should refer. Where a heading has been marked by the symbol □ there is no new information.

Within each chapter, updating information is referenced to the relevant paragraph in the main volume.

# PREFACE

All law books suffer from obsolescence, but the level of change affecting Civil Costs is unprecedented. The second edition was published in November 1999 and within six months there had been huge changes wrought in the field of costs by the Access to Justice Act 1999 and its attendant Rules and Regulations. The most fundamental changes are to litigation funding, with the introduction of recoverable success fees and insurance premiums, not to mention the demise of the Legal Aid Board and the introduction of the Legal Services Commission and the Community Legal Service. These changes were accompanied by other changes to Appeals, Security for Costs and Group Litigation. The Costs Practice Direction had to be completely revised and updated, resulting in a fifty per cent increase in length. The old schedule of costs forms was replaced with new precedents and the prescribed forms have now been incorporated.

The result of all this change was to make the publication of a supplement a necessity if Civil Costs was to remain of any real use. The supplement, I hope, covers all the changes adequately, but I would be happy to learn of any errors or omissions through the publishers.

P. T. Hurst
Senior Costs Judge
Supreme Court Costs Office
London
August 23, 2000.

# TABLE OF CASES

# TABLE OF STATUTES

# TABLE OF STATUTORY INSTRUMENTS

# TABLE OF CIVIL PROCEDURE RULES

# CHAPTER 1—INTRODUCTION



## D. TYPES OF COST

### Solicitor and client costs 1–005

### Delete the first sentence of the second paragraph and substitute:

In the case of costs arising out of contentious business (except where the bill is to be paid out of the Community Legal Service Fund under the Legal Aid Act 1988 or the Access to Justice Act 1999) the costs are assessed on the indemnity basis. (CPR rule 48.8 as amended by the Civil Procedure Amendment Rules 2001).

### Insert after footnote 26: 1–006

If a judge considers that a party has acted unreasonably in connection with the litigation in breach of a direction of the court, there might come a time when it was appropriate to make an order for indemnity costs against that party or to exercise the power to award interest on damages at a much higher rate than usual (*Baron v. Lovell, The Times,* 14 September, 1999 CA). Where a party discontinues proceedings and becomes liable for the other party's costs, the costs order is deemed to have been made on the standard basis. However the court's power to order otherwise, granted by rule 38.6(1), includes a discretion to determine the basis upon which costs should be paid. Where the circumstances were exceptional a court could order that the costs should be paid on the indemnity basis. (*Atlantic Bar & Grill Ltd v. Posthouse Hotels Ltd,* November 2, 1999, Rattee J. (unreported)). Where an unsuccessful party had conducted itself throughout the proceedings on the basis that its commercial interests took precedence over the rights and wrongs of the situation, and that it was prepared to risk the outcome of litigation, it was appropriate for the court to order costs on the indemnity basis. In particular the party had embarked on, or brought upon itself and pursued, large scale litigation and suffered a resounding defeat involving the rejection of much of the evidence adduced in support of the case: *Omoko (UK) Exploration Co v. British American Off-Shore Ltd* [2001] EWHC QBD November 22, Langley J. The usual order for costs is one on the standard basis unless there is some element of the party's conduct of the case which deserves some mark of disapproval; but it is not just to penalise a party for running litigation which is lost. Advancing a case which was unlikely to succeed or which fails in fact is not sufficient reason for an award of costs on the indemnity basis: *Shaina Investment Corp v. Standard Bank London Ltd* [2001] EWHC Ch November 2, Mr M Kallipetis Q.C.

Successful defendants sued in relation to a management agreement submitted after judgment that, having regard to the Articles of Association of each of the claimant's companies it was contractually entitled to be indemnified from the assets of each of the companies against the costs incurred in defending the proceedings. The application was dismissed since no application had been made at the time when the judgment was handed down for deferment of the issue of costs. The court had exhausted its jurisdiction under section 51 of the Supreme Court Act 1981. It was however open to the applicant to seek to recover the costs in separate proceedings: *John v. Pricewaterhousecoopers* (Costs) *The Times*, August 22, 2001, Ferris J.

## 1–006 Insert at end:

If the ulterior motive for a company commencing and continuing proceedings was not one of good faith, the court could express its disapproval, under section 394 of the Companies Act 1985, by making an order for costs on the indemnity basis against those responsible. (*Jarvis Plc v. Pricewaterhouse Coopers,* July 13, 2000, Lightman J. (unreported)).

## 1–006 Footnote 28, add:

and see *John & Ors v. Pricewaterhouse & Anor* [2001] EW HC CH, July 12, Ferris J. *The Times*, August 22, 2001.

## Legal aid costs

### Delete 1–007 – insert: 1–007

## Costs out of the Community Legal Service Fund

The Access to Justice Act 1999 introduced the Community Legal Service Fund as a replacement for legal aid under the Legal Aid Act 1988. Although this work does not concern itself with legal aid or CLS funding, it is necessary to understand the effect of certificates issued under the funding code and under the Legal Aid Act. Legal aid certificates issued under the Legal Aid Act will continue to be dealt with under the Civil Legal Aid (General) Regulations 1989 as amended. The Legal Services Commission will issue certificates under the funding code certifying the decision to fund services for the client. The Civil Legal Aid (General) Regulations 1989 as amended also apply to those certificates. Where a contract entered into by the Commission before April 1, 2003, provides that the procedures for assessing remuneration payable by the Commission will be the same as those set out in the above General Regulations, the Legal Aid in Civil Proceedings (Remuneration) Regulations 1994, or the Legal Aid in Family Proceedings (Remuneration) Regulations 1991, the court will assess the remuneration. (Community Legal Service (Funding) Order 2000, article 6). The Legal Aid Board ceased to exist on April 2, 2001 (The Legal Aid Board (Abolition) Order 2001, S.I. 2001 No.779).

## Costs out of central funds

### Insert at end: 1–008

Where a legal representative has represented an assisted person or a "client" (a "client" means an individual who has received funded services), (article 2, Community Legal Service (Funding) Order 2000) the legal representative has a statutory right to the costs of representation and they can only be claimed and paid for out of the Community Legal Service Fund. Under the Civil Legal Aid (General) Regulations 1989, as amended, it is possible to recover from an opposing party more than the amount recoverable out of the CLS Fund, by virtue of the Legal Aid in Civil Proceedings (Remuneration) Regulations 1994 and the Legal Aid in Family Proceedings (Remuneration) Regulations 1991. The assisted person's/client's legal representatives are not prevented from recovering from the paying party the full amount of costs and interest awarded, by any rule of law which limits the costs recoverable by a party to proceedings to the amount which he is liable to pay his legal representatives (the indemnity principle). Subject to reimbursement of the CLS Fund in respect of any costs and interest which it has paid out, any costs recovered from the paying party in addition belong to the solicitor (Civil Legal Aid (General) Regulations 1989, regulation 107B(3)).

## 1–008 In Footnote 40 add reference: [1994] 1 EC 22.

## Add at end of first paragraph:

Notwithstanding the decision of the House of Lords, a Trade Association having successfully applied for the Restricted Practices Court to recuse itself as a consequence of the apparent bias of one of its members, calculated that about £1 million worth of costs had been thrown away because the proceedings had had to begin again. The Association sought its costs relying on the Human Rights Act 1998 and alleging breach of their rights under Article 6(1) of the European Convention on Human Rights. The Court of Appeal found that the Trade Association was not a victim within Article 3(4) of the ECHR and since there was no breach of Article 6(1) there could be no entitlement to wasted costs as part of the compensation. Had the court decided otherwise it is not clear whether an order for costs out of Central Funds would have been made or whether the order would have been made against the Lord Chancellor. (*Director General of Fair Trading v. Proprietary Association of Great Britain* [2001] EWCA Civ 1217; [2002] 1 All E.R. 853 CA).

## 1–009 Insert new paragraph after 1–008:

Although it is possible to recover from an opposing party costs of an amount more than prescribed under the Regulations, the Court of Appeal has decided (under an earlier version of the Regulations), that an unsuccessful defendant could not be ordered to pay costs on the indemnity basis to a legally aided claimant, since the Regulations specified that costs were to be paid by the Legal Aid Board on the standard basis. Accordingly it was a wrong exercise of discretion to direct the paying party to pay costs on the indemnity basis to a claimant who had been legally aided throughout the proceedings. It is arguable that the court would have decided the case differently under the 1994 Remuneration Regulations (*Willis v. Redbridge HA* [1996] 3 All E.R. 114, CA).

# CHAPTER 2—THE CIVIL PROCEDURE RULES 1998



## A. THE OVERRIDING OBJECTIVE

### Add at end: 2–003

Proportionality has always been a target which courts should aim at, it is now part of the overriding objective. The Court of Appeal has expressed the view that case management powers will allow a Judge to exercise the power of limiting costs either indirectly or even directly so that they are proportionate to the amount involved (*Solutia (U.K.) Ltd v. Griffiths* [2001] EWCA Civ 736). As to the correct approach to proportionality, see paragraph 4–020/1.

It is a lawyer's duty to further the overriding objective. If parties turn down alternative dispute resolution out of hand they will suffer the consequences when costs come to be decided. Where a successful defendant refused ADR because it had been confident of winning no order for costs was made: *Dennett v. Railtrack Plc* [2002] EWCA Civ. February 2.

## C. TRANSITIONAL ARRANGEMENTS

### Add at end: 2–007

Where a bill was taxed before April 26, 1999 but the review took place after that date the court held that paragraphs 57.6 and 57.7 of the Costs

Practice Direction were intended to keep the application of the two sets of rules separate. Accordingly the review was conducted under the earlier rules: *Morris v. Wiltshire* [2001] EWHC QBD, November 30, Roderick Evans J.

2–007 **Delete footnote 11a — insert:**

*Biguzzi v. Rank Leisure Plc* [1999] 4 All E.R. 934, CA, and see *Axa Insurance Co Ltd v. Swire Fraser Ltd, The Times,* January 19, 2000, CA.

## D. THE COURT'S CASE MANAGEMENT POWERS

### Estimates of costs

2–009 **Add:**

The Court of Appeal has expressed the hope that Judges conducting cases will make full use of their powers under Costs Practice Direction, section 6 to obtain estimates of costs and to exercise their powers in respect of costs and case management to keep costs within the bounds of the proportionate in accordance with the overriding objective. Section 6.1 of the Costs Practice Direction expressly indicates that the amount of costs should play an important part both in the court's orders about costs and in its orders about case management (*Solutia (U.K.) Ltd v. Griffiths* [2001] EWCA Civ 736).

### Judgment without trial after striking out

2–011 **Footnote 17:**

Renumber CPR rule 3.5(4), r. 3.5(5).

### Default judgment

2–014 **Delete first sentence – insert:**

The claimant may not obtain a default judgment if the defendant has applied to have the claimant's statement of case struck out under rule 3.4

or for summary judgment under Part 24 and in either case the application has not been disposed of.

## J. THE MULTI TRACK

### Estimates of costs

**Insert new paragraphs after 2–032:** 2–032/1

### Group Litigation

CPR Part 19 deals with Group Litigation Orders (GLO). Where a judgment is given in a claim on the group register, in relation to a (GLO) issue, that judgment is binding on all the parties to all other claims that are on the group register at the time the judgment is given, unless the court orders otherwise (r. 19.12). Unless the court orders otherwise, any order for common costs against group litigants imposes on each group litigant several liability for an equal proportion of those common costs. Normally where a group litigant is ordered to pay costs he will, in addition to any costs which he is liable to pay to the receiving party, be liable for the individual costs of his claim and an equal proportion (together with all the other group litigants) of the common costs. When making an order about costs the court will direct the proportion of the costs that is to relate to the common costs and the proportion that is to relate to the individual costs. If the court fails to do so the Costs Judge or District Judge will make the apportionment (r. 48.6A).

2–032/2 It is of fundamental importance that any claimant who decides to compromise or discontinue can do so and establish definitively what he is entitled to receive or obliged to pay rather than being exposed to a contingent liability for adverse costs. In group litigation involving over 1,000 claimants the Master made a costs sharing order which provided for the liability of each party for costs to be several not joint, for individual costs to be those incurred in respect of each claimant, excluding costs in respect of a claim which was selected as a lead case and for the common costs to be the costs which were not individual costs. In the event of compromise by a claimant on terms that the defendants were to pay the claimants costs then the claimant would be entitled to individual costs and his share of common costs incurred up to the end of that quarter. Similarly if a claimant discontinued, or the claim was dismissed on terms that the claimant was to pay the defendant's costs, the claimant would be liable for individual costs and his share of the common costs incurred by the defendants up to the end of that quarter. Directions were given for statements of case with supporting medical reports to be served in eight lead cases to be selected by the parties. On appeal the Master's order was upheld on the basis that although it did have a pre-emptive effect between opposing parties, it did so only where agreed terms provided for a defendant to pay a claimant's costs, or where a claimant decided to discontinue (knowing the costs consequences), or the court decided to order a dismissed claimant to pay a defendant's costs (*Sayers v. Smithkline Beecham Plc* [2000] EW HC QBD November 6, Bell J.).

## K. OFFERS TO SETTLE AND PAYMENTS INTO COURT

2–033 **Insert at end of footnote 14:**

See *Jones (Marilyn) v. Jones (Margaret), The Times,* November 11, 1999 CA, and *Burgess v. British Steel, The Times,* 29 February, 2000, CA.

2–033 **Insert at end of paragraph 2—033:**

A defendant's disclosure of a medical report containing an allegation that the claimant was malingering (thereby causing the claimant to pursue the claim in order to rid himself of that charge) was not sufficient to permit a judge to depart from the normal rule as to costs following a payment in (*Burgess v. British Steel, The Times,* 29 February, 2000, CA. Although the Court of Appeal decision was given under the CPR, the payment in and trial had taken place pre-CPR). In a personal injury action the defendant adduced video evidence and late medical evidence with the permission of the judge. In the course of the judgment the judge absolved the claimant of any dishonesty but concluded that her ability to manage was significantly greater than she was prepared to concede. When the evidence had been disclosed, the claimant offered to settle by accepting the amount already paid into court together with the costs up to the date of the disclosure of the video. The defendant however insisted that they should be paid their costs after the date of payment in. The judge at first instance found that the defendants ought to have obtained their evidence earlier and that the late disclosure had prevented the claimant from assessing the merits of the payment in. The judge awarded the claimant all of her costs even though she had failed to beat the payment in. On appeal the Court of Appeal found that the judge was required to take into account all relevant aspects of the litigation including late disclosure, late service of evidence or the development of unanticipated contentions. The judge was to consider whether or not the parties had conducted the litigation in accordance with the system of litigation which had been designed to enable the parties to know where they stood at the earliest possible stage and at the lowest practicable cost so that they might make informed decisions about their prospects and the sensible conduct of their cases. In personal injury litigation where a defendant was asserting that the claimant was a malinger or was exaggerating the symptoms, fairness demanded that the claimant should be given a reasonable opportunity to deal with those allegations. On the facts of the particular case, the claimant having been found not to have been acting dishonestly and to have reacted reasonably to the disclosure of the evidence, there was no proper basis for interfering with the judgment at first instance (*Ford v. G.K.R. Construction Ltd* [2000] 1 All E.R. 802, CA).[15a] The power to award enhanced interest is designed to make a material difference to the final award and to force the parties to concentrate on the likely outcome of their dispute (*Little v. George Little Sebire & Co* (enhanced interest), *The Times*, November 17, 1999, David Foskett Q.C.).[15B]

The entitlement to enhanced interest does not apply where a defendant is found liable for a figure greater than that contained in the claimant's Part 36 offer, where summary judgment is obtained against the defendant. (*Petrotrade Inc v. Texaco Ltd.*, [2001] 4 All ER, C.A.).

2–033 In *Petrotrade Inc v. Texaco Ltd* above the Court of Appeal explained why an order for the payment of indemnity costs made under Rule 36.21 should not be regarded as penal.

> "It would be wrong to regard the rule as producing penal consequences. An order for indemnity costs does not enable a claimant to receive more costs than he has incurred. Its practical effect is to avoid his costs being assessed at a lesser figure" (*per* Lord Woolf M.R.)

The effect of the rule is that, in a case where a claimant who has made a Part 36 offer which has not been accepted was successful at trial the court is required to consider whether the defendant has been held liable for more than the amount for which the claimant has offered to settle. If the outcome of the trial is that the claimant has beaten his own Part 36 offer then Rule 36.21 applies and the court is required to make an order for payment of interest under paragraph (2) and for the payment of costs under paragraph (3) unless it considers it is unjust to do so.

In a libel trial where the claimant's Part 36 offer was successful the Judge refused to order interest on damages or to make an order for indemnity costs. That was a question for the Judge to determine in the exercise of his discretion and the Court of Appeal could only interfere if satisfied that the decision was so perverse that the Judge must have fallen into error. In his judgment the Judge referred to "the modern presumption in favour of indemnity costs which still carries something of a stigma and is bound to be interpreted as a indication of the court's disapproval of the defendant's conduct". The decision in Petrotrade quoted above was not available to the Judge. The court allowed the appeal and awarded the claimant costs on the indemnity basis with interest at rate of 4 per cent above base rate from the date upon which the work was done or liability for a disbursement was incurred. Interest was to run until the date of judgment, and thereafter interest on damages and costs would be payable at the judgment rate under section 17 of the Judgments Act 1838 (*McPhilemy v. Times Newspapers Ltd (No.2)* [2001] EWCA Civ 933, [2001] 4 All E.R. 861.

2–033 Rule 36.21 applies to costs and other consequences where a claimant does better than proposed in the claimant's Part 36 offer. There is no alternative for a successful defendant's Part 36 offer. In considering what costs were payable there is a need to review CPR Part 44 including the conduct of the parties, whether a party has succeeded in part of its claim and whether a payment into court was made. It is incorrect for the Judge to be guided by the pre CPR cases. In a case other than one covered by Part 36, the award of costs on the indemnity basis was normally reserved to cases where the court wished to indicate its disapproval of the conduct of the party against whom costs are awarded: *Reid Minty v. Gordon Taylor* [2001] EWCA Civ October 29.

Lord Woolf explained in Petrotrade that part of the culture of the CPR is to encourage parties to avoid proceedings if it is reasonable to do so. The Part 36 offer is aimed at a genuine offer to settle and not some tactical ploy for the purpose of advancing a claim for enhanced interest and costs on the indemnity basis: *Utankio Ltd v. P & O Nedlloyd BV*; *East West Corp v. DKMS* AF 1912 and AKT [2002] EWHC 253 Comm, Thomas J.

The underlying rationale of Rule 36.21 to encourage claimants to make offers has simply no counterpart with regard to defendants. Conduct, albeit falling short of misconduct deserving of moral condemnation can be so unreasonable as to justify an order for indemnity costs. Such conduct would need to be unreasonable to a high degree; unreasonable in this context does not mean merely wrong or misguided in hindsight. An indemnity costs order made under Rule 44 (unlike one made under Rule 36) does carry at least some stigma. It is of its nature penal rather than exhortatory: *Kiam v. MGN Ltd* [2002] EWCA Civ February 6.

2–033/1 Where a Part 36 payment relating only to part of a claim is accepted, Rule 36.15(3) makes it clear that unless the parties agree the costs, liability for costs will be decided by the court. The overall intention of the Rules is unmistakably clear, that the court should have a discretion except where the Part 36 payment covers the whole of the proceedings and brings the proceedings to an end (*Clark Goldring & Page Ltd v. ANC Ltd* [2001] *The Times*, March 27, Mr John Martin Q.C.).

2–033/2 There are are compelling reasons of principle and policy why those prepared to make genuine offers of monetary settlement should do so by way of Part 36 payments rather than written offers. Part 36 payments offer greater clarity and certainty about genuineness, ability to pay, whether the offer is open or without prejudice and the terms on which the dispute could be settled. In a case where a claimant sues for the cost of work done the defendant wrote offering settlement plus costs, and stating that it would be paid into court if the offer was not accepted. The offer was rejected. It was not until some 10 months later that the defendant made a Part 36 payment, and then only for half the original offer. A further payment in was made subsequently. A total of £3,000 had been paid into court. At trial the defendant's counterclaim was dismissed and the claimant was awarded £2,321. At first instance the Judge ordered the claimant to pay the defendant's costs from the date of the original written offer. On appeal it was held that the Judge had erred in law in making the same costs order as he would have done if the defendant had made the payment in at the start of the period and succeeded on all issues at trial. Given the Recorder's conclusions as to the unreasonableness of the claimant's conduct in relation to the proceedings an order that the claimant pay half of the defendant's costs from the date of the written offer to the date of the Part 36 payment was appropriate (*Amber v. Stacey* [2001] 2 All E.R. 88 CA). The general rule is that the unsuccessful party should be ordered to pay the successful party's costs but different orders may be made. Relevant factors include: payments in, offers to settle, the conduct of the parties and whether a party has lost an issue. Where a defendant made two Part 36 payments and a written offer to settle and the award of damages exceeded the total paid in, the claimant was entitled to all its costs up to the date of the second payment in and to 70 per cent thereafter because of the way it had conducted the litigation (*Firle Investments Ltd v. Datapoint International Ltd* [2001] EW CA Civ 1106).

A Part 36 payment or offer should be regarded as the best to which a party is prepared to go and if the claimant recovers more than the payment he is entitled to his costs and should not be deprived of them by reason of a comparison with his Part 36 offer. The costs order should reflect the fact that the claimant had not been frank about material matters but where the claimant has not exaggerated its claim, which was not unreasonable or too large, it being put forward in good faith and where there were reasonable grounds for advancing it, the court would not reduce the claimant's ordinary entitlement to costs on the basis that it had not been successful. On the particular facts of the case, reflecting the defendant's success on one issue and the claimant's conduct and its effect on the course of the trial, the claimant was awarded 80 per cent of its costs: *Quorum A-S v. Schramm* [2001] EWHC Comm November 21, Thomas J.

**2–033/3** A Part 36 offer terminates on its rejection and can no longer be accepted unless the party making the offer makes it clear that the offer remains open notwithstanding its rejection. Rule 36.5(8) expressly contemplates that a Part 36 offer might be withdrawn, although in the partiuclar case the offer had not been withdrawn it ceased to be capable of acceptance once it had been rejected. Even if an offer is not terminated by rejection it lapses after a reasonable period of time. In the particular case the court held that that period expired when the parties received the draft judgment (*Pitchmastic Plc v. Burse Construction Ltd* (No.2) [2000] EW HC TCC May 19, Dyson J.). In complex litigation where a detailed Part 36 offer or payment is made in the course of intensive preparation for trial, a period longer than 21 days may be required to consider whether or not to accept the offer or payment. In a case where a party accepted a Part 36 payment after the expiry of the time for accepting, the court extended the period for which the party making the payment in had to pay the costs in relation to some of the issues. Thereafter the claimant had to pay the other party's costs (*R v. Secretary of State for Transport ex p. Factortame Ltd* [2000] The Times, August 22, TCC H.H.J. Toulmin Q.C.).

On appeal the court held that the presumption that a claimant who fails to better a payment in should be treated as the unsuccessful party from the date fixed for acceptance can be dislodged in special circumstances, for example where the defendant has withheld material and has not allowed the claimant to make a proper appraisal of the defendant's case. There is no principle that a defendant at fault for failing to amend his case timeously should in fact provide the claimant with additional time for accepting payment in: *Factortame Ltd v. Secretary of State for Transport* [2002] EWCA Civ 22.

# CHAPTER 3—THE RELATIONSHIP WITH THE CLIENT



## A. SOLICITORS

### Retainer

### Footnote 2:

3–002

Insert correct reference *J H Milner & Son v. Percy Bilton Ltd* [1966] 1 W.L.R. 1582.

### Oral retainer

3–004

### Add at end:

"On this question of retainer, I would observe that where there is a difference between a solicitor and his client on it, the courts have said for the last 100 years or more that the word of the client is to be preferred to the word of the solicitor, or, at any rate more weight is to be given to it: see *Crossley v. Crowther* per Sir George J Turner V.-C.; re *Paine per* Warrington J. The reason is plain. "It is because the client is ignorant and the solicitor is, or should be, learned. If the solicitor does not take the precaution of getting a written retainer, he has only himself to thank for being at variance with his client over it and must take the consequences." *per* Denning L.J. *Griffiths v. Evans* [1953] 2 All E.R. 1364 at 1369.

### Termination of retainer

### Insert after footnote 36

3–007

It is for the client to establish that the solicitor is in possession of potentially relevant confidential information and for the solicitor to establish the heavy burden of showing that there is no risk of inadvertent disclosure (*Re Solicitors* [2000] 1 Lloyd's Rep. 31, Timothy Walker J.).

# CHAPTER 4—GENERAL PRINCIPLES



## A. SOLICITORS

### Legal aid costs

### Delete existing text — Insert: 4–006

### Community Legal Service funded costs

Costs payable out of the Community Legal Service Fund are payable to the legal representative who has earned them and not to the client. To the extent that there is a shortfall between the amount payable by the CLS Fund to the legal representative and the amount recovered from an opposing party, the client may, by virtue of the statutory charge, have to pay some or all of that shortfall (section 10(7) Access to Justice Act 1999). The statutory charge operates on any contribution paid by the client and also on any property which is recovered or preserved for the client in the proceedings. Although a party to proceedings may have been funded by the CLS Fund it is still possible for the court to make an order for costs against that person with respect to those proceedings, but the liability of the funded client will not exceed the amount, if any, which is a reasonable one for him to pay having regard to all the circumstances, including the financial resources of all the parties and their conduct in connection with the dispute (section 11 Access to Justice Act 1999).

In certain circumstances, in proceedings to which a funded client is a party, and which are finally decided in favour of an unassisted party, the court may make an order for the payment out of the CLS Fund to the unassisted party of the whole or any part of the costs incurred by him in the proceedings (section 11 Access to Justice Act 1999).

Where the solicitor nominated in the legal aid certificate ceases to act for an assisted person, even though the certificate has not been discharged, the Court of Appeal has held that the legally assisted person ceases to be such for the purposes of sections 17 and 18 of the Legal Aid Act 1988 since the person is no longer receiving advice, assistance, mediation or representation under the Act. In consequence the former legally assisted person loses the protection provided by section 17 in respect of his own liability for costs and the Legal Aid Board ceases to be liable for him under section 18 (*Burridge v. Stafford; Khan v. Ali* [1999] 4 All E.R. 660, CA).

## B. COUNSEL

### Legal aid costs

**4–009** **Delete existing text—insert:**

### Community Legal Service funded costs

Where counsel has undertaken work in respect of which he is entitled to be paid out of the Community Legal Service Fund, it is the duty of the solicitor to prepare and submit a bill for detailed assessment in the normal way (Civil Legal Aid (General) Regulations 1989 regulation 107). Where no application for detailed assessment has been made, or the client's certificate is discharged before assessment, the Legal Services Commission may authorise the making of the application for detailed assessment on his behalf and the costs of the application and of the assessment are deemed to be costs in the proceedings to which the certificate related (Civil Legal Aid (General) Regulations 1989 regulation 108). The Civil Procedure Rules enable the Commission to put pressure on a solicitor who has delayed in putting in his bill for assessment, by applying to the court for an order that detailed assessment proceedings be commenced within a certain time (r. 47.8(4)). The funded client's solicitor must, within seven days after the detailed assessment, notify counsel in writing where the fees claimed on his behalf have been reduced or disallowed and must endorse the bill of costs with the date on which the notice was given, or that no such notice was necessary (*ibid.* regulation 112(1)). Once the bill is endorsed that no notice is necessary the costs officer may issue the certificate; where a notice has been given, the costs officer may not issue the certificate until 14 days have elapsed from the date when the notice was endorsed (*ibid.* regulation 112(2)).

# C. COSTS BETWEEN PARTIES

## The court's discretion and circumstances to be taken into account when exercising its discretion as to costs

### Insert at end of paragraph 4–010:

4–010

There has been a number of decisions concerning the way in which the court should exercise its discretion as to costs. Where the ordinary costs order is departed from it is incumbent upon the judge to give reasons, albeit short, for that departure (*London Borough of Brent v. Anienobe*, November 24, 1999, CA (unreported)). The task for the judge is to take an overview of the case as a whole and reach a conclusion based on two questions: (1) who has succeeded in the action?; and (2) what order for costs does justice require? Where the honours are even it is appropriate for there to be no order for costs (*BCCI SA v. Ali* (No.4) [1999], 149 N.L.J. 1734, Lightman J.). Lord Woolf M.R. explained the most significant change of emphasis of the new rules is to require courts to be more ready to make separate orders which reflect the outcome of different issues. In doing this the new rules are reflecting a change in practice which has already started (before the coming into force of the CPR). It is now clear that a too robust application of the "follow the event principle" encourages litigants to increase the cost of litigation since it discourages litigants from being selective as to the points they take. If you recover all your costs as long as you win you are encouraged to leave no stone unturned in your effort to do so. (*AEI Rediffusion Music Ltd v. Phonographic Performance Ltd* [1999] 1 W.L.R. 1507, CA). A subsequent case in which Lord Woolf's judgment was drawn to the attention of the court the judge found it difficult to detect in r. 44.3 what Lord Woolf M.R. had called the "change of emphasis" for the courts to make different costs orders to reflect the outcome of the issues. The judge felt that the judgment of the Court of Appeal in *Re: Elgindata* (No.2) [1992] 1 W.L.R. 1207 still afforded a good working guide as to the just disposal of costs (*per Rimer J. Deg-Deutsche Investitions Und Entwicklungsgesellschaft Mbh v. Thomas Koshy* [2001] *The Times*, February 20, CA. Lord Woolf M.R. subsequently emphasised that costs could be awarded on the basis of the issues actually involved (see r. 44.3(4)) so as to encourage good litigation practice. In the particular case under appeal this appeared to have been the basis on which the judge had made the costs order having sought to reflect the amount of time spent on the substantive issues. But such an approach could go too far (see In *Re: Elgindata (No.2)* above) (*Universal Cycles Plc v. Grangebriar Ltd*, February 8, 2000, CA (unreported)).

## 4–010/1 Insert new paragraphs after 4–010:

Where a claimant obtained interim relief in the form of an injunction which was extended until trial of the preliminary issue between the parties the court found that the judge's decision, to order the defendant to pay the costs of the application which had been summarily assessed, was inherently unjust since the judge had decided the issue on the balance of convenience until the dispute could be properly decided at a full hearing. It was inconsistent with such a basis that there could be any successful or unsuccessful parties. The proper exercise of the discretion would have been to reserve the costs of the application to the trial judge (*Richardson v. Desquenne et Giral UK Ltd*, November 23, 1999, CA (unreported)). It was subsequently held that it could be right to depart from that general approach if, on the balance of convenience, it was so clearly a case in favour of the claimant that the defendant should have a costs order against them for wasting time and money in fighting the issues. (*Picnic at Ascot Inc v. Derigs*, February 9, 2000, Neuberger J. (unreported)). The Court of Appeal in allowing a defendants' appeal from a case management decision nonetheless ordered the defendants to pay the costs in any event because of the way the matter had been conducted in the court below (*Daniels v. Walker*, May 3, 2000, CA (unreported)).

In a case where at first instance the Judge held that the defendant had unreasonably pursued two discrete issues in its counterclaim which it lost, although it was successful on the remainder of the counterclaim, the Judge ordered the defendant to pay 10 per cent of its costs and those of the claimant. The Court of Appeal held that although the defendant had not succeeded on the two issues it had not acted unreasonably in pursuing them. Exercising the Judge's discretion anew the Court of Appeal was satisfied there was nothing in the facts of the case which justified departure from the general rule that a successful party should be awarded the whole of its costs: *Spice Girls Ltd v. Aprilia World Service BV* [2002] EWCA Civ 15.

In a case in which the defendant succeeded on its counterclaim, which was the major monetary issue in the proceedings, and also enjoyed significant success in relation to its defence of the claimant's claim, and taking into account the defendants open offer of settlement which had been made, the Court of Appeal ordered that the claimant should have two thirds of its costs of the issue of repudiation of contract but that the defendant should have the balance of the costs of the proceedings: *Dick Van Dijk v. Wilkinson* [2002] EWCA Civ 1780.

## 4–010/2 Delete last sentence on page 47 and insert:

It may be inappropriate to make such an order where the paying party is a funded client because there will not have been a determination of that person's liability to pay those costs under section 11 of the Access to Justice Act 1999.

## Insert new paragraphs after paragraph 4–010/2:

**4–010/3** The grounds upon which the court may depart from the usual order (that the successful party is to be awarded its costs) are set out in rule 44.3(4) & (5). That list is not exhaustive and the Court of Appeal has held that it is wrong for the court to deprive a successful defendant of part of its costs on the grounds that the judgment might be of assistance to it in the future because it was a test case. Where litigation had been conducted at arms length the only approriate order was for the successful defendant to have its costs (*Pexton v. The Wellcome Trust* [2000] EW CA Civ, October 10).

A party who meets with "substantial" success is not necessarily entitled to all his costs. The situation has changed with the coming into force of the CPR. The new rules enable the court to do greater justice in cases where a successful party has caused an unsuccessful party to incur costs on an issue which later fails. In the partiuclar case the court ordered that the claimant should pay the defendant's costs on an issue which failed, to be set off against the claimant's costs on the issue which succeeded (*Winter v. Winter* [2000] EW CA Civ November 10). Where a claimant brought a money claim against the defendant in respect of which there were four principal issues the defendants were successful on a single determinative issue but lost on the other three issues. The court held that the award of costs to the defendant should be reduced by one quarter. The Judge found that the unsuccessful points that were argued were not unreasonable and were inter-related with the determinative issue. If the points had not been taken the number of witnesses would not have been reduced, although the amount of evidence would have been. In deciding to reduce the award of costs the Judge applied the following criteria:

(a) the reasonableness of taking the point;
(b) the extra time taken up prior to trial in preparing to argue the point;
(c) the extra time taken in court to argue the point;
(d) the extent to which it was just in all the circumstances to deprive the successful party of its costs; and
(e) the extent to which the unsuccessful point was related to any successful point (*Antonelli v. Alan* [2000] EWHC Ch.D., November 29, Neuberger J.).

It is no longer necessary to establish that a successful party acted unreasonably or improperly in raising an issue to be deprived of its costs and to be ordered to pay the unsuccessful party's costs of that particular issue. The issue based approach requires the court to consider issue by issue where costs in each discrete issue fall: *Summit Property Ltd v. Pitmans* [2001] EWCA Civ November 19. Where a claimant had fundamentally altered its particulars of claim shortly before trial, resulting in the costs of the case substantially exceeding the original amount claimed in the case, the award of two thirds of the costs against the unsuccessful party was upheld: *Professional Information Technology Consultants Ltd v. Jones* [2001] EWCA Civ December 7.

## Add new paragraph after paragraph 4–010/3:

## Costs of Disclosure

4–010/4 The Court of Appeal held that Rule 44.3 did not apply where a claimant applied to discover the identity of a person posting information on the defendant's internet discussion board (a Norwich Pharmacal application). Such applications are not really *inter partes* disputes. The defendant had not resisted the court making the order, its attitude was neutral. Such applications are akin to proceedings for pre-action disclosure under Rule 48.3. In general the costs incurred should be recovered from the wrongdoer, not from the party from whom disclosure was sought. In a normal case the applicant should be ordered to pay the costs of the party making disclosure, including the costs of disclosure: *Totalise Plc v. Motley Fool Ltd* [2001] EWCA Civ December 19.

## The conduct of the parties

## Add at end:

4–011 Claimants took proceedings against their former solicitors for failing to serve a claim within the limitation period. The claimants claimed in excess of £1 million plus interest. Judgment was finally entered for the claimants and damages of £190,000 awarded. The defendants argued that they should not have to pay all the costs because the claim had been substantially exaggerated. The court found that the claim had not been exaggerated and that when the court was deciding whether or not to make an alternative order it had to have regard to all the circumstances of the case, including the conduct of the parties, the degree of success of the parties, any offers made and whether the claimant had exaggerated his claim. In the particular case the claimants recovered 25 per cent of the figure claimed but there was no evidence to show that the level of the claim had added to the cost or length of the case. Any suggestion that the decision in *Elgindata* was still good practice needed to be approached with great caution (*Harrison & Anor v. Bloom Camillin* [2001] EWHC Ch.D., March 13, Neuberger J.). In deciding what order to make about costs where a party had succeeded on part of the case, even though not wholly successful, the other party's reasonableness in raising, pursuing or contesting a particular allegation was not necessarily relevant or a pre-condition to taking that factor into account. (*Stocznia Gdanskasa v. Latvian Shipping Co* [2001] The Times, May 8, Thomas J.).

## Orders which the court may make

### Insert after footnote 41:

4–012

Where a claimant was predominately successful on the trial of preliminary issues, the court refused to make an order for the costs of that trial and for payment on account as there might have been a payment into court in respect of the substantive trial and the costs should therefore be reserved to the conclusion of that trial or other disposal of the remaining issues in the action (*Amec Process and Energy Ltd v. Stork Engineers and Contractors BV*, December 7, 1999, H.H.J. Hicks Q.C. (unreported)).

### Insert at end of paragraph 4–012:

4–012

In a case where the claimant succeeded on some issues, failed on others and abandoned still others the Court of Appeal held that it was open to the judge to award the claimant a proportion of the costs in respect of those issues on which it had succeeded, but in respect of the abandoned issues, these should have been left to the costs judge. Those costs should be disallowed on detailed assessment as costs unreasonably incurred in the litigation. (*Shirley v. Caswell, The Independent*, July 24, 2000, C.A.).

## Judicial Review

4–012/1

The Administrative Court has considered what costs orders should be made where judicial review proceedings are concluded without a full hearing. The following principles were identified:

(i) the court has power to make a costs order where the substantive proceedings have been resolved without a trial but the parties have not agreed about costs;
(ii) it will normally be irrelevant that the claimant is LSC funded;
(iii) the overriding objective is to do justice between the parties without incurring unnecessary court time and consequently additional costs;
(iv) at each end of the spectrum there will be cases where it is obvious which side would have won had the substantive issues been fought to a conclusion. In between the position will, in differing degrees, be less clear. How far the court will be prepared to look into the previously unresolved substantive issues which depend on the cir-

cumstances of the particular case, not least the amount of costs at that stage and the conduct of the parties;

(v) in the absence of a good reason to make any other order the fall-back is to make no order as to costs;

(vi) the court should take care to ensure that it does not discourage parties from settling judicial review proceedings, for example by a local authority making a concession at an early stage (*Boxall v. London Borough of Waltham Forest* [2000] EWHC Admin., December 21, Scott-Baker J.).

Since it is now open to a defendant in judicial review proceedings to resist the application for permission the court has held that if a defendant incurs costs in submitting an acknowledgment of service as required by the new rules, and in putting forward objections to the claim, the defendant ought to be able, if he succeeded, to recover his costs of so doing (*R. (Leach) v. Commissioner for Local Administration* [2001] The Times, August 2, Collins J.).

4–012/2 Where a claimant obtained without notice a freezing order in an excessive amount which was the subject both of an application to discharge by the defendant and an application to vary by the claimant which failed, the claimant being ultimately successful in the smaller sum at the trial, the court ordered that there should be no order as to costs in respect of the initial application of the freezing order, that the claimant should pay the defendant's costs of the application to discharge the order, that there be no order as to the costs in respect of the claimant's unsuccessful application to vary and that the defendant should pay the claimant two thirds of its costs of the trial (*Mr Biss v. Sox Ltd* [2001] EWHC QBD, May 3, Holland J.).

## Set-off

## Add:

4–015 Where a claimant entered into a conditional fee agreement with his solicitors, and the solicitors entered into a conditional retainer agreement with counsel, and where in the course of the proceedings the claimant obtained certain pre-trial costs orders in his favour, and the defendants obtained an order in their favour, the claimant sought to set-off the opposing orders so as to extinguish any liability. The defendants argued that because of the CFA no costs had become due and therefore nothing was recoverable by the claimant. The court held that this argument was wrong. The word "recover" was used in the agreement to mean: obtain an order for payment as distinct from actually obtaining payment. The same applied to counsel's fees. "Winning" under the CFA included the client recovering costs during the litigation. Thus counsel and solicitors were entitled to their costs when the client obtained a pre-trial order for costs (*Arkin v. Brochard Lines Ltd* [2001] EWHC QBD, June 19, Colman J.).

## Cost orders deemed to have been made

## Add at end:

4–017 In a libel action the claimant discontinued where his claim became worthless, not through any fault of his own but due to the defendant's supervening bankruptcy. The court held that the discontinuance could not be equated with defeat or an acknowledgement of likely defeat; permission was granted to discontinue with no order as to costs: *Etherton v. WPBSA (Promotions) Ltd & Ors* EWHC QBD [2001] December 12, Gray J.

## Special situations

## Add at end:

4–018 The Administrative Court is entitled to order a coroner to pay costs when ordering a coroner to hold an inquest. Such an order was held to be consistent with the power in Section 13(2)(b) of the Coroner's Act 1988 (*R. v. H. M. Coroner for Inner London North, ex p. Touche* [2001] EW CA Civ, March 23).

## Remuneration of receivers

## Delete final sentence—insert:

4–019 An appeal in relation to such an assessment is in accordance with Part 52.

## Basis of assessment

## Add new section after paragraph 4–020:

## Proportionality

4–020/1 The Court of Appeal quoted with approval the judgment of H.H.J. Alton in the Birmingham County Court in an unnamed case where the Judge said:

> "In modern litigation, with the emphasis on proportionality, it is necessary for parties to make an assessment at the outset of the likely value of the claim and its importance and complexity, and then to plan in advance the necessary work, the appropriate level of person to carry out the work, the overall time which would be necessary and appropriate to spend on the various stages in bringing the action to trial, and the likely overall cost. While it is not unusual for costs to exceed the amount in issue, it is, in the context of modern litigation such as the present case, one reason for seeking to curb the amount of work done, and the cost by reference to the need for proportionality."

The Court of Appeal added that it is helpful for a Judge carrying out summary assessment to express his reasoning in some detail for the figures allowed: *Jefferson v. National Freight Carriages Plc* [2001] EWCA Civ, February 7.

## Proportionality

4–020/2 The Court of Appeal has given guidance on proportionality. The court stated that the requirement of proportionality now applies to decisions as to whether an order for costs should be made and to the assessment of costs which should be paid when an order has been made. The Court suggested that the considerations to be taken into account by the Court when making an order for costs under Rule 44.3 are 'redolent of proportionality'.

Because of the central role that proportionality should have in the resolution of civil litigation it is essential that courts attach the appropriate significance to the requirement of proportionality when making orders for costs and when assessing the amount of costs.

> '. . . what is required is a two stage approach. There has to be a global approach and an item by item approach. The global approach will indicate whether the total sum claimed is or appears to be disproportionate having particular regard to the considerations which Part 44.5(3) states are relevant. If the costs as a whole are not disproportionate according to that test then all that is normally required is that each item should have been reasonably incurred and the costs for that item should be reasonable. If on the other hand the costs as a whole appear disproportionate then the court will want to be satisfied that the work in relation to each item was necessary and, if necessary, that the cost of the item was reasonable. If, because of lack of planning or due to other causes, the global costs are disproportionately high, then the requirement that the costs should be proportionate means that no more should be payable than would have been payable if the litigation had been conducted in a proportionate manner. This in turn means that reasonable costs will only be recovered for the items which were

necessary if the litigation had been conducted in a proportionate manner.'

4–020/3 The Court expressed the view that Costs Judges are well equipped to assess which approach a particular case requires. In a case where proportionality is likely to be an issue a preliminary judgment as to the proportionality of the costs as a whole must be made at the outset. This will ensure that the Costs Judge applies the correct approach to the detailed assessment.

> 'In considering that question the Costs Judges will have regard to whether the appropriate level of fee earner or counsel has been deployed, whether offers to settle have been made, whether unnecessary experts had been instructed and the other matters set out in Part 44.5(3). Once the decision is reached as to proportionality of costs as a whole, the Judge will be able to proceed to consider the costs, item by item, applying the appropriate test to each item.'

In considering what was necessary a sensible standard of necessity has to be adopted. This is a standard which takes fully into account the need to make allowances for the different judgments which those responsible for litigation can sensibly come to as to what is required. The danger of setting too high a standard with the benefit of hindsight has to be avoided. The threshold required to meet 'necessity' is higher than that of 'reasonable' but it is still a standard that a competent practitioner should be able to achieve without undue difficulty. When a practitioner incurs expenses which are reasonable but not necessary he may be able to recover his fees and disbursements from his client but the extra expense which results from conducting litigation in a disproportionate matter cannot be recovered from the other party.

In deciding what is necessary the conduct of the other party is highly relevant. A party who is unco-operative may render necessary, costs which would otherwise be unnecessary and it is acceptable that he should pay the costs for the expense which he has made necessary.

4–020/4 Dealing with the situation where a claimant recovers significantly less than he has claimed the court stated that the following approach should be followed:

> 'Whether the costs incurred were proportionate should be decided having regard to what it was reasonable for the party in question to believe might be recovered, thus:
>
> (i) the proportionality of the costs incurred by the claimant should be determined having regard to the sum that it was reasonable for him to believe that he might recover at the time he made his claim;
>
> (ii) the proportionality of the costs incurred by the defendant should be determined having regard to the sum it was reasonable for

him to believe that the claimant might recover should his claim succeed.

This is likely to be the amount that the claimant has claimed, for a defendant will normally be entitled to take a claim at its face value.

The rationale for this approach is that a claimant should be allowed to incur the cost necessary to pursue a reasonable claim but not allowed to recover costs increased or incurred by putting forward an exaggerated claim and a defendant should not be prejudiced if he assumes the claim which was made was one which was reasonable and incurs costs in contesting the claim on this assumption.'
(*Home Office v. Lownds* [2002] EWCA Civ 365)

## Costs payable by or to particular persons

### Add at attend:

4–021 There is a presumption under Rule 48.1 that the court will award costs to the person against whom the order for production of documents is sought. The court is entitled as a matter of discretion to deprive that party of its costs on the basis that the application has been unreasonably and unsuccessfully resisted (*Bermuda International Securities Ltd v. KPMG* [2001] EW CA Civ 26).

## Costs order in favour of or against non-parties

### 4–022 Delete footnote 64—insert:

This rule does not apply where the court is considering whether to make an order against the Legal Services Commission; to make a wasted costs order; or in proceedings for pre commencement disclosure under r. 48.1: r. 48.2(2).

### 4–022 Delete two footnote references and replace with:

*National Justice Compania Naviera SA v. Prudential Assurance Co Ltd* [2000] 1 All E.R. 37 CA. *Robertson Research International Ltd v. ABG Exploration, The Times,* 3 November, 1999, Laddie J.

### Delete footnote 76 reference and replace with:

*Globe Equities Ltd v. Globe Legal Services Ltd* [1999] B.L.R. 232, CA. The Director and owner of a company in winding up proceedings could be ordered to pay the costs personally where he was the only person behind the company, he had not co-operated with the Secretary of State, the scheme run by his company was a swindle and he was responsible for the proceedings being contested. (*Secretary of State for Trade and Industry v. Aurum Marketing Ltd, The Times,* 10 August, 2000, C.A.).

## Insert to text after footnote 78: 4–022

When considering whether a non party insurer should be ordered to pay costs it does not necessarily always have to be shown that the insurer has acted out of self interest unless there is sufficient conflict of interest (*Cormack v. Excess Insurance Co Ltd, The Times,* 30 March 2000, CA.

**Footnote 80:** After *T. G. A. Chapman Ltd v. Christopher* insert *Cormack v. Washbourne*, 16 March, 2000, CA.

**Footnote 81:** *Murphy v. Young & Co's Brewery Plc*—insert reference [1997] 1 W.L.R. 1591, CA and see *Fulton Motors Ltd v. Toyota (GB) Ltd*, July 23, 1999, CA (unreported).

14 lines from the end delete "insolvement" substitute "insolvent". 4–022

## Insert at end of footnote 83:

and see *Quadrant Holdings (Cambridge) Ltd v. Quadrant Research Foundation* (Costs) [1999] F.S.R. 918, Pumfrey J.

## Insert new paragraphs after paragraph 4–022:

4–022/1 In relation to defamation cases the court has to have particular regard to the Convention right of freedom of expression. In a case where a unsuccessful claimant had been supported by others the court refused to make an order against the non parties in favour of the defendant stating that none of the respondents had played any active part in the litigation. Donations towards the claimant's funds were not made as a result of any obligation but as an act of charity through sympathy with his predicament and in some cases affinity to the Conservative Party. Until the last minute emergence of certain evidence the claimant had had some realistic prospect of success; it was in the public interest and in the interests of justice that a litigant of limited means could assert a right against a rich opponent. A rich philanthropist who wished to act as a charity to achieve effective access and a measure of equality of arms should not be discouraged and it was in the public interest that these matters be decided by a jury (*Hamilton v. Al-Fayed* [2001] *The Times*, July 25, Morland J.). The Court of Appeal upheld this decision, adding that the interests of justice did not generally require such a funder to contribute to the costs which the defendant was unable to recover from the claimant alone. *Hamilton v. Al Fayed*, *The Times*, June 17, 2002, C.A.

4–022/2 A party believing the constitution of the Restrictive Practices Court was biased appealed to the Court of Appeal from the refusal of the lower court to recuse itself. The appeal was successful and the appellant submitted that their right to a fair trial under Article 6(1) the ECHR had been infringed and that they were entitled to be compensated for the wasted costs by the Lord Chancellor who was the emanation of the State responsible for providing impartial tribunals to conduct trials of civil litigation. The court held that the appellant could not properly be regarded as a victim for the purpose of making a claim and since the court had remedied the situation by providing an impartial tribunal to determine the party's civil rights and obligations there had been no violation of the party's right to a fair trial. The application was refused: In *Re Medicaments and Related Classes of Goods (No.4)* [2001] EWCA Civ, July 26, *The Times*. July 26, 2001 CA.

## Legal aid

4–024 **Delete first paragraph and substitute:**

### Orders for costs against the Legal Services Commission

Under section 51(1) of the Supreme Court Act 1981 the court has jurisdiction to make an order for costs even against the Legal Services Commission provided that, exceptionally, the circumstances are such as to make it appropriate.

## Other parties

4–026 **Insert at end of paragraph 4–026:**

In the case of a director of an insolvent company an order that that director should pay the costs personally would not normally be made unless it could be shown that the director had caused the company to bring or defend the proceedings improperly. The fact that the director might have benefited personally if the litigation had been successful is not enough by itself to justify an order under section 51 of the Supreme Court Act 1981. Something more is required such as deliberately misleading evidence, even if that evidence is not ultimately relied upon in court (*Gardiner v. F.X. Music Ltd* [2000] All E.R. (D) 144, Geoffrey Vos Q.C., Deputy High Court Judge).

Following a complaint by a member of a pension scheme to the Pensions Ombudsman, the Ombudsman required the trustee and employer of the complainant to secure the provision of additional benefits for him. The employer appealed to the High Court, as did the scheme's insurer. Both were separately represented on appeal. The complainant took no part in the appeals because of lack of means. The Ombudsman appeared by solicitors and counsel and the two appeals were successful. The court held that since the Ombudsman had made himself a party to the proceedings he put himself at risk as to an order for costs. In the case of appeals from tribunals other than the Pensions Ombudsman there was a settled practice that if the tribunal took no part in the appeal an order for costs would not be made against it, but if it did appear and make representations it made itself at least potentially liable for costs in the event that its decision was reversed. The court held that there was no reason to distinguish the position of the Ombudsman from that of other tribunals. There was no reason to depart from the general rule that the unsuccessful party should be ordered to pay the costs of the successful party, but on the facts of the case there was no justification for ordering the Ombudsman to pay two sets of costs. The Ombudsman was ordered to pay the employers' costs of the appeal: *Moore's (Wallisdown) Ltd v. Pensions Ombudsman* [2002] 1 All E.R. 737, Ferris J.

## Champerty

### Insert at end of paragraph 4–029:

4–029

In proceedings where there were related actions, the claimant was being funded by a third party in relation to the litigation and the defendant in separate winding-up proceedings was also being funded by a third party, the Court of Appeal held that there were two questions for decision. The court stated that the law relating to champerty could now be found in the Court of Appeal decision of *Faryab v. Smyth*, August 28, 1998 (unreported). The questions were:

(1) whether the agreements were unlawful and contrary to public policy on the ground of champerty;
(2) if so whether further proceedings should be stayed on that ground.

If the court decided that the proceedings should not be stayed, even if the agreements were champertous, it was unnecessary to resolve the first question. The question of whether the court's process was affected or threatened by an agreement for the division of spoils was one to be considered in the light of the facts of each case. In coming to its conclusion the court stressed that where a subsidiary company involved in litigation is funded by its parent company, the nature of the parent company's interest in the proceedings is the key to the question whether the company may be made liable in costs as a non party (*Stocznia Gdanska SA v. Latreefers Inc*, February 9, 2000, CA (unreported). The court confirmed that *Globe Equities Ltd v. Globe Legal Services Ltd* [1999] B.L.R. 232, CA, was the leading authority on non party costs. The court also stated that *Kommunar (No.3)* [1997] 1 Lloyd's Rep. 22, Colman J. laid down no general rule).

## Group actions

4–030 **Insert at end of second paragraph:**

Where it is clear that the claimants and their advisers intend that the costs of the lead action should be borne proportionately by all claimants, all claimants should contribute to the costs of defendants who have been successful in a test case [footnote 32—delete previous reference to *Ochwat v. Watson Burton,* substitute *Ochwat v. Watson Burton,* December 10, 1999, CA (unreported)]. In group litigation a costs order in favour of the successful party is generally to be adopted as being calculated to achieve the end of justice. The overriding objective of the court is to make the order which justice requires, but the court in a particular case may make a different order if on the facts of the case justice required, and the court should have regard to the success of the parties on parts only of their cases. It is no longer necessarily the case that a party who establishes, for example a breach of contract but is unable to prove loss, would be held to have lost and be subject to an adverse order for costs (*Bank of Credit & Commerce International SA (in liquidation) v. Ali (No.4) The Times,* 2 March, 2000, Lightman J. At a subsequent hearing it was decided that the costs of five test cases should be borne by all the employees of the Bank who were affected rather than the five individuals whose cases had been litigated. *BCCI v Ali,* April 13, 2000 Park J. (unreported); and see *Re Elgindata* (No.2) [1992] 1 W.L.R. 1207).

4–030/1 **Insert new paragraph after 4–030:**

The court refused to make an order to the effect that if the claim was ultimately successful only those claimants still involved in the litigation should be entitled to their costs and if it failed all the claimants who had been involved at any stage should be liable to pay any costs order on a pro rata basis. The court held that the proposal was not suitable as it encouraged claimants with weaker cases to continue at all costs. The order should provide that both liability for and the benefit of costs in relation to the issues common to all claimants should be several rather than joint. It was not yet clear what would happen to an unsuccessful claimant at the end of group litigation conducted under a conditional fee agreement (*Hodgson v. Imperial Tobacco Ltd (No.2)* [1998] 2 Costs L.R. 27 Wright J.).

The Court of Appeal has stated that both the recoverability of common costs and the liability, if any, of discontinuing claimants for costs should be determined at the same time as orders for common costs were made in respect of those common issues. The court would then have a full picture and could make whatever order was just in all the circumstances. A rule that any discontinuing claimant should have a crystallised inability to recover common costs and a potential liability for the common costs of the defendants at the end of a quarter in which he discontinued was too blunt an instrument and unnecessarily favourable to defendants, when it was as yet unknown whether the claimants as a whole were to be successful in the common issues which were to be tried: *Sayers & Ors v. Smith Kline Beecham Plc*; *XYZ & Ors v. Schering Health Care Ltd*; *Afrika & Ors v. Cape Plc* [2001] *The Times*, December 21, CA.

## Legal expenses insurance

## Delete footnote 35 reference and substitute:

4–031

*Murphy v. Young & Co's Brewery Plc* [1997] 1 W.L.R. 1591, CA.

## Other principles applicable to costs between the parties

### Cost payable pursuant to a contract

## Add at end:

4–035

The claimant and defendant entered into a series of contracts which contained an English jurisdiction clause. The claimant commenced proceedings in England against the defendant for sums due under the contracts. The defendant issued its own proceedings in New York. The claimant successfully applied in New York for those proceedings to be struck out as being in breach of the jurisdiction clause. No application was made to the New York court for costs since costs are not recoverable in New York in such circumstances. The claimant subsequently added a further claim to the English proceedings seeking to recover the costs of the New York proceedings as damages for breach of contract. The Court of Appeal held that absent a separate cause of action the costs of foreign proceedings could not be recovered in separate proceedings in England. In this case the claimant had a separate cause of action and there were no policy reasons why it should not be entitled to pursue that cause of action. In particular:

(i) international comity would not be breached by permitting such recovery;
(ii) there was no issue of *res judicata* because there was an independent cause of action and there had been no adjudication by the New York court;
(iii) the principle in *Henderson v. Henderson* [1843] 3 Hare 100 (issue estoppel) was manifestly inapplicable to the facts of the present case; and
(iv) the mere fact that the English courts had for many years proceeded on the presumption that such costs were not recoverable was no reason for permitting one party to a contract to escape liability for damages that he had caused by attempting to sue in a country where a different costs regime prevailed: *Union Discount Co Ltd v. Robert Zoller* [2001] EWCA Civ, November 21 [2002] 1 All E.R. 693 CA.

4–035 **Insert at end of footnote 46:**

*Fairview Investments Ltd v. Sharma*, October 14, 1999, CA (unreported).

**Orders for costs against justices**

## Delete paragraph 4–038 and substitute:

4–038 **Orders for costs under particular statutes**

**The Justices and Justices Clerks' (Costs) Regulations 2001 and the General Commissioners of Income Tax (Costs) Regulations 2001**

The above Regulations give the court power to make an order that the Lord Chancellor should pay the costs of proceedings under section 53A of the Justices of the Peace Act 1997 or under section 2A of the Taxes Management Act 1970. The amount of costs payable is determined in accordance with the Regulations and is a separate procedure to that laid down under the CPR. When making the order for costs the court will normally determine the amount it considers sufficient reasonably to compensate the receiving party for any costs properly incurred by him in the proceedings and specify that amount in the order; but the court may direct the amount of costs to be determined by a Costs Judge where the hearing has lasted more than one day or there is insufficient time for the court to determine the costs on the day of the hearing, or the court considers that there is

other good reason for the Costs Judge to determine the amount of the costs.
The Regulations (Appendix V) set out the procedure to be followed. The time for filing a claim for costs in the Supreme Court Costs Office is three months from the date on which the order was made. The Costs Judge has the power in exceptional circumstances to extend that period. The claim must be made on Form N258D which must be filed at the Supreme Court Costs Office accompanied by copies of: the order of the court giving the right to costs; the bill of costs; a copy of all the orders made by the court relating to the costs of the proceedings which are to be determined; any fee notes of counsel, receipts or accounts or other disbursements relating to items claimed; and, the relevant papers in support of the bill. No fee is prescribed in respect of determinations under these Regulations.

4–038/1 In determining the claim for costs the Costs Judge is required to take into account all the relevant circumstances of the case, including the nature, importance, complexity or difficulty of the work and the time involved. The Costs Judge will allow such costs in respect of:

(a) such work as appears to him to have been actually and reasonably done; and
(b) such disbursements as appear to him to have been actually and reasonably incurred,

as he considers sufficient reasonably to compensate the receiving party for any expenses properly incurred by him in the proceedings.

4–038/2 Any doubt which the Costs Judge may have as to whether the costs were reasonably incurred or were reasonable in amount must be resolved against the receiving party. When the Costs Judge carries out a determination of the claim for costs he will also determine any claim for the costs of drawing the bill and attending upon the determination.

4–038/3 There is no power under section 53A(3) of the Justices of the Peace Act 1997 or Section 2A(3) of the Taxes Management Act 1970 to enable the Costs Judge to order that the costs of the proceedings before the Costs Judge should be paid by the receiving party. The Costs Judge does however have the power where a receiving party has behaved unreasonably to disallow some or all of the costs of the proceedings before the Costs Judge. The provisions of CPR Part 52 (Appeals) apply in respect of the proceedings before a Costs Judge under these Regulations.

**Admiralty**

4–039/1 The Secretary of State ordered a rehearing of the formal investigation under section 269 of the Merchant Shipping Act 1995 into the loss of the MV Derbyshire. The ship builder, ship owner and classification society each claimed their costs of attending and assisting the investigation. The court found that the ship owner was not involved in any continuing litigation arising out of the casualty and was exposed to the risk of adverse criticism. The owners were found to be free of fault, their evidence did make a contribution to the investigation and report. They played an important part in the meeting of experts. They were awarded 30 per cent of the aggregate of their solicitors' overall profit costs and disbursements, including counsel's fees from public funds. The ship builders had been made a party to the investigation by the court's order. They were exposed to the risk of criticism. They provided important evidence to the investigation. They played an important part in the meetings of experts. They were awarded 75 per cent of their costs. The classification society occupied a unique position in the Inquiry since its existence was directed to the objective of ship safety which underlay the investigation. It contributed substantially to the investigation and report but the time and money involved had been in the course of performing its function as a classification society. The society was awarded 15 per cent of its costs: Re-hearing of formal investigation into the loss of NV Derbyshire [2001] EWHC (Admiralty) October 22, Colman J.

## D. LITIGATION IN PERSON

### Footnote 64: Add:

4–040 The scope of the 1975 Act was extended to Magistrates' Courts in England and Wales in relation to civil proceedings before those courts by the Litigants in Person (Magistrates' Courts) Order 2001 (S.I. 2001 No. 3438).

# CHAPTER 5—AGREEMENTS AS TO COSTS



## D. CONTINGENT FEE AGREEMENTS

### Delete paragraphs 5–008—5–022 and insert:

5–008

## D. LITIGATION FUNDING

In 1995, the Government, realising that many potential litigants were not eligible for legal aid and not wealthy enough to contemplate undertaking litigation at their own expense and risk, introduced conditional fee agreements with a view to taking a large portion of the risk away from the client and transferring it to the legal representatives. The statutory provisions enabled the legal representative to reflect the risk being taken by charging a success fee by way of an uplift on the fees charged to the client. Originally the success fee was borne by the successful client and not by the other party to the litigation. The maximum uplift was set at 100 per cent which was intended to enable lawyers to take cases with a risk up to 50 per cent. Lord MacKay of Clashfern, the Lord Chancellor, made it clear that he did not intend 100 per cent to become the standard uplift, stating:

> "... the availability of detailed assessment will help to ensure that uplifts reflect the true risks in individual cases".

Although the Rules of the Supreme Court and latterly rule 48.9 make provision for detailed assessment of the costs of conditional fee agreements, so far as can be ascertained, no client has ever applied for detailed assessment under this provision.

5–009 The Court of Appeal in 1998 came to the view that there was nothing unlawful in a solicitor acting for a party to litigation agreeing to forego all or part of his fee if he lost, provided that he did not seek to recover more than his ordinary profit costs and disbursements if he won. (*per* Millett L.J. *Thai Trading Co v. Taylor*, [1998] 3 All E.R. 65, CA). That judgment fundamentally altered the perception of what was and what was not lawful in relation to contingent fees, maintenance and champerty. The Access to Justice Act 1999 gives statutory effect to the judgment (see sections 27 to 31).

5–010 The Divisional Court in a subsequent case disagreed with the Court of Appeal decision and did not follow it (*Hughes v. Kingston-Upon-Hull City Council* [1999] 2 All E.R. 49, DC). That court held that the Solicitors Practice Rules 1990 (r. 8(1)) imposed a mandatory prohibition on entering into any arrangement to receive a contingency fee in respect of proceedings and that provision had the force of statute (*Swain v. The Law Society* [1982] 2 All E.R. 827, HL). Following this the Law Society altered its Practice Rules to permit any agreement between solicitor and client which was not contrary to the law. A differently constituted Court of Appeal considering itself bound by the House of Lords decision in *Swain v. The Law Society*, found that an oral arrangement, partly reflected in writing entered into in 1993 was unenforceable as being both contrary to legislation and common law (*Geraghty v. Awwad* [2000] 1 All E.R. 608, CA).

5–011 The Access to Justice Act 1999 and the Statutory Instruments made under it provide that conditional fee agreements, including Thai Trading type agreements, are enforceable provided they comply with the Regulations. There remains some uncertainty for agreements signed between January 1 1999 (when the Law Society's Practice Rules were altered) and April 1 2000 (when the Access to Justice Act came into force).

5–012 The 1999 Act permits the recovery of costs under a conditional fee agreement, including one which provides for a success fee (Access to Justice Act 1999 section 27). The Act also provides for recovery of insurance premiums by way of costs and recovery of an additional amount where a membership organisation undertakes to meet liabilities which members of the organisation, or other persons who are party to the proceedings, may incur to pay the costs of other parties to the proceedings (sections 29 and 30).

## At the end of paragraph 5–012/1, add the following:

5–012/1 The introduction of recoverable success fees and insurance premiums as part of the costs between the parties has given rise to considerable problems. The issue came before the Court of Appeal which considered four main questions:

(i) the time at which it is appropriate to enter into a CFA and take out an ATE policy;
(ii) the reasonableness of the success fee when a claim is quickly resolved without the need for court proceedings;
(iii) whether the claimants are entitled to recover an ATE premium where there has been no need to commence proceedings;
(iv) the reasonableness of ATE premiums.

After a hearing at which representatives of interested bodies were also allowed to make representations the court found:

(i) it is in principle permissible for a claimant to enter into a CFA with a success fee and to take out ATE insurance when he first consults his solicitor and before the solicitor writes a letter of claim and receives the prospective defendants' response;
(ii) in relation to modest and straightforward claims for compensation resulting from road traffic accident cases where a CFA is agreed at the outset, 20 per cent is the maximum uplift that can reasonably be agreed in such a case;
(iii) ATE premiums are in principle recoverable as part of a claimant's costs even though his claim is quickly resolved without the need for proceedings;
(iv) the court requested a Costs Judge to investigate and report on the reasonableness of ATE premiums.

The court also considered that it is open to a solicitor and to a client to agree a two stage success fee at the outset of proceedings. It gave an example of an uplift agreed at 100 per cent subject to a reduction to a maximum of 5 per cent should the claim settle before the end of the period fixed by a pre-action protocol. Such an uplift would normally reflect the risks of the individual case. The court suggested that once the necessary data became available, consideration would need to be given to the question whether the requirement to act reasonably mandates the agreement of a two stage success fee in a case where a CFA with a success fee is agreed at the outset (*Callery v. Gray* [2001] EW CA Civ, 1117, [2001] 1 W.L.R. 2112, CA.).

The Court of Appeal subsequently held that the words "insurance against the risk of incurring a costs liability" in section 29 of the Access to Justice Act 1999 mean "insurance against the risk of incurring a costs liability that cannot be passed on to the opposite party". In the particular case a small element of cover for "own costs insurance" could be regarded as falling within the description of insurance against the risk of liability within section 29 and the premium of £350 in the particular case was held to be reasonable.

The circumstances in which and the terms upon which "own costs" cover would be reasonable in relation to other policies, so that the whole premium could be recovered as costs, would have to be determined by the courts when dealing with individual cases. Other issues mentioned in the

Costs Judges report would fall to be judicially determined as and when they arose in individual cases. A copy of the report was annexed to the Court of Appeal judgment with the warning that views expressed might be helpful but were not definitive (*Callery v. Gray (No.2)* [2001] E.R. CA Civ, 1246, [2001] 1 W.L.R. 2142, CA.).

**Before the event insurance**

5–012/2 The Court of Appeal subsequently dealt with a case of a passenger who suffered injury in a road traffic accident for which the driver of the car in which he was travelling was responsible. He took out after the event insurance and the claim settled for a comparatively small sum without proceedings having been commenced. During the course of the subsequent costs only proceedings the defendant's insurers disclosed that the defendant's policy contained a provision for legal expenses insurance which covered a claim made by a passenger in the car against the insured driver. The Court of Appeal stated:

> "45. In our judgment proper modern practice dictates that a solicitor should normally invite a client to bring to the first interview any relevant motor insurance policy, any household insurance policy and any stand alone BTE insurance policy belonging to the client and/or any spouse or partner living in same household of the client . . ."

The court went on to say that if the claim was likely to be less than about £5,000 and there were no features of the cover which made it inappropriate, the solicitor should refer the client to the BTE insurer without further ado. A solicitor is not obliged to embark on a treasure hunt in case by chance an insurance policy belonging to a member of the client's family contains relevant BTE cover. The Court of Appeal held that on the facts of the case the BTE policy did not provide the claimant with appropriate cover in the circumstances of the case. Representation arranged by the insurer of the opposing party, to which the claimant had never been a party, and of which he had no knowledge at the time it was entered into and where the opposing insurer through its chosen representative reserved to itself the full conduct and control of the claim, was not a reasonable alternative to representation by a lawyer of the claimant's own choice backed by an ATE policy: *Sarwar v. Alam* [2001] EWCA Civ 1401; [2002] 1 WLR 125 CA.

5–012/3 In a simple clinical negligence case where the claimant undergoing dental treatment swallowed a reamer, which was passed naturally during the course of the next few days, the claimant suffering no injury other than shock and upset, the claim settled before proceedings and in the costs only proceeding the court allowed a success fee of 20 per cent as against the 50 per cent claimed: *Bensusan v. Freedman* [2001] September 20, Senior Costs Judge.

# E. CONDITIONAL FEE AGREEMENTS

5–013 The Access to Justice Act 1999 makes provision for conditional fee agreements by substituting new sections 58 and 58A in the Courts and Legal Services Act 1990. A conditional fee agreement is defined as an agreement with a person providing advocacy or litigation services, which provides for his fees and expenses, or any part of them, to be payable only in specified circumstances; and a conditional fee agreement provides for a success fee if it provides for the amount of any fees to which it applies to be increased in specified circumstances (usually success in the action), above the amount which would otherwise be payable (Courts & Legal Services Act 1990 section 58(2)). All proceedings may be the subject of an enforceable conditional fee agreement except specified family proceedings and criminal proceedings other than those under section 82 of the Environmental Protection Act 1990. A conditional fee agreement must relate to proceedings of a description specified by order made by the Lord Chancellor. The Lord Chancellor has specified all proceedings, except proceedings under section 82 of the Environmental Protection Act 1990 (Conditional Fee Agreements Order 2000 Article 3). The maximum percentage success fee specified by the Lord Chancellor is 100 per cent (*ibid.* article 4).

5–014 A conditional fee agreement must be in writing, it must not relate to proceedings which cannot be the subject of an enforceable conditional fee agreement; and it must comply with any requirements prescribed by the Lord Chancellor (Courts & Legal Services Act 1990 section 58(3)). If the conditional fee agreement provides for a success fee it must relate to proceedings of a description specified by order made by the Lord Chancellor; it must state the percentage increase of the success fee; and that percentage must not exceed the maximum prescribed by the Lord Chancellor (*ibid.* section 58(4)). If the conditional fee agreement is a non contentious business agreement within section 57 of the Solicitors Act 1974 it is not unenforceable (*ibid.* section 58(5)).

5–015 A costs order made in any proceedings may, subject to Rules of Court, include provision requiring the payment of any fees payable under a conditional fee agreement which provides for a success fee (*ibid.* section 58A(6)).

## Requirements of a Conditional Fee Agreement

5–016 The agreement must specify:

(a) the particular proceedings or parts of them to which it relates;
(b) the circumstances in which the legal representative's fees and expenses are payable;
(c) what payment, if any, is due:

(i) if those circumstances only partly occur;
(ii) irrespective of whether those circumstances occur; and
(iii) on the termination of the agreement for any reason; and

(d) the amounts which are payable in all the circumstances and cases specified, or the method to be used to calculate them, and in particular whether the amounts are limited by reference to the damages which may be recovered on behalf of the client (Conditional Fee Agreements Regulations 2000 regulation 2).

5–017 If the conditional fee agreement provides for a success fee, it must briefly specify the reasons for setting the percentage increase at the level stated in the agreement and must specify how much of the percentage increase, if any, relates to the cost to the legal representative of the postponement of the payment of his fees and expenses (*ibid.* regulation 3(1)).

**Add:**

5–017 Any percentage which relates to the cost of postponement of payment is not recoverable from a paying party but is recoverable from the client. The reason for this is that the cost of funding litigation has never been a recoverable item between the parties (see *Hunt v. R M Douglas (Roofing) Ltd* [1987] EW CA Civ, November 18).

5–018 If the conditional fee agreement relates to court proceedings, it must provide that where the percentage increase becomes payable as a result of those proceedings, then: if any fees subject to the increase are assessed and the legal representative or the client is required by the court to disclose the reasons for setting the percentage increase at the level stated in the agreement, he may do so; if any such fees are assessed and any amount in respect of the percentage increase is disallowed on the assessment on the ground that the level at which the increase was set was unreasonable in view of the facts which were or should have been known to the legal representative at the time it was set, that amount ceases to be payable under the agreement, unless the court is satisfied that it should continue to be so payable. If the legal representative agrees with the paying party that a lower success fee than the amount payable in accordance with the conditional fee agreement is to be paid, the amount payable under the agreement in respect of those fees will be reduced accordingly, unless the court is satisfied that the full amount should continue to be payable under it (*ibid.* regulation 3(2)(c)).

## Information to be Given Before Conditional Fee Agreement is Made

5–019 Before the conditional fee agreement is made the legal representative must inform the client about certain matters and provide such further explanation, advice or other information about those matters as the client reasonably requires (regulation 4(1)). The matters to be explained are:

(a) the circumstances in which the client may be liable to pay the costs of the legal representative in accordance with the agreement;
(b) the circumstances in which the client may seek assessment of the fees and expenses of the legal representative and the procedure for doing so;
(c) whether the legal representative considers that the client's risk of incurring liability for costs in respect of the proceedings to which the agreement relates is insured against under an existing contract of insurance;
(d) whether other methods of financing those costs are available and if so how they apply to the client and the proceedings in question;
(e) whether the legal representative considers that any particular method or methods of financing those costs is appropriate, and, if he considers that a contract of insurance is appropriate or recommends a particular insurance policy, his reasons for doing so and whether he has an interest in doing so (*ibid.* regulation 4(2)).

5–020 Before a conditional fee agreement is made the legal representative must explain its effect to the client. Information given to the client must be given orally whether or not it is also given in writing, but information required to be given in connection with any particular method or methods of financing the costs and whether or not he considers the contract of insurance as appropriate must be given both orally and in writing, as must the explanation, of the effect of the agreement, to the client (*ibid.* regulation 4(3) & (5)). These requirements do not apply in the case of an agreement between a legal representative and an additional legal representative (*ibid.* regulation 4(6)). A conditional fee agreement must be signed by the client and the legal representative, although this requirement does not apply to an agreement between a legal representative and an additional legal representative (*ibid.* regulation 5).

## The position of legal representatives acting under conditional fee agreements

5–021 The Court of Appeal has considered the position of solicitors acting on behalf of claimants under conditional fee agreements. The court held that:

> "The existence of a conditional fee agreement does not alter the relationship between the legal adviser and his client. The solicitor or counsel still owes to the client exactly the same duties that would be owed if there were no conditional fee agreement. A solicitor or client acting under a conditional fee agreement remains under the same duty to the

client to disregard his own interests in giving advice to the client and in performing his other responsibilities on behalf of the client. This extends to advising the client of what are the consequences to the client of the client entering into the conditional fee agreement. The lawyer also still owes the same duties to the court.

The fact that there is a conditional fee agreement cannot justify the legal adviser coming to any additional or collateral arrangement which would not be permissible if there were no conditional fee agreement.

The lawyer, as long as he puts aside any consideration of his own interests, is entitled to advise the client about commencing, continuing or compromising proceedings but the decision must be that of the client and not of the lawyer. The lawyer has however, the right, if the need should arise, to cease to act for the client under a conditional fee agreement in the same way as a lawyer can cease to act in the event of there being a conventional retainer.

There is no reason why the circumstances in which a lawyer acting under a conditional fee agreement can be made personally liable for the costs of a party other than his client should differ from those in which a lawyer who is not acting under a conditional fee agreement would be so liable.

The existence of a conditional fee agreement should make the legal adviser's position as a matter of law no worse, so far as being ordered to pay costs is concerned, than it would be if there were no conditional fee agreements. This is unless the conditional fee agreement is outside the statutory protection.

[. . .] the [claimant's] lawyers are in no different position because they are acting under a conditional fee agreement than they would be acting for a legally aided client with a nil contribution.

[. . .] the court has a limited additional jurisdiction to make an order for costs against legal advisers personally in circumstances in which it would be possible to make a wasted costs order [. . .] The limited additional jurisdiction can arise under two heads. First there is the court's inherent jurisdiction to make such an order at least against solicitors [. . .] The second area of additional jurisdiction is that which arises under the general jurisdiction of the court as to costs contained in Section 51(1) and (3) of the Supreme Court Act 1981. This is a jurisdiction which cannot arise where a legal representative is acting only in that capacity in the context of legal proceedings.

What we intend to make clear is that lawyers acting under conditional fee agreements are at no more risk of paying costs personally than they would be if they were not so acting. In addition whether or not conditional fee agreements are properly the subject of professional privilege they are not normally required to be disclosed."[66]

[66] per Lord Woolf M.R. *Hodgson & Others v. Imperial Tobacco Ltd & Ors* [1998] 1 W.L.R. 1056, CA.

**aragraphs 5—022 to 5–024/1 have been deleted from the upplement and the following substituted:**

## Detailed Assessment of Conditional Fee Agreement with a uccess Fee

5–022 to 5–024/1 (sup)

Where the solicitor and client have entered into a conditional fee agreement he client may apply for assessment of the base costs or of the percentage ncrease or both. The base costs will be assessed in the same way as any other bill from a solicitor to his client (in accordance with Rule 48.8(2)) as f the solicitor and client had not entered into a conditional fee agreement. Where the court is considering a percentage increase (whether on the application of the legal representative under Rule 44.16 or on the application of the client) it will have regard to all the relevant factors as they reasonably appeared to the solicitor or counsel when the conditional fee agreement was entered into or varied (CPR 48.8(3)).

The Court of Appeal has allowed a claimant who had no prospect of funding the prosecution of his action in a foreign jurisdiction, which was the most natural forum for its trial, to proceed in England, which was not an inappropriate forum, by means of a conditional fee agreement with his solicitors. The court held that the interests of justice weighed in favour of the English forum where he could assert his rights. The solicitor gave an undertaking in relation to legal aid (the previous legal aid certificate had been discharged and it was unlikely that a new certificate would be granted) (*Connelly v. RTZ Corp Plc & Anor, The Times*, July 12, 1996 CA).

## Recovery of Insurance Premiums

5–025

Where an order for costs is made in favour of a party who has taken out an insurance policy against the risk of incurring a liability in proceedings, the costs payable to him may, subject to Rules of Court, include costs in respect of the premium of the policy (Access to Justice Act 1999 section 29).

## Recovery of Additional Amount by Membership Organisation

5–026

Where a prescribed body or membership organisation undertakes to meet liabilities which its members, or other persons who are parties to proceedings, may incur to pay the costs of other parties to the proceedings, if the court makes a costs order in favour of the member or other person the costs may, subject to Rules of Court, include an additional amount in respect of any provision made by or on behalf of the body in connection with the proceedings against the risk of having to meet those liabilities. The additional amount must not exceed the likely cost to the member or other person of the premium of an insurance policy against the risk of incurring a liability to pay the costs of other parties to the proceedings (Access to Justice Act 1999 section 30).

### Requirements for Arrangements to Meet Costs Liabilities

5–027 Where a membership organisation or body specified by the Lord Chancellor (the Lord Chancellor has approved a number of organisations, including many Trade Unions, Police Federations and motoring organisations), undertakes to meet liabilities which members of the body or other persons who are party to the proceedings may incur, to pay the costs of other parties, the arrangements which are made must satisfy certain conditions. The arrangements must be in writing and must contain a statement specifying:

(a) the circumstances in which the member or other party may be liable to pay costs of the proceedings;
(b) whether such a liability arises if those circumstances only partly occur, irrespective of whether those circumstances occur, and, on the termination of the arrangement for any reason;
(c) the basis on which the amount of the liability is calculated; and
(d) the procedure for seeking assessment of costs.

A copy of that part of the arrangement containing the above statement must be given to the member or other party to the proceedings whose liabilities the body is undertaking to meet as soon as possible after the undertaking is given (The Access to Justice (Membership Organisations) Regulations 2000, regulation 3).

### Recovery of Additional Amount for Insurance Costs

5–028 Where an additional amount is included in costs in respect of any provision made by or on behalf of the body in connection with the proceedings against the risk of having to meet the specified liabilities, the additional amount must not exceed the likely cost to the member or other person of the premium of any insurance policy against the risk of incurring a liability to pay the costs of other parties to the proceedings (*ibid.* regulation 4).

## F. LITIGATION FUNDING AGREEMENTS

5–029 The Access to Justice Act 1999 inserts a new section 58B into the Courts & Legal Services Act 1990. A litigation funding agreement is an agreement under which the funder agrees to fund, wholly or partly, the provision of advocacy or litigation services (by someone other than the funder) to the litigant and the litigant agrees to pay a sum to the funder in specified circumstances (Courts & Legal Services Act 1990 section 58B(2)). At the time of writing the provisions of this section have not been brought into force).

## Conditions Applicable to a Litigation Funding Agreement

5–030 The funder must be prescribed by the Lord Chancellor, the agreement must be in writing, and it must not relate to criminal proceedings or family proceedings, apart from proceedings under section 82 of the Environmental Protection Act 1990, or to such proceedings as may be prescribed by the Lord Chancellor. The agreement must comply with any requirements which may be prescribed. The sum to be paid by the litigant must consist of any costs payable to him in respect of the proceedings to which the agreement relates together with an amount calculated by reference to the funder's anticipated expenditure in funding the provision of the services, and that amount must not exceed the percentage of the anticipated expenditure prescribed by the Lord Chancellor in relation to proceedings of the description to which the agreement relates (Courts & Legal Services Act 1990 section 58B(3)).

The Lord Chancellor may require the funder to have provided prescribed information to the litigant before the agreement is made and may impose different requirements for different descriptions of litigation funding agreements (*ibid.* section 58(b)(5)).

5–031 A costs order made in any proceedings may, subject to Rules of Court, include provision requiring the payment of any amount payable under a litigation funding agreement, and Rules of Court may make provision with respect to the assessment of any costs which include fees payable under a litigation funding agreement (ibid. section 58B(8)&(9). (At the time of writing these provisions are not in force.)

## Other agreements as to costs

## Costs payable to a solicitor by his client: r. 48.8

5–032 Where the relationship of solicitor and client exists, Part III of the Solicitors Act 1974 deals with the remuneration of solicitors. Where the court makes an order for the assessment of costs payable to a solicitor by his client the solicitor is required to serve a breakdown of costs within 28 days of an order for costs to be assessed. The client is required to serve points of dispute within 14 days thereafter, and if the solicitors wish to serve a reply that must be done within 14 days after that. Either party may request a

hearing date after points of dispute have been served but a limit of thre
months after the date of the order to be assessed is imposed.[91]

Except where the bill is to be paid out of the legal aid fund, or there i
a conditional fee agreement, costs will be assessed on the indemnity basi
and are presumed to have been reasonably incurred if they were incurre
with the express or implied approval of the client, and to be reasonable i
amount if their amount was expressly or impliedly approved by the client
Costs will be presumed to have been unreasonably incurred if they are o
unusual nature or amount and the solicitor did not tell the client that, as
result, they might not be fully recoverable from the other party.[92] Tha
information must have been given to the client before the costs wer
incurred.[93] If a party fails to comply with the requirement to serve a break
down of costs or points of dispute any other party may apply to the cour
for an order requiring it may make it subject to conditions, including th
condition to pay a sum of money into court and specify the consequenc
of failure to comply with that order or condition.[94]

Solicitors acting for a client, where there is no specific contract to pa
the sums claimed as fees, are entitled to reasonable and fair remuneratio
for the work which they have done. In a case where the time for applyin
for detailed assessment of the solicitors' costs had passed, the Court o
Appeal held that the solicitor (who had sued for their costs) could no
simply ask the court, without any further investigation, to underwrite th
amount which they had chosen to claim:

> "Where a *quantum meruit* for work done, the benefit of which ha
> been obtained under a contract, but where the contract sum has no
> been agreed, is claimed, there may be an order for judgment to b
> entered for the [claimant] with the quantum to be assessed."

The court went on to state that the judicial assessment should be carrie
out by a costs judge since they have the requisite expertise for that purpose.[95]

Where a client had been provided by the solicitor with an estimate o
costs on the basis of an hourly state shortly prior to trial it was not ope
to the solicitor subsequently to charge him a higher rate than he was led t
believe he should be charged. In the particular case the correspondenc
amounted to a clear and considered indication of the client's maximu
liability to the solicitor upon which the client relied. Where an estimate i
given, the final amount payable should not vary substantially from th
estimate unless the client has been informed of the changed circumstance

[91] CPR, r. 48.10. the Direction Relating to Part 48 effectively repeats the rule. The Direction
to Part 48, paras 2.18 to 2.36 give detailed guidance as to the procedure.
[92] CPR, r. 48.8.
[93] Direction relating to Part 48, para. 2.9.
[94] Direction relating to Part 48, para. 2.12.
[95] *Thomas Watts & Co. v. Smith*, March 16, 1998, CA (unreported).

in writing.[96] The court reduced the amount allowed to the solicitors to the amount of the solicitor's estimate.[97]

The presumption of reasonableness which arises from the express or implied approval of the client cannot and does not arise unless the information given by the solicitors to the client was sufficient to enable the client to give "informed" approval or consent (*MacDougall v. Boote Edgar Esterkin* [2002] EWHC QBD, October 12, Holland J.).

## Agreement of costs between parties

5–033

It is open to the parties to agree to a figure for costs, either in a lump sum settlement, or separately from the damages, or even after judgment has been given in favour of a party awarding costs. If the agreement is reached before a request for a detailed assessment hearing has been made, no fee is payable to the court. Once such a request is made and the fee is paid it is not refundable.[98] Where a defendant consented to judgment on a personal injury action with costs, it was not then open to the defendant to apply for leave to appeal to set aside the costs order on the grounds of mistake as to the terms on which the claimant's solicitors have been retained. The order could be challenged by a fresh action, but not by appeal to the Court of Appeal.[99] Where the parties agreed the damages payable with "Costs to be paid in full" this was held to mean something more than costs assessed on the standard basis. In the circumstances the court found that there was no final agreement between the parties in relation to costs, and that the action had not therefore been settled.[1]

Where it appears to the Lord Chancellor that the payment of any fees specified in the Fees Order would, owing to the exceptional circumstances of the particular case, involve undue financial hardship hardship, the Lord Chancellor may reduce or remit the fee in that case. This power is delegated to the Court Managers of district registries and county courts and to the finance officer of the Royal Courts of Justice.[2]

Where there was an agreement between the parties for consideration, that an appeal would be dismissed, and the respondent on the face of the agreement had acted to his detriment, it was a bar to the exercise of the court's discretion as the the payment of the parties' litigation costs. The court was precluded from considering the orders it had made on the merits so as to redress the injustice.[3]

Where parties to litigation agreed orders as to costs between the claimant

[96] See the Law Society's guide to the Professional Conduct of Solicitors 7th ed., para. 13.07.
[97] *Wong v. Vizards* [1997] 2 Costs L.R. 46, Toulson J.
[98] Supreme Court Fees Order, 1999, County Court Fees Order 1998, Family Proceedings Fees Order 1999.
[99] *Skinner v. The Thames Valley & Aldershot Co. Ltd,* July 7, 1995, CA (unreported).
[1] Gannon v. Chubb Fire Ltd [1996] P.I.Q.R. P1808, CA.
[2] Supreme Court Fees Order 1999, art. 6; County Court Fees Order 1999, art. 6.
[3] *Neville v. Wilson (No. 2), The Times,* July 28, 1997, CA.

and the first and third defendants and the first defendant became unable to pay the claimant sought indemnity from the third defendant on the basis that it had discovered that the third defendant had funded the first defendant. The court held that it did not have jurisdiction to revisit the consent order. The contract between the parties had been embodied in a court order, which, in the absence of fraud, misrepresentation or mistake could only be set aside or amended in the most exceptional circumstances. In the instant case the litigation had been settled on contractual terms and a very good reason would be required to add to the liability of the third defendant. Secondly, it was right as a matter of principle that there was finality to the proceedings (*Centerhigh Ltd v. Amen & Ors* [2001] EWHC CHD, July 18, Neuberger J.).

## CLS Funded

5–034 It is now possible to agree costs between parties in a case funded out of the Community Legal Service Fund without having to have the whole bill assessed, provided that the agreed costs have been paid (Civil Legal Aid (General) Regulations 1989 regulation 106A).

Where proceedings (other than where the funded client is a child or patient) (r. 48.5) are settled without any direction of the court as to costs on terms, including a provision for the payment of agreed costs in favour of the funded client, the provisions relating to assessment set out below will apply (Civil Legal Aid (General) Regulations 1989 regulation 106A(2)(a)). Similarly where proceedings have been brought to an end by judgment, decree or final order and there has been agreement as to the costs to be paid in favour of the funded client (*ibid.* regulation 107A(2)(b)), and in circumstances where the retainer of a funded client's solicitor or counsel is determined (in circumstances to which Civil Legal Aid (General) Regulations 1989 regulation 105(2) refers) before proceedings are actually begun and there is an agreement for the payment of agreed costs in favour of the funded client those provisions also apply (*ibid.* regulation 106A(2)(c)).

5–035 The provisions relating to assessment referred to above are:

(a) the funded client's solicitor may apply to the Area Director for an assessment limited to costs payable from the Community Legal Service Fund only, if of the opinion that the amount of the costs, including counsel's fees, will not be more than £1,000; (*ibid.* regulation 106A(3)
(b) the solicitor may apply for a detailed assessment (*ibid.* regulation 107A(2) limited to costs payable from the Community Legal Service Fund only, if of the opinion that the amount of costs, including counsel's fees, would be more than £500 (*ibid.* regulation 106A(4));

(c) before any assessment, the solicitor must confirm in writing to the relevant authority that the agreed costs have been paid (*ibid.* regulation 106A(6).

The authority may require the production of any information which it considers relevant to the determination (*ibid.* regulation 106A(6).

## Children and patients

5–036 In general the court must order a detailed assessment of the costs payable by any party who is a child or patient to his solicitor. On the assessment of those costs, the court must also assess any costs payable to that party in the proceedings unless the court has issued a default costs certificate.[15]

The court does not need to order detailed assessment of costs payable by any party who is a child or patient where there is no need to do so to protect the interests of the child or patient or his estate. Detailed assessment need not be ordered where another party has agreed to pay a specified sum of money in respect of the costs and the solicitor acting for the child or patient has waived the right to claim any further costs. The same applies where the court has decided the costs payable to the child or patient by summary assessment and the solicitor has waived the right to further costs. If an insurer or other person is liable to discharge the costs which the child or patient would otherwise be liable to pay, and the court is satisfied that the insurer or other person is financially able to discharge those costs, detailed assessment need not be ordered.[16]

## Offers to settle without prejudice save as to costs of the detailed assessment proceedings

5–037 This is the old Calderbank procedure revised for use under the new cost rules. Either party may make a written offer to settle the cost of the proceedings, which is expressed to be without prejudice, save as to the costs of the detailed assessment proceedings. There is no time-limit for making such an offer but the earlier it is made the more effective it is likely to be. The court will take the offer into account in deciding who should be liable to pay the costs of the assessment proceedings.[17] The prohibition against making such offers where the receiving party was an assisted person was deleted by the Rule Committee but the Legal Aid Board and the LCD were not prepared to allow that situation to continue and the Practice Direction provides that r. 47.19 does not apply where the receiving party is an assisted person unless the court so orders.

[15] i.e. Under Rule 47.11 see para. 7–009. R. 48.5(1) and (2).
[16] Direction relating to Part 48, para. 1.2.
[17] r. 47.19(1) and (2). Direction relating to Part 47, paras 7.4–7.6.

# CHAPTER 7—CONTENTIOUS COSTS



## A. SUMMARY AND DETAILED ASSESSMENT

### Factors to be taken into account in deciding the amount or costs

### Add:

7–002 Where separate actions between several claimants against several defendants were tried together, even though the actions had not been consolidated, some costs incurred by the defendants were common to all four actions, others were specific to each claim. The actions were dismissed by the trial Judge who decided to carry out a summary assessment. The court held that the unsuccessful claimants were jointly and severally liable for the common costs (*Bairstow v. Queens Moat Houses Plc* [2000] EW QBD, April 14, Nelson J.).

## B. ASSESSMENT OF COSTS

### Summary Assessment

### Delete penultimate paragraph—Insert: 7–003

The court will consider whether or not to order a payment on account in accordance with r. 44.3(8). The question of whether an interim payment on account of costs prior to formal assessment should be ordered, is within the discretion of the court. If the issue is considered broadly as a matter of principle there is no good reason why a successful party should have to wait to receive their costs following judgment. Any delay is simply attributable to the assessment process itself. In the interests of justice it may therefore be right and proper to make an order for an interim payment of a sum approximating to an amount which the successful party was almost certain to recover on a detailed assessment. In deciding whether or not such an order should be made the court should have regard to all the circumstances of the case including the likelihood of an appeal, the parties' respective financial positions and the overall interests of justice (*Mars UK Ltd v. Teknowledge Ltd (No.2)* [1999] 2 Costs L.R. 44, Jacob J.).

The failure of a party to file and serve a copy of the statement of costs not less than 24 hours before the date fixed for the hearing does not warrant the wholesale disallowance of costs. Where the only factor against awarding costs is merely the failure to serve a statement of costs without aggravating factors, a party should not be deprived of all his costs, the court will take the matter into account but its reaction should be proportionate. The court should ask itself what if any prejudice there had been to the paying party and how that prejudice should be dealt with *e.g.* by allowing a short adjournment or adjourning the summary assessment to another date or directing detailed assessment (*MacDonald v. Taree Holdings Ltd* [2000] *The Times*, December 28, Neuberger J.).

In carrying out a summary assessment the Judge is required to analyse the statement of costs and not to apply his own tariffs as to what costs were appropriate *e.g.* for a one day paper only appeal, that approach is wrong in principle (*One-800 Flowers Inc v. Phonenames Ltd* [2001] *The Times*, July 9, CA).

Only the Judge who has heard a case is in the position to make a summary assessment of the costs of that case, otherwise the issue of costs should be sent to a Costs Judge for consideration: *Mahmood v. Penrose* [2002] EWCA Civ 15 March.

The court has a discretion under Rule 44.3 as to when costs are to be paid. Unless otherwise ordered however the costs become payable within 14 days of the date of the order by virtue of Rule 44.8. If a party seeks an extension of time in which to pay costs it is for that party to make such an application supported by evidence. In the absence of any alternative order costs are payable within 14 days (*Pepin v. Watts & The Chief Constable of Surrey Police* [2000] EW CA Civ, October 4).

**7–005 Delete text and insert:**

Decisions on summary assessment are appealable in accordance with the ordinary rules as to appeals. Permission is required (Part 52).

# C. DETAILED ASSESSMENT

## Add at end of first paragraph:

7–006

In a passing off action, which failed at the interim injunction stage, the court ordered that the defendant should have their costs in any event and that the costs should not be assessed and paid forthwith but should await the outcome of the proceedings. Since there was a real prospect that the proceedings would go no further the defendant was given liberty to apply to convert the order into an order that the costs be assessed forthwith: *Local Sunday Newspapers Ltd v. Johnston Press Ltd* [2001] June 19, Neuberger J., unreported.

## Procedure

## Add:

7–008

Many claims are settled on terms which are confidential and the terms are contained in a schedule to the order concluding the proceedings (Tomlin Order) but, unless the order itself contains a provision for costs to be paid and assessed if not agreed, the right to detailed assessment does not arise. The fact that the terms of the schedule deal with the position with regard to costs is insufficient.

**Privileged documents and disclosure**

## Delete the last paragraph.

7–014

## Add:

7–014

The views of Hobhouse J in *Pamplin v. Express Newspapers Ltd* (above) were held to be still valid. The court was not persuaded that the client care letter and payment calculations were privileged but if anything in them had been privileged the documents could have been redacted. The basic principle is that if a party wishes to prove his version of a disputed issue of fact by reference to certain documents those documents must be disclosed to the opposing party: *Dickinson v. Rushmer* [2001] EWHC ChD. December 21, Rimer J. The court did not suggest that the Costs Judge may potentially put the receiving party to its election in respect of every document relied on. It was expected that in the majority of cases the paying party would be content to agree that the Costs Judge alone should see the privileged documents. Only where it is necessary and proportionate should the receiving party be put to his election. The redaction and production of privileged documents or the adducing of further evidence would lead to additional delay and increase costs. Detailed assessment is litigation without discovery or disclosure. The rule that the other party is entitled to see the material even if the party which possesses it does not deploy it can have no application when the material is privileged. The principle is an absolute one, privilege will not be overridden by the court and must be waived by the party entitled to assert it. Paragraph 40.14 of the Costs Practice Direction is consistent with the requirements of ECHR. The protection which is afforded to the receiving party by the rule that the waiver is for the purpose of the assessment only, and that the document remains otherwise privileged, should play a much more significant role than it appears to in the decision whether or not to waive privilege in a proper case: *South Coast Shipping Co Ltd v. Havant Borough Council* [2001] EWHC Ch, December 21, Pumphrey J. The court has indicated that it should be standard practice where a client care letter is affirmatively relied on that it should be produced to the paying party: *Adams v. MacInnes* [2001] EWHC QBD, November 8, *per* Gray J.

# CHAPTER 8—APPLICATION FOR AND ATTENDANCE UPON DETAILED ASSESSMENT



## A. SOLICITOR AND CLIENT

### Statutory requirements of a delivered bill

**Footnote 4: Insert after** ***Haigh v. Ousey—Eversheds v.*** *Osman*, April 7, 1998, CA (unreported). 8–002

**Footnote 5: insert** *Aaron v. Okoye* [1998] 2 Costs L.R. 6 CA. 8–002

### Interim and final bills

**Insert at end of paragraph 8–009** 8–009

A natural break cannot simply mean a date thought by the claimant solicitors to be a convenient date upon which to deliver a bill, since otherwise the concept of a natural break would be meaningless and section 65(2) of the Solicitors Act 1974 would be rendered largely redundant. The law does provide for the possibility of interim bills being payable by virtue of an inferred agreement, such an agreement can be inferred from the conduct of the parties. (In the particular case the defendant had paid the first 26 of 42 bills rendered monthly.) [*Penningtons (a firm) v. Abedi*, March 23, 2000, CA (unreported)].

## In the High Court

### Application by the solicitor

8–013 **Delete text of footnote 59 and insert:**

*O. Palomo SA v. Turner & Co* [1999] 4 All E.R. 353, CA.

## Legal Aid

8–023 **Delete text of paragraphs 8–023 and 8–024 down to footnote number 26 in the latter. Replace with:**

### Costs out of the Community Legal Service Fund

The detailed assessment of the costs of proceedings to which a funded client is a party, must be in accordance with any direction or order given or made in the proceedings, irrespective of the interest of the funded client in the detailed assessment.

Costs will be assessed on the standard basis subject to the Legal Aid in Civil Proceedings (Remuneration) Regulations 1994, the Legal Aid in Family Proceedings (Remuneration) Regulations 1991, the Community Legal Service (Funding) Order 2000 and the Community Legal Service (Funding) (Counsel in Family Proceedings) Order 2001.

Any certificate or notice of revocation or discharge must be made available on the detailed assessment (*ibid.* regulation 107(2)). In cases where a notice of discharge has been issued or the certificate has been revoked the costs of the funded client will be assessed on production of a copy of the notice of discharge or revocation at the appropriate office (*ibid.* regulation 107(4)).

8–024 **Basis of detailed assessment**

With the introduction of prescribed rates for work funded by the Community Legal Service Fund, the costs recoverable will be assessed on the standard basis subject to the appropriate remuneration regulations. Where the retainer of a funded client's solicitor or counsel is determined before proceedings have actually been commenced, and there is no subsequent change of solicitor or counsel under the certificate, the amount of costs is assessed by the Area Director. "Assessment" in this context means an assessment of costs with a view to ensuring that the amounts of costs to be allowed are those which would be allowed on a detailed assessment in accordance with the Regulations (Civil Legal Aid (General) Regulations 1989 Regulations 105(1), (2) and 107A(2)).

Where proceedings have been commenced and the solicitor is of the opinion that the total amount which he and counsel would receive after detailed assessment would be not more than £500, the costs must be assessed by the Area Director (*ibid.* regulation 105(2A)). Where the solicitor is of the opinion that the total amount which he and counsel would receive after detailed assessment would be not more than £1,000, or there are special circumstances where the detailed assessment would be against the interests of the funded client, or would increase the amount payable from the Fund, or the solicitor incurs costs after a direction that there should be a detailed assessment of costs in recovering monies payable to the CLS Fund, the solicitor may apply to the Area Director for an assessment (*ibid.* regulation 105(3)).

Where solicitors represent a number of clients, only some of whom are funded by the Legal Services Commission, when the bill of costs comes to be assessed the overriding principle for the court is that each client is to be charged only with the costs of his own case. The general costs which cannot be attributed to particular clients on the basis of separate claims/ defences or distinct issues must be apportioned pro rata (*Baylis v. Kelly, The Times*, June 6, 1997 Chadwick J.).

Where judgment is signed in default, or the court gives final judgment, the judgment must include a direction for the costs of any funded client to be assessed on the standard basis (Civil Legal Aid (General) Regulations 1989 regulation 107(3)).

### Delete final paragraph of 8–024 and insert:

8–024

It is the duty of a funded client's solicitor to safeguard the interests of the Community Legal Service Fund on any detailed assessment between the parties, pursuant to an order for costs made in favour of the funded client, where that person may himself have no interest in the result of the detailed assessment. The solicitor is required to take such steps as may appear to be necessary to appeal the detailed assessment.

## B. COUNCIL

### Legal Aid

### Delete text of paragraph 8–027 down to footnote number 38. Replace with:

8–027

### Costs out of the Community Legal Service Fund

**Assessment/Detailed Assessment**

The onus is upon the solicitor to have the costs, including counsel's fees, assessed by the Legal Services Commission. The solicitor must, within seven days after an assessment or review, notify counsel in writing whether the fees claimed on his behalf have been reduced or disallowed (Civil Legal Aid (General) Regulations 1989 regulation 105(8)). There is a similar duty in respect of detailed assessment or provisional assessment (*ibid.* regulation 112(1)).

Counsel's fees will always be included in the solicitor's bill for detailed assessment in a case funded out of the Community Legal Service Fund. The solicitor must endorse the bill with the date on which notice was given to counsel of any reduction or disallowance, or a statement that no such notice was necessary (*ibid.* regulation 112(1)).

Where the bill of costs is endorsed to the effect that no notice was necessary the costs officer may issue the final certificate but where a notice has been given, the certificate may not be issued until 14 days have elapsed from the date of the endorsement (*ibid.* regulation 112(2)).

## Add after paragraph 8–028/1:

8–028/1 Although the Costs Practice Direction enables a claim for the reasonable costs of preparing a bill to be allowed, where a claim is made subject to the Legal Aid in Family Proceedings (Remuneration) Regulations 1991 or similar provisions which do not allow for such an item, the statutory provision is not overridden by the Practice Direction. Accordingly the amount to be allowed is the figure specified in the Regulations. The costs of drawing up a bill may be distinguished from the costs of preparing for and attending the assessment hearing, and an additional figure may be allowed in respect of it (*A Local Authority v. A Mother and Child (Family Proceedings: Legal Aid Assessment)* 2000 EW CA Fam. December 20).

## D. LITIGANTS IN PERSON

### Form of Bill

8–029 **Delete first sentence—substitute**

The information required from a litigant in person to be included in a bill of costs should, so far as possible, follow the requirements of the Rules and Practice Direction. The court will normally accept a bill in any form so long as it sets out clearly what is being claimed and details of the work done set out in chronological order with details of the time, costs and disbursements claimed against each item.

## Insert at the end of penultimate paragraph: 8–029

A Costs Judge should keep in mind that it is appropriate in a proper case to allow a litigant in person more time for a particular task than would be allowed to a solicitor. A solicitor's charging rate takes account of the fact that he has support staff, secretaries and messengers. "The time spent reasonably doing the work . . ." permits a reasonable assessment of the time spent by the litigant in person and should reflect matters such as posting letters, taking files to court and photocopying documents (*Mealing-McLeod v. Common Professional Examination Board*, March 30, 2000, Buckley J. (unreported)).

## Footnote 46, add:

See also *London & Scottish Benefit Society v. Chorley* [1884] 13 QBD 872 and *Stubblefield v. Kemp* [1999] EWHC Ch.D, November 10, Arden J., [2001] 1 Costs L.R. 30. 8–029

## Add at end:

Where a litigant in person succeeded in judicial review proceedings and was awarded costs, the court at first instance decided that he was not entitled to costs for research (1200 hours). The Court of Appeal decided that in principle the litigant in person was entitled to his time for researching his case at the rate fixed by statute subject to a cap of two thirds of what he would have recovered if legally represented. The Court of Appeal found no reason to disbelieve the litigant's assertion that he had spent 1200 hours on the case and decided that he was entitled to be paid for it. The court held that the starting point was the cap of two thirds and took the figure of £15,000 as a rough estimate (from information supplied by solicitors). The litigant was entitled to two thirds of that figure plus expenses for photocopying and travel. He was accordingly awarded £10,460: *R. v. Legal Services Commission (formerly Legal Aid Board) ex p. Wulfshon* [2002] EWCA Civ, February 8. 8–029

## Insert new paragraph after 8–032: 8–033

## McKenzie Friends

The Court of Appeal has summarised the way in which McKenzie Friends are to be treated as follows:

1. In relation to proceedings in public, a litigant in person should be allowed to have the assistance of a McKenzie Friend unless the judge is satisfied that fairness and the interests of justice do not require the litigant in person to have that assistance.
2. The position is the same where the proceedings are in Chambers unless the proceedings are in private.
3. Where the proceedings are in private then the nature of the proceedings which makes it appropriate for them to be heard in private may make it undesirable in the interests of justice for a McKenzie Friend to assist.
4. A judge should give reasons for refusing to allow a litigant in person the assistance of a McKenzie Friend.
5. The assistance of a McKenzie Friend is available for the benefit of the litigant in person and whether or not a McKenzie Friend is paid or unpaid for his services he has no right to provide those services; the court is solely concerned with the interests of the litigant in person (*R. v. Bow County Court ex parte Pelling* [1999] 4 All E.R. 751, CA. As to granting permission for a litigant in person to have an advocate who has no right of audience, see: *Clarkson v. Gilbert, The Times,* July 4, 2000, CA).

# CHAPTER 9—REVIEW AND APPEAL



## Delete existing chapter 9 and insert the following:

# Appeals

## Appeals generally

9–001 Part 52 governs appeals from all decisions except appeals against decisions of an authorised court officer in detailed assessment proceedings. Part 52 applies in respect of appeals against summary assessment as well as against detailed assessment. An appellant or respondent requires permission to appeal in every case. The application for permission to appeal may be made to the lower court at the hearing at which the decision to be appealed against was made or to the appeal court in an appeal notice (r. 52.1 and r. 52.3).

Appeal lies to the next level of judge in the court hierarchy. Thus in the County Court appeal lies from a District Judge to a Circuit Judge and from a Circuit Judge to a High Court Judge; and in the High Court appeals lie from a Costs Judge or District Judge of the High Court to a High Court Judge and from a High Court Judge to the Court of Appeal. The court hearing a first appeal is described in Part 52 as the appeal court and the court from whose decision an appeal is brought is described as the lower court (*per* Brooke L.J. in *Tanfern Ltd v. Cameron-MacDonald*, May 12, 2000, CA (unreported)).

Brooke LJ subsequently amended what he had said in Tanfern to read (at paragraph 17):

> "A final decision includes the assessment of damages or any other final decision where it is "made at the conclusion of part of a hearing or trial which has been split up into parts and would if made at the conclusion of that hearing or trial be a final decision": Article 1(3) of the

Order of 2000; it does not include a decision only on the detailed assessment of costs."

*Dooley v. Parker* [2002] EWCA Civ, February 7.

**9–001.1** The proper approach of the court on an appeal from a costs judge was considered by Buckley J.:

> "Broadly speaking a judge will allow an appeal . . . if satisfied that the decision of the Costs Judge was wrong . . . that is easy to apply to matters of principle or construction. However where the appeal includes challenges to the details of the assessment, such as hours allowed in respect of a particular item, the task in hand is one of assessment or judgment, rather than principle. There is no absolute answer. Notwithstanding that the judge to whom the appeal is made may sit with assessors . . . the appeal is not a re-hearing and, given the nature of the Costs Judge's task and his expertise, I would usually regard it as undesirable for it to be so. . . .
>
> . . . [S] ince the appeal is not a re-hearing I would regard it as inappropriate for the judge on appeal to be drawn into an exercise calculated to add a little here or knock off a little there. If the judge's attention is drawn to items which, with the advice of his assessors, he feels should in fairness be altered, doubtless he will act. That is a matter for his good judgment. Permission to appeal should not be granted simply to allow yet another trawl through the bill, in the absence of some sensible and significant complaint. If an appeal turns out to be no more than such an exercise the sanction of costs may be used."

(*Mealing-McLeod v. The Common Professional Examination Board*, March 30, 2000, Buckley J. (unreported).

## Add the following paragraphs after paragraph 9–001:

**9–001/2** The approach of the court was further clarified by the Court of Appeal in *Tanfern v. Cameron-McDonald* [2000] 1 W.L.R. 1311 as follows: "The first ground of interference speaks for itself. The epithet "wrong" is to be applied to the substance of the decision made by the lower court. If the appeal is against the exercise of a discretion by the lower court the decision of the House of Lords in *G v. G (Minors: Custody Appeal)* [1985] 1 W.L.R. 647 warrants attention. In that case Lord Fraser of Tullybelton said at page 652: "certainly it would not be useful to enquire whether different shades of meaning are intended to be conveyed by words such as "blatant error" used by the President in the present case, and words such as "clearly wrong", "plainly wrong" or "simply wrong" used by other Judges in other cases. All these various expressions were used in order to emphasise the point that the Appellate Court should only interfere when they consider that the Judge at first instance has not merely preferred an imperfect solution, which is different from an alternative imperfect solution which the Court of Appeal might or would have adopted, but has exceeded the generous ambit within which such a reasonable disagreement is possible."

9–001/3 Rule 52.4(2) provides that the appellant must file the appellant's notice at the appeal court within such period as may be directed by the lower court, or, where that court makes no such direction, 14 days after the date of the decision of the lower court that the appellant wishes to appeal. In detailed assessment proceedings the 14 days starts from the date of the particular decision complained of, even if the detailed assessment hearing continues over a number of days. The time does not run from the conclusion of the detailed assessment hearing (*Kasir v. Darlington & Simpson Rolls Mills Ltd*, March 1, 2001, Popplewell J. unreported).

## Appeals from authorised court officers in detailed assessment proceedings

9–002

Any party to detailed assessment proceedings may appeal against a decision of an authorised court officer without having to obtain either permission or request reasons. The appeal is to a Costs Judge or District Judge of the High Court (r. 47.20, 47.21). The appeal is a re-hearing of the proceedings which gave rise to the decision appealed against and the court may make any order and give any direction it considers appropriate (r. 47.23). Permission to appeal is required from a decision made by a Costs Judge or District Judge of the High Court in such proceedings because the exception to the requirement to obtain permission applies only to appeals in detailed assessment proceedings against the decision of an authorised court officer and not at this higher level of appeal in such proceedings. Where costs are summarily assessed by a judge as part of a final decision in a multi track claim the principles relating to appeals against final decisions in multi track claims will be applied (*per* Brooke L.J. in *Tanfern Ltd v. Cameron-MacDonald*, May 12, 2000, CA (unreported)).

## Assessors

9–003

Earlier rules made provision for the court to appoint assessors under section 70 of the Supreme Court Act 1981 or section 63 of the County Courts Act 1984. Part 52, which now governs appeals, makes no separate provision for assessors, but rule 35.15 deals with the court's ordinary power to appoint assessors. As a matter of practice, on appeals from decisions in the Supreme Court Costs Office each appeal will be considered by the Senior Costs Judge or another Costs Judge appointed by him to decide whether assessors should be appointed and if so how many and whether a barrister or a solicitor. The fees of assessors form part of the costs of the proceedings (r. 35.15). The court will give notice to the parties of the intention to appoint assessors giving the name of the proposed assessor, the matter in respect of which the assistance of the assessor will be sought and the qualifications of the assessor to give that assistance. Any party may object in writing to the proposed appointment within seven days of receipt of the notification. The objection will be taken into account by the court in deciding whether or not to make the appointment (PD 35 paragraphs 6.1 to 6.4). The court may order any party to deposit in the court office a specified sum in respect of the assessor's fees and where it does so the assessor will not be asked to act until the sum has been paid (r. 35.15).

## Appeals relating to costs out of the Community Legal Service Fund

9–004 A funded client's solicitor may appeal against a decision in detailed assessment proceedings in accordance with Part 52 (or in the case of appeal from an authorised court officer, rules 47.20 to 47.23) and if counsel, acting for the funded client, notifies the solicitor that he is dissatisfied with the decision, the solicitor must appeal, but the costs of any such appeal are deemed to be costs to which the funded client's certificate relates only to the extent that the court hearing the appeal so orders (Civil Legal Aid (General) Regulations 1989 regulation 113(2)).

9–005 The funded client is not required to make any contribution to the fund on account of the costs of any appeal against a decision in detailed assessment proceedings and the charge created by section 10(7) of the Access to the Justice Act 1999 does not apply in relation to any increase in the net liability of the fund in consequence of any order made in such an appeal.

9–006 Where permission to appeal is obtained, the funded client's solicitor is required to give written notice to the Lord Chancellor and must send to the Lord Chancellor with that notice, copies of the bill of costs and the request for permission to appeal. When filing the notice of appeal the solicitor must file with the court a copy of the notice given to the Lord Chancellor. The notice of appeal must be sent without delay to the Lord Chancellor once it has been filed (*ibid.* regulation 113(4) to (7)).

# CHAPTER 10—WASTED COSTS SANCTIONS AND THE COURTS INHERENT JURISDICTION



## A. PERSONAL LIABILITY OF LEGAL REPRESENTATIONS FOR WASTED COSTS

### Add at beginning:

10–001 Rule 48.7 sets out the personal liability of legal representatives for wasted costs under Section 51(6) of the Supreme Court Act 1981. The court cannot act as an appellate court in respect of its own order for costs except where fraud has been shown in the original application for the order (*Commissioners for Customs & Excise v. Anchor Foods* [1999] EW Ch.D, July 8, Neuberger J.). This decision was distinguished in a case where the Defendant was successful and an order was made for costs as between the parties. Prior to the detailed assessment the defendant sought a wasted costs order against the claimants' legal representative. On appeal it was held that the court did have jurisdiction to make a wasted costs order. The case was not concerned with revisiting costs with a view to a wasted costs order under section 51(6) of the 1981 Act but with revisiting a decision on costs as between the parties under section 51(1). This involved the exercise of two separate discretions and the discretion in relation to a possible wasted costs order could be exercised at any time until detailed assessment (*Melchior v. Vettivel* [2001] EW CA, May 25, Patten J.).

It is open to a litigant to seek a wasted costs order against the legal representatives of any party including his own representatives: *Brown v.*

*Bennett* EWHC Ch.D, November 16, Neuberger J. *The Times*, Novembe
21, 2001.

The court does not have jurisdiction to make a wasted costs order agains a legal representative who is not within the definition of "persons exercisin a right to conduct litigation" *e.g.*, because the representative has not issue proceedings: *Byrne v. South Sefton Health Authority* [2001] EWCA Ci 1904.

Delay in the conduct of proceedings can give rise to a wasted costs order When considering making a wasted costs order the Judge is obliged to carr out some enquiry into the costs incurred, although not a detailed enquiry Provided that a reasoned assessment of the costs wasted is made the Judg may make an order in broad terms: Kilroy v Kilroy [1997] PNLR 66 CA.

## Decided cases in wasted costs

## Add at end of first paragraph:

10–002 The Code of Conduct of the Bar imposes a personal duty on counsel no to make allegations of fraud or other dishonest or dishonourable conduc without the evidence to make good the allegations. The material upo which such allegations are founded has to be material which may be pu before the court. In a case in which allegations should never have bee made with the authority of counsel it was held that the wasted costs juris diction existed to compensate those who had incurred costs unnecessaril as well as providing a sanction. A wasted costs order was accordingly mad against counsel (*Medcalf v. Mardell* [2000] EW CA Civ, November 24).

## 10–004 Insert at end of paragraph 10–004:

Care must be exercised to avoid the fallacy that the proper inference fron what proved to be a hopeless case is that the conduct of the legal represent atives must have been improper or unreasonable (*Jones v. Chief Constabl of Bedfordshire*, July 30, 1999, CA (unreported)).

## 10–005 Delete text—substitute:

*Legal Aid/CLS funded work:* The Court of Appeal has set out the proced ure to be adopted where a funded client has been unsuccessful and the unassisted party seeks to recover costs against the Legal Services Commis sion or under the wasted costs jurisdiction (re *O (a minor) (costs: liabilit as a Legal Aid Board)* [1977] 1 F.L.R. 465, CA). In relation to the issue o legal aid, it was held that the effect of section 31(1) of the Legal Aid Act 1988 was that the existence of legal aid did not affect the client/representative relationship nor the rights of other parties to the proceedings or the principles on which any discretion was exercised. It was incumbent on the courts to which wasted costs applications were made to bear prominently in mind the peculiar vulnerability of legal representatives acting for funded clients (*Symphony Group Plc v. Hodgson* [1993] 3 W.L.R. 830 at 842). It would subvert the benevolent purposes of the legal aid legislation if such representatives were subject to any unusual personal risks. The court should also bear prominently in mind that the advice and conduct of legal representatives is not to be tempered by the knowledge that their client is not their paymaster and so not in all probability liable for the costs of the other side.

In considering whether or not to make a wasted costs order in a LSC funded case the court should be slow to supplement statutory or regulatory duties by placing a higher standard on the parties. Where the wasted costs would effectively be recovered by the Community Legal Service Fund, the consent of the Commission should be obtained before embarking on proceedings for a wasted costs order (*Tate v. Hart, The Independent*, March 8, 1999, CA).

## Insert at the end of paragraph 10–007: 10–007

Since the decision in *Ridehalgh v. Horsefield* the House of Lords has again considered the immunity of advocates (*Arthur J. S. Hall & Co v. Simons; Barratt v. Woolf Seddon; Harris v. Schofield, Roberts & Hill* [2000] 3 W.L.R. 543, HL). In each of the three cases the Judge at first instance had concluded that solicitors enjoyed an advocate's immunity and struck out the claims as an abuse of process. The Court of Appeal decided that in none of the cases were the solicitors immune and restored the client's claim. The House of Lords decided that it was appropriate to reconsider the issue of advocate's immunity and went on to find that none of the reasons said to justify immunity had sufficient weight to sustain immunity in relation to civil proceedings. The House of Lords found that the powers of the courts and the CPR were such as to restrict the ability of clients to bring unmeritorious and vexatious claims against advocates, and accordingly public interest in the administration of justice no longer required that advocates should enjoy immunity from suit for alleged negligence in the conduct of civil proceedings. There was a similar finding in respect of criminal proceedings.

## Add the following paragraphs:

10–008 The liability of a barrister for a wasted costs order is not limited to his conduct of the proceedings in court. A barrister is within the definition of a person "exercising a right of audience or a right to conduct litigation" under Section 51(13) of the Supreme Court Act 1981: *Brown v. Bennett*

[2001] EWHC Ch.D, November 16, Neuberger J. *The Times*, November 21, 2001.

Whilst a barrister cannot be asked to reveal the contents of his instructions or brief, or be asked to answer a question which would in practice reveal part of the contents of the brief, the barrister could be asked, in respect of non privileged documents, whether he saw or knew of the particular document, provided that the purpose of the question was merely to find out specifically whether counsel had seen or knew of those documents. If the purpose of the question was to find out if a particular document was in his instructions that question would be impermissible even if the document was not privileged: *Brown v. Bennett (No.3)* [2001] EWHC Ch.D, December 17, Neuberger J., *The Times*, January 4, 2002.

A material factor in deciding the culpability of legal representatives' conduct is whether the client has waived legal professional privilege. If not the court must make assumptions in favour of those legal representatives: *Daly v. Hubner* [2001] EWHC Ch.D, Etherton J.

**10–008 Delete last sentence and footnote.**

**10–010 Insert at the end of paragraph 10–010:**

A solicitor, representing litigants who gave evidence in other proceedings rendering their pleaded defence untenable, could not escape liability for wasted costs on the basis that the defence had been settled by counsel. The court found that the solicitor knew about his clients' evidence in the other proceedings and it was startlingly clear that the pleaded defence was not a true statement of the defence case. The court found the solicitor's conduct had been unreasonable and had caused the wasted costs (*General Mediterranean Holdings SA v. Patel*, January 27, 2000, Curtis J. (unreported)).

**Add:**

10–012 In family proceedings where the husband changed his legal advisers which required the wife's solicitors to seek discovery of documents held by his original solicitors, the trial being vacated without directions either being sought or given, it was appropriate to hear the wife's application for a wasted costs order against the husband's former legal team before the main trial began: *B v. B (Wasted costs: abuse of process)* [2001] 1 F.L.R. 843 Wall J.

## After CPR Part 48.7(2) insert:

10–014

(The Costs Practice Direction Section 53 relating to rule 48.7 sets out the procedure and the approach which the court will adopt when considering such an application)

## Other examples of wasted costs

## Add at end:

10–018

Where proceedings before the Restricted Practices Court had to be abandoned by reason of the appearance of bias by a member of the court, an application was made for payment of the wasted costs by the Lord Chancellor who was the emanation of the State responsible for providing impartial tribunals to conduct trials of civil litigation and that there had been a breach of Article 6 of the European Convention on Human Rights. The Court of Appeal held there had been no breach of the article because the situation had been remedied by providing an impartial tribunal. The applicant was unable to show any authority for the contention that the Lord Chancellor should have to pay the wasted legal costs as compensation (*In Re Medicaments and Related Classes of Goods (No.4)* [2001] *The Times*, August 7, CA).

## Wasted costs in cases concerning children

## Insert at end of pargraph 10–019:

10–019

Different considerations arise in non-adversarial care proceedings when contrasted with litigation, and the court has a special role in initiating wasted costs enquiries in such proceedings should this be necessary, *e.g.* where legal representatives failed to arrange for expert witnesses to have access to all relevant documents in breach of the guidance given by Family Division Practice Directions. ((Children) (G Care Proceedings: Wasted Costs) [2000] 2 W.L.R. 1007; [1999] 4 All E.R. 371, Wall J).

## C. INHERENT JURISDICTION

## Add:

10–023

Where the court was persuaded that a solicitor had not acted negligently in continuing to act for a company which had been struck off the register, nonetheless the court was able to make an award of costs against the solicitor under its inherent jurisdiction on the basis that the solicitor had been acting without authority. The award was however reduced on the basis that the defendants were clearly in a position to know the status of the company (*Padhiar v. Patel*, November 23, 2000, Miss H Heilbron Q.C. (unreported)).

## E. THE LAW SOCIETY'S POWERS IN RESPECT OF INADEQUATE PROFESSIONAL SERVICES

10–025 **Delete first paragraph—Insert:**

If the Council directs compensation to be paid by the solicitor the amount awarded may not exceed £5,000 (Solicitors Act 1974 Schedule 1A paragraph 3, as amended by the Solicitors (Compensation for Inadequate Professional Services) Order 2000 S.I. 2000 No.644).

# CHAPTER 11—ARBITRATION COSTS

PARA.



## C. COSTS IN THE COPYRIGHT TRIBUNAL

### Insert at the end of paragraph 11–010: 11–010

The Copyright Tribunal has power to make such order as it determines to be reasonable in all the circumstances in relation to costs. (Section 135D of the Copyright Designs & Patents Act 1988). The determination of the Tribunal is far more likely than ordinary civil litigation to produce an outcome in which there is no clear winner and loser and the Tribunal's discretion is not fettered by any reference to the outcome of the application (*AEI Rediffusion Music Ltd v. Photographic Performance Ltd* [1999] 1 W.L.R. 1507, CA).

## D. INSOLVENCY

### Insert at the end of pargraph 11–011: 11–011

As to the principles to be considered when setting aside a statutory demand see *Bayoil SA* [1999] 1 W.L.R. 147. Provided the judge properly directs himself upon the matters to be considered costs are always discretionary (*Re: A Debtor (No.87 of 1999)* January 17, 2000, Rimmer J. (unreported), as to setting aside statutory demands in relation to costs in family proceedings see *Levy v. Legal Aid Board*, February 4, 2000, Evans-Lombe J. (unreported)).

The limitation period in respect of an order for costs begins to run when the order becomes enforceable by action which is at the date of certification, not on the date the costs order was made (*Times Newspapers Ltd v. Chohan* [2001] *The Times*, August 1).

Where it is sought to enforce an order for summarily assessed costs by invoking the bankruptcy regime the policy considerations of the CPR favouring summary assessment of costs and their early recovery has to be weighed against the operation of a bankruptcy regime including the fact that the court could set aside a statutory demand whether the debtor appeared to have a counterclaim set off or cross demand. The court ordered the application to set aside would be adjourned until after judgement in the substantive proceedings and ordered that no bankruptcy proceedings should be commenced in the meantime: *Cohen v. TSB Bank Plc* [2001] EWHC Ch.D, November 29, Etherton J.

## Costs Paid Otherwise than out of the Insolvent Estate

11–015 **Insert at the end of paragraph 11–015:**

Where petitioning creditors agreed a compromise with the debtor after the appointment of the trustee in bankruptcy and agreed to the setting aside of the statutory demand and to the annulment of the bankruptcy, the court ordered both the creditors and the debtor to be jointly liable for the trustee's costs. This was on the basis that it was the least unjust way of dealing with the matter since both parties were legally aided (*Butterworth v. Soutter*, February 8, 2000, Neuberger J. (unreported)).

11–020 **Insert paragraphs 11–020 and 11–021 after paragraph 11–019:**

## E. EMPLOYMENT APPEAL TRIBUNAL

On a complaint of racial discrimination the claimant was successful and the Tribunal rejected the respondent's claim for an award of costs based on the applicant's amended claim for compensation. The Employment Appeal Tribunal found that the decision not to award costs could not be said to be perverse and awarded the applicant the costs of the appeal. The court observed, in considering the award of costs on appeal, that the fact that a case had been allowed through at a preliminary hearing was not a bar to arguing that the appeal was "unnecessary" (*Tesco Stores Ltd & Anor v. Wilson*, January 12, 2000, HHJ Peter Clark EAT).

## F. SPECIAL EDUCATIONAL NEEDS TRIBUNAL

**11–021** In deciding whether or not a child with special needs could go to a particular school the Tribunal erred in preferring the effect of the Education (Special Schools) Regulations 1994 over the provisions of section 9 of the Education Act 1996. On appeal the Education Authority did not contest the issue. The Treasury Solicitor wrote to the court stating that the Tribunal would not be represented and drew the court's attention to the fact that new Regulations had been made: Education (Maintained Special Schools) (England) Regulations 1999. The Tribunal did however seek to oppose the order to pay the costs of the appeal. The court found that the Tribunal should have consented to the appeal being allowed in conformity with the overriding objective of the CPR. Nevertheless the Tribunal's error fell well short of the perversity or flagrant disregard of the principles of justice which was the threshold for a costs order to be made against Justices or tribunals (see *R. v. Lincoln Justices, Ex P. Count* [1996] 8 Admin L.R. 233). The Tribunal's conduct fell just short of the stringent criteria for a costs order (*S v. Metropolitan Borough of Dudley*, [1999] 149 N.L.J. 1904).

# CHAPTER 12—COSTS OF TRUSTEES, PERSONAL REPRESENTATIVES AND UNDER CONTRACT



## A. GENERAL PRINCIPLES

### Add after first paragraph:

Sir Andrew Morritt V.C. issued a Practice Statement (Trust Proceedings: Prospective Costs Orders) on May 12001 (see Appendix U) dealing with the costs of proceedings brought by trustees or beneficiaries or other persons concerned in relation to the administration of a trust including questions of construction, questions relating to the exercise of powers conferred on the trust, or questions as to the validity of the trust. 12–001

### Footnote 4—insert reference:

1893 1 Ch 547 CA. 12–001

## B. COSTS PAYABLE PURSUANT TO A CONTRACT

### Insert at end of second paragraph: 12–006

Where there is a contractual right to costs the discretion under section 51 of the Supreme Court Act 1981 should be exercised so as to reflect that right (*Fairview Investments Ltd v. Sharma*, October 14, 1999, CA (unreported)).

## C. PRE-EMPTIVE COSTS ORDERS IN RESPECT OF TRUSTEES AND OTHER FIDUCIARIES, BENEFICIARIES, DERIVATIVE ACTIONS AND PENSION FUNDS

**Add at end:**

12–007 A policy holder objecting to a proposed scheme of re-organisation of an insurance company was entitled to a pre-emptive costs order in his favour because his position was closely analogous to that of a shareholder bringing a derivative action against the controllers of a company on behalf of the company as a whole, in that he had given consideration in exchange for his interest. The application also enabled the proposed reorganisation to be fully tested by the court (In Re Axa Equity & Law Life Assurance Society Plc; *In Re Axa Sun Life Plc* [2000] EW Ch.D, November 1, Evans-Lombe J.).

12–007 **Delete footnote number 32—substitute:**

CPR rule 19.9 (derivative claims).

### The Special Principle—costs out of a fund

12–010 **Insert at end of paragraph 12–010:**

Under the CPR the court may take a more robust view about costs to be paid out of the trust fund. Where trustees are able and willing to bring proceedings themselves a successful claimant who is a beneficiary will not necessarily be awarded costs out of the fund. (*D'Abo v. Paget (No 2), The Times,* August 10, 2000, Lawrence Collins Q.C.

**Footnote 36—insert reference:**

12–010 1907 2 Ch 406.

**Add at end:**

12–010 The court should avoid the temptation to be swayed by a comparison between the costs of a potential appeal and the funds in a scheme so as to be generous with the money of another. Trusts did not exist to fund litigation by a minority group of members at the expense of its members as a whole but to use its assets for the benefit of all those members in accordance with the rules that defined its existence and purpose: *Chessels v. British Telecommunications Plc* [2001] EWHC Ch.D, December 20, Laddie J. (pre emptive costs order refused).

## Add new paragraph:

## Other Orders for the Costs of Trustees

**12–011** Whilst it is normal practice on an application to the court for directions by trustees for the costs to be paid out of the trust funds, the court has a discretion to diverge from that practice where appropriate. Such a course was held to be appropriate where the trustees had decided to adopt a partisan role, where they had argued positively for a specific outcome in the interests of one class of beneficiary against the interests of another class. In those circumstances the court held that the role adopted by the trustees was not neutral and the trustees had to accept that they might be subject to costs consequences. The existence of an exoneration clause within the trustees' terms of office was no protection against a court order, nor was it a factor which inclined the court to exercise its discretion in the trustees favour (*Breadner v. Granville and Grossman* [2000] EWHC Ch.D, July 17, Park J.).

Where the Charity Commission appointed a receiver and manager of the charity, and subsequently on his advice appointed new trustees and removed the former chairman of trustees, under section 18 of the Charities Act 1993, the former trustee appealed against the appointment of the receiver and applied for an order indemnifying him out of the charity's property in respect of the costs of the appeal. The trustees' application was dismissed and permission to appeal refused by the Court of Appeal on the basis that the trustee had not been acting for the benefit of the charity (by refusing to compromise an earlier action) and was therefore liable to pay the costs (*Weth v. H M Attorney General* [2001] EWHC Ch.D, February 23).

# CHAPTER 13—LIEN AND RECOVERY OF COSTS



## B. THE RETAINING LIEN

### Change of solicitor

### Add at end of first paragraph:

The principles which can be extracted from the authorities include the following: 13–003

(i) the solicitor is entitled to a general lien in respect of his costs on any property belonging to his client which came into his possession in his capacity as a solicitor;
(ii) however a solicitor who has discharged himself is not allowed so to exert his lien as to interfere with the course of justice;
(iii) where a solicitor terminates his retainer his lien does not affect the client's entitlement to an order that papers required for the conduct of pending litigation be delivered to the new solicitor against an undertaking to return them at the end of the litigation, although in exceptional cases the court could attach conditions to such an order;
(iv) the refusal by a solicitor to act unless he was put in funds is generally treated by the court as an effective discharge of his retainer (*Ismail v. Richards Butler* [1996] 2 All E.R. 506).

### Insert at end of paragraph 13–003 13–003

On the question of whether the court has power to override a solicitor's lien where the client has terminated the retainer, as opposed to the solicitor discharging himself, it appears that the jurisdiction does exist and that the court has discretion under rule 25.1(1)(m). On the particular facts of the case an order was made for delivery up of documents notwithstanding the lien and the client was required to pay the amount in dispute into court (*Paragon Finance Plc v. Rosling King*, May 26, 2000, Hart J. (unreported)).

There is no reason in principle why, in appropriate circumstances, a court should not be able to interfere in the enforcement of a common law lien on equitable principles even where it was the client and not the solicitor who had terminated the retainer. The court must be satisfied that there were matters affecting the relationship between the solicitor and the client which, as a matter of conscience, make it inappropriate for the lien to continue and be enforced in particular circumstances: *Slatter v. Ronaldsons* [2001] EWHC Ch.D, December 14, Patten J.

# CHAPTER 14—CHARGING ORDERS



## A. UNDER THE SOLICITORS ACT 1974, s. 73

**Add:**

14–001 Where a claimant brought proceedings for infringement of two chemical processes and was unsuccessful in respect of one of the processes, the claimant was ordered to pay the defendant's costs. The defendant was ordered to take certain steps in relation to the other process which it failed to do. The defendant subsequently went into receivership and its assets were sold to another company. Its solicitors obtained a charging order under the 1974 Act to protect their fees. The claimant sought judgment in default in respect of the process in respect of which the defendant had failed to comply with the directions. The claimant also sought to set off its costs against the costs which it had been ordered to pay the defendant in respect of the other process. The court refused to order set off since, although there would be no prejudice to the defendant in allowing a set off, the existence of the charging order meant that there would be prejudice to the defendant's solicitors. The protection afforded by charging orders under section 73 of the 1974 Act should be upheld unless there were good reasons to come to a contrary decision: *Rohm & Hass Co v. Collag Ltd* [2001] EWHC Ch.D, November 14, Pumfrey J.

### Legal Aid

### Delete title and text—substitute: 14–003

### Community Legal Service Fund

By virtue of section 10(7) of the Access to Justice Act 1999 there is a first charge for the benefit of the CLS Fund on any property, wherever situated.

which is recovered or preserved on behalf of a funded client in the proceedings to which the funding relates.

## B. UNDER THE CHARGING ORDERS ACT 1979

14–006 **Insert at end of second paragraph:**

A charging order takes effect and is enforceable as an equitable charge, so that the holder of a charging order is entitled to add to his security the costs of obtaining possession and sale as against the mortgagor and any third party claiming an interest (*Parker-Tweedale v. Dunbar Bank Plc* (No.2) [1991] Ch 26 and *Ezekiel v. Orakpo* above). The argument that a charging order cannot be made for unassessed costs confuses the jurisdiction to make a charging order under section 1(1) of the 1979 Act, with the rights of the holder of a charging order to add further sums for interest and costs to the security as a result of the terms of section 3(4). In the particular case the court ordered the costs of the proceedings to be paid to the claimants out of the proceeds of sale of the property (*Holder v. Hupperstone* [2000] 1 All E.R. 473 Evans-Lombe J.).

# CHAPTER 15—SECURITY FOR COSTS IN LITIGATION



**Delete first paragraph—substitute:** 15–001

In certain circumstances (Part 25, Part 2) a defendant (or a person who is in the position of a defendant in respect of a Part 20 claim) may apply to the court for security for his costs of the proceedings. (r. 25.12(1)). The application must be supported by written evidence and, where the court makes an order for security it will determine the amount and direct the manner in which and the time within which the security must be given (r. 25.12(2) and (3).

The court will make an order for security if it is satisfied, having regard to all the circumstances of the case, that it is just to do so, one or more of the conditions set out below applies or an enactment permits the court to require security for costs (r. 25.12 and r. 25.13(1)). The conditions to be fulfilled before the court will make an order for security are:

(a) that the claimant is an individual who is ordinarily resident out of the jurisdiction (and is not a person against whom a claim can be enforced under the Brussels Conventions or the Lugano Convention as defined by section 1(1) of the Civil Jurisdiction and Judgments Act 1982);

(b) the claimant is a company or other incorporated body which is ordinarily resident out of the jurisdiction (and is not a body against whom a claim can be enforced under the Brussels Conventions or the Lugano Convention);

(c) the claimant is a company or other body (whether incorporated inside or outside Great Britain) and there is reason to believe that it will be unable to pay the defendant's costs if ordered to do so; (the fact that the claimant's poor financial situation may be due to the defendant's breach of contract may be a reason for not ordering security. *Fernhill Mining Ltd v. Kier Construction Ltd* January 27, 2000 CA (unreported).

(d) the claimant has changed his address since the claim was commenced with a view to evading the consequences of the litigation;

(e) the claimant failed to give his address in the claim form or gave an incorrect address in that form;

(f) the claimant is acting as a nominal claimant (other than as a representative claimant under Part 19) and there is reason to believe that he will be unable to pay the defendant's costs if ordered to do so;

(g) the claimant has taken steps in relation to his assets that would make it difficult to enforce an order for costs against him (r. 25.13(2)).

Where the court makes an order for security it will determine the amount of the security and direct the manner in which and the time within which the security must be given (CPR rule 25.12(3)).

The court may make an order for security for costs against someone other than the claimant on the defendant's application if it is satisfied that it is just to make such an order and one or more of the following conditions applies. The conditions are: that the person has assigned the right to the claim to the claimant with a view to avoiding the possibility of a costs order being made against him; or has contributed or agreed to contribute to the claimant's costs in return for a share of any money or property which the claimant may recover in the proceedings; and is a person against whom a costs order may be made (r. 25.14(1) and r. (2)).

15–001 The purpose of Rule 25.13 is to eliminate any covert discrimination against nationals of other convention states. In the context of the rule "claim" is to be construed as including any claim whether or not a money claim and not limited to an order for costs. The conditions in the rule: (a) confine the jurisdiction to individuals who are not ordinarily residents either in the U.K. or another convention state. Such a claimant cannot deprive the court of jurisdiction by placing an asset in a convention state. The court has jurisdiction under Rule 25.13 to order security to be given by a claimant by reason of the fact that he was an individual claimant who was ordinarily resident out of the jurisdiction and not ordinarily resident in a convention state. On the particular facts of the case in which the claimant had assets in Switzerland, although there was in principle no reason to suppose an order for costs might not be fully enforceable in Switzerland, the court had to take into account the ease with which the assets held there could be moved, including the most valuable asset which was some shares in a U.S. company. Bearing in mind the nature and potential size of the risk security was ordered to be given (*De Beer v. Kanaar & Co* [2001] EW CA Civ, August 9).

The wording of Rule 25.13 was introduced in order to abolish the discriminatory effect under Community Law of the language of the old Rule

*Cheque Point SARL v. McClelland* [1997] QBD 51). Against that background the Rule is to be interpreted as being confined to persons who were nationals or residents of other convention countries. As a matter of discretion it was not just to make an order for security against a foreign company whose ships came so regularly to the ports of the U.K. and of other convention countries that the whereabouts of the vessels could easily be tracked and a judgment easily enforced in the U.K. or another convention country if a vessel owned by the claimant was there. In the circumstances no order for security was made (*White Sea & Omega Shipping v. International Transport Workers Federation* [2001] EW CA Civ, March 7).

The discretion under CPR 25.13 and 25.15 to award security for costs against an individual not resident in a contracting state of the enforcement conventions is to be exercised only on objectively justified grounds relating to obstacles to or the burden of enforcement in the context of the particular individual or country concerned. If there are likely to be no obstacles to or difficulty about enforcement but simply an extra burden in the form of costs or moderate delay the appropriate course is to limit the amount of the security ordered by reference to that potential burden. The mere absence of reciprocal arrangements or legislation providing for enforcement of foreign judgments cannot of itself justify an inference that enforcement would not be possible: *Nasser v. United Bank of Kuwait* [2001] EWCA Civ 556; [2002] 1 All E.R. 401 CA.

## Add to footnote:

15–001

As to ordering security against a claimant who has taken steps in relation to his assets that would make it difficult to enforce an order for costs against him see *Chandler v. Brown* [2001] CP Rep 103 Park J.

## Delete text from footnote 8 to footnote 9 and from footnote 18 to footnote 20.

## Insert at end of paragraph 15–001:

It is appropriate for a judge to have regard to the possibility that a claimant would recover a substantial sum in another action before the time for costs arose in the action in which the application for security is made. The court was right to consider the interrelationship between the two actions when deciding what order for security, if any, to make. (*Cripps v. Heritage Distribution Corporation The Times*, November 10, 1999, CA). An order for security should normally, within its terms, deal with failure to pay and the consequence of that failure would result in a dismissal of the claim without further order of the court (*Clive Brooks & Co Ltd v. Baynard, The Times*,

April 30, 1998, CA and *CTSS Management Services Ltd v. Charism Records,* January 18, 2000, Jacob J. (unreported)).

## Security for costs in the Court of Appeal

**15–002** **Delete text—substitute:**

## Security for costs on an appeal

The court may order security for costs of an appeal on the same ground as it may order security for costs against a claimant under Part 25. Th order may be made against an appellant and/or a respondent who als appeals. Such an order may be made where the person against whom th order is sought is a limited company and there is reason to believe that i will be unable to pay the costs of the other parties to the appeal should it appeal be unsuccessful (r. 25.15(1) and r. (2)). Where, on an appeal th court ordered the claimant to pay security for costs, and the claimant com plied with the order by borrowing that amount from her bank but sub sequently withdrew the appeal, the court found that the money was hel on trust, that it would be returned to the bank if the appeal was successfu or even paid by the claimant under the terms of the loan agreement if th appeal was unsuccessful. The court allowed the money to be repaid to th bank. The court also held that the reasonable costs of complying with th order for security for costs included both the arrangement fee and the inter est payable on the loan, because when the order for security was made i was obvious that the order could not be met out of the claimants ow funds (*R. v. Common Professional Examination Board ex p. Mealing McCleod,* May 2, 2000, CA (unreported)).

## Statutory powers to award security for costs

**15–003** **Delete text—substitute:**

Certain enactments empower the court to require security to be given for the costs of any proceedings. The relevant Acts are: The Companies Act 1985 section 726(1) and the Arbitration Act 1996 section 38(3). The court may make an order for security against someone other than the claimant if it is satisfied, having regard to all the circumstances of the case, that it is just to do so and one or more of the following conditions applies. Those conditions are that the person:

(a) has assigned the right to the claim to the claimant with a view to avoiding the possibility of a costs order being made against him; or

(b) has contributed or agreed to contribute to the claimant's costs in return for a share of any money or property which the claimant may recover in the proceedings; and is a person against whom a costs order may be made (r. 25.14).

## 'he Companies Act 1985, s. 726(1)

### nsert at end of second paragraph: 15–004

'here are well established principles, in the context of liquidators, to the ffect that an adverse costs order made against a company being wound up 'ould be paid in full and in priority to virtually every other claim against ıe insolvent's estate. These principles are based on fairness and justice 'hich also apply to provisional liquidators. A provisional liquidator is xpressly appointed by the court in order to produce a resolution of a ompany's financial problems and has the power to expend the assets of ıe company as seen fit without further order of the court. If a provisional quidator in the pursuance of his powers as officer of the court embarks n litigation, justice requires that the costs should come out of the assets f the company (*Smith v. UIC Insurance Co Ltd*, January 19, 2000 Dean . (unreported)).

The new regime relating to appeals and the requirement to obtain perıission does not alter the approach of the court to security for costs. Vhether an appeal has much merit or not may be a relevant factor but it oes not follow that because permission has been granted therefore security ɔr costs should not be ordered. The real concern is whether it is appropri-te for an appellant to be able to pursue an appeal without running a risk f actually having to pay the costs of the other side if unsuccessful (*Federal ank of the Middle East v. Hadkinson, The Times,* December 7, 1997, A).

## . INTERNATIONAL CONVENTIONS

### 'hird paragraph—amend to read: 15–006

'he Court of Appeal has held that CPR Schedule 1 RSC, Order 23 (see ow Part 25, Part II) does not offend against . . .

**Add at end:**

15–006 There is no inflexible assumption that a person not resident in a Brusse or Lugano state should provide security for costs. The question is wheth security is objectively justified having regard to the difficulties of enforc ment in relation to this particular foreign claimant and country concerne Impecuniosity might be relevant to the issue of enforcement. The absen of reciprocal enforcement arrangements does not justify an inference th enforcement will not be possible (*Nasser v. United Bank of Kuwait* [200 EW CA Civ, April 11).

Security in the form of a charge over property is in principle adequate fulfill an order for security for costs. In the ordinary course of events how ever if a property were valuable enough there would be no difficulty obtaining a secured bank guarantee. In a commercial case the court woul wish to know why undertakings could not be given, or why no secure bank guarantee was possible: *AP (U.K.) Ltd v. West Midlands Fire & Ci Defence Authority* [2001] EWCA Civ, November 16.

# CHAPTER 16—RECOVERY, INTEREST AND REIMBURSEMENT OF COSTS



## INTEREST ON COSTS AND DISBURSEMENTS

### Interest on judgment debts

### Insert at end of first paragraph: 16–007

Interest payable under section 17 of the Judgments Act or under section 74 of the County Courts Act 1984 begins to run from the date that judgment is given, unless a rule of court or Practice Direction makes a different provision or the court orders otherwise. The court has the power to order that interest shall begin to run from a date before the date that judgment is given (r. 40.8(1) and r. (2)).

Where an order is made by a county court requiring the payment of a sum of money, that judgment is registered in the Register Of County Court Judgments. An order for a sum of money to be paid following a summary assessment, other than the final decision in the proceedings, is exempt from registration. (Register of County Court Judgments Regulations 1985).

16–007 Where the Court of Appeal made an order setting aside the costs order made in the lower court, and this had the effect of ordering that interest should run from the date of the Court of Appeal order, the Court of Appeal could not order that the interest should be recoverable on all costs from the date of the Judge's order because the slip rule could not enable the court to have second or additional thoughts. The slip rule did however enable the court to amend an order to give effect to the intention of the court. The court had not intended to alter the general right to interest on costs which had already been ordered. The Court of Appeal order was amended accordingly (*Bristol Myers Squibb Co v. Baker Norton Pharmaceuticals Inc* [2001] EW CA Civ, March 28).

# CHAPTER 17—GENERAL PRINCIPLES OF ASSESSMENT



## THE INDEMNITY PRINCIPLE

### Insert at end of paragraph 17–001: 17–001

There is a presumption that if a party has a solicitor on the record that party is liable to pay the solicitor's costs (*R. v. Miller; R. v. Glennie* [1983] 1 W.L.R. 1056). The party seeking to recover costs does not have to adduce evidence to support the presumption. If the paying party puts the receiving party to proof of his entitlement to costs, the presumption could be relied upon, but where a genuine issue was raised as to whether or not the receiving party has incurred costs, the receiving party should be given notice of the issue and the court should decide whether it requires proof of the liability to pay or whether the paying party's case was insufficient to displace the presumption (*Hazlett v. Sefton Metropolitan Borough Council* [1999] 149 N.L.J. 1869, DC).

### Bailey v. IBC Vehicles Ltd

### Delete footnote number 10—substsitute: 17–003

*Nederlandse Reassurantie Groep Holding NV v. Bacon & Woodrow* (No.4) [1998] 2 Costs L.R. Tucker J.

## B. THE BASIS OF CHARGE

### Add after third paragraph:

17–008 The case of Eastwood quoted above established that the convention method appropriate to assessing a bill of a solicitor in private practice wa also appropriate for the bill of an in-house solicitor in all but special case where it was reasonably plain that that method would infringe the inden nity principle. This had the merit of simplicity and of avoiding the burde of detailed enquiry. A special case could arise under the principles in *Eas wood* where a sum could be identified different from that produced by th conventional approach, which was adequate to cover the actual co incurred in doing all the work done. Such a sum might be identified b concession or by factual assessment of the assessing tribunal itself, but tha possibility did not justify a detailed investigation in every case (*Cole British Telecommunications Plc* [2000] EW CA Civ, July 4).

## D. HOURLY RATES

### Footnote 25: Add:

17–010 and see *Solutia (U.K.) Ltd v. Griffiths* [2001] EW CA Civ 736.

### Advocates

### Add at end of first paragraph footnote:

17–014 See the Higher Courts Qualification Regulations 2000.

### Rights of audience on detailed assessment

### Add:

17–015 The existence or otherwise of a right of audience is determined exclus ively by Part 2 of the Courts & Legal Services Act 1990. If the perso attending is not a solicitor or barrister, or a member of any other authorise body and does not have rights granted by some statute, he may only hav a right of audience in relation to proceedings if "granted by that court i relation to those proceedings". The grant of rights of audience is only t be exercised in exceptional circumstances. The courts should pause lon efore granting rights to individuals who make a practice of seeking to epresent otherwise unrepresented litigants.

With regard to MacKenzie Friends the only right is that of the litigant o have reasonable assistance. A MacKenzie Friend has no right to act as uch. A MacKenzie Friend is not entitled to address the court. If he does o he becomes an advocate and requires the grant of a right of audience. As a general rule a litigant in person who wishes to have a MacKenzie riend should be allowed to do so unless the Judge is satisfied that fairness nd the interests of justice do not so require. The court can prevent a MacKenzie Friend from continuing to act in that capacity where the assistance he gives impedes the efficient administration of justice: *Noueiri v. Paragon Finance Ltd* [2001] EWCA Civ September 19.

## CLAIM AND COUNTERCLAIM

### nsert at end of paragraph 17–016:

17–016

Where a claimant was successful on the claim and a defendant successful n a counterclaim it has been usual for the claimant and the defendant to e awarded the costs of their respective claims (*Chell Engineering v. Unit Tool & Engineering Co* [1950] 1 All E.R. 378). Costs could also be warded on the basis of the issues actually involved in accordance with r. 4.3(4) so as to encourage good litigation practice. It is one thing to award successful claimant a proportion of the costs, it was quite another to order him to pay the defendant's costs. In deciding what order about costs o make it is relevant to good litigation practice to consider the ways in which both sides could have protected themselves as to costs. (*Universal Cycles Plc v. Grangebriar Ltd*, February 8, 2000, CA (unreported)).

### Footnote 36—insert at end:

17–016

nd see *Cartonneries De Thulin SA v. CTP White Knight Ltd* (Costs) 1999] F.S.R. 922, Neuberger J.

## G. COUNSEL'S FEES

### Brief fee and refreshers

### Add after paragraph 17–022:

17–022/1

The court has indicated that the correct approach for assessing brief fees and skeleton argument fees for counsel in the Court of Appeal is in three stages. Stage 1 – the fee for the skeleton argument should be assessed. This will be done largely by reference to the amount of time which counsel has reasonably and proportionately devoted to reading the document researching the law and drafting the skeleton argument. Stage 2 – the bri fee should be assessed. This involves considering both the amount of tim properly spent and many other factors (see rule 44.5). The guidance give by Hobhouse J. in *Loveday v. Renton (No.2)* [1992] 3 All E.R. 184 at 19 is still effective. In relation to a brief fee for the Court of Appeal it i important to avoid double payment. In so far as counsel has prepare whilst drafting the skeleton argument that preparation time should not b paid for in the brief fee. Stage 3 – having arrived at an appropriate skeleto argument fee and brief fee a cross check should then be done, the tw figures should be aggregated to see whether the total is too large or to small for the overall conduct of the case in the Court of Appeal. If the tota figure seems to be disproportionately large or disproportionately small the an appropriate adjustment should be made to the brief fee or the skeleto argument fee (*per* Jackson J. in *Hornsby v. Clarke Kenneth Leventha* [2000] EWHC QBD, June 19).

## H. EXPERTS

### Add after paragraph 17–026

**17–026/1** In general the work of a party's employees in investigating, formulatin and prosecuting a claim by legal proceedings does not qualify for an orde for the payment of costs of and incidental to those proceedings. The excep tion to the general rule is in Re: *Nossen's Letter Patent* [1969] 1 W.L.R 638 where the court held that the reasonable actual and direct costs o employed experts conducting experiments for the purpose of the proceed ings were recoverable. More recently the court has found that the reason able costs of claimant's expert employees in investigating, formulating an presenting claims against a defendant are potentially recoverable from th time that the claimant formed its suspicions that the defendant was com mitting the wrongs which were the subject of the claim. The costs coul not include any element of overhead recovery or of profit. Whether th work of the claimant's employees qualifies for inclusion in an order fo costs depends on whether the employees are truly experts and on the natur of the work carried out: *Admiral Management Services Ltd v. Para Protec Europe Ltd* [2002] EWHC Ch.D, 233 Stanley Burnton J.

# SUPPLEMENTARY MATERIALS

# APPENDIX C

**elete paragraph C-002 and substitute with:**

**ontents of the claim form**

.2 Where the claimant uses the Part 8 procedure the claim form must state— C–002

(a) that this Part applies;
(b) (i) the question which the claimant wants the court to decide; or
(ii) the remedy which the claimant is seeking and the legal basis for the claim to that remedy;
(c) if the claim is being made under an enactment, what that enactment is;
(d) if the claimant is claiming in a representative capacity, what that capacity is; and
(e) if the defendant is sued in a representative capacity, what that capacity is.

Part 22 provides for the claim form to be verified by a statement of truth)
(Rule 7.5 provides for service of the claim form)
(The costs practice direction sets out the information about a funding arrangement to be provided with the claim form where the claimant intends to seek to ecover an additional liability)
("Funding arrangement" and "additional liability" are defined in rule 43.2)

**ssue of claim form without naming defendants**

**.2A**

(1) A practice direction may set out the circumstances in which the court may give permission for a claim form to be issued under this Part without naming a defendant.
(2) An application for permission must be made by application notice before the claim form is issued.
(3) The application notice for permission —

(a) need not be served on any other person; and
(b) must be accompanied by a copy of the claim form that the applicant proposes to issue.

(4) Where the court gives permission it will give directions about the future management of the claim.

**elete paragraph C-003 and substitute with:**

**cknowledgment of service**

**.3** C–003

(1) The defendant must—

(a) file an acknowledgment of service in the relevant practice form not more than 14 days after service of the claim form; and
(b) serve the acknowledgment of service on the claimant and any other party.

(2) The acknowledgment of service must state—

(a) whether the defendant contests the claim; and
(b) if the defendant seeks a different remedy from that set out in the clai form, what that remedy is.

(3) The following rules of Part 10 (acknowledgment of service) apply—

(a) rule 10.3(2) (exceptions to the period for filing an acknowledgment c service); and
(b) rule 10.5 (contents of acknowledgment of service).

(4) Part 11 (disputing the court's jurisdiction) applies subject to the modifica tion that in rule 11(4)(a) and (5)(b) (time limit for application disputin court's jurisdiction) references to the period for filing a defence are treate as if they were references to a period of 14 days from the filing of a acknowledgment of service.

(The costs practice direction sets out the information about a funding arrangemer to be provided with the acknowledgment of service where the defendant intends t seek to recover an additional liability)

("Funding arrangement" and "additional liability" are defined in rule 43.2)

# APPENDIX D

**Delete 2.2 and substitute:**

D–002

**2.2** Where a claimant uses the Part 8 procedure, the claim form (practice form N208) should be used and must state the matters set out in rule 8.2 and, if paragraphs 1.2 or 1.3 apply, must comply with the requirements of the practice direction in question. In particular, the claim form must state that Part 8 applies; a Part 8 claim form means a claim form which so states.

(The Costs Practice Direction supplementing Parts 43 to 48 contains details of the information required to be filed with a claim form to comply with rule 44.15 (providing information about funding arrangements))

**Delete existing claim form and substitute:**

**Claim form**

D–013

**A.3** The claimant must use the Part 8 claim form.

**Table 1**

| | |
|---|---|
| RSC 0.17, r.3(1) | Interpleader (Mode of application) |
| RSC 0.50, r.9A | Charging orders, Stop orders etc., Enforcement of charging order by sale |
| RSC 0.50, r.10(2) | Charging orders, Stop orders etc., Funds in court: Stop order |
| RSC 0.50, r.14(4) | Charging orders, Stop orders etc., Withdrawal etc. of Stop Notice |
| RSC 0.50, r.15(2) | Charging orders, Stop orders etc., Order prohibiting transfer, etc., of securities |
| RSC 0.71, r.2(1) | Reciprocal Enforcement of Judgments and Enforcement of European Community Judgments and Recommendations etc. under The Merchant Shipping (Liner Conferences) Act 1982 (I Reciprocal Enforcement: The Administration of Justice Act 1920 and the Foreign Judgments (Reciprocal Enforcement) Act 1933 - Application for registration) |
| RSC 0.71, r.38 | Reciprocal Enforcement of Judgments and Enforcement of European Community Judgments and Recommendations etc. under The Merchant Shipping (Liner Conferences) Act 1982 (III Reciprocal Enforcement: The Civil Jurisdiction and Judgments Act 1982 - Enforcement of United Kingdom Judgments in other Parts of the United Kingdom: Non-money Provisions) |
| RSC 0.71, r.41 | Reciprocal Enforcement of Judgments and Enforcement of European Community Judgments and Recommendations etc. under The Merchant Shipping (Liner Conferences) Act 1982 (IV Enforcement of Recommendations etc. under the Merchant Shipping (Liner Conferences) Act 1982 – Application for registration) |

Table 1—*continued*

| | |
|---|---|
| RSC 0.77, r.11 | Proceedings by and against the Crown (Interpleader: Application for order against Crown) |
| RSC 0.77, r.16(2) | Proceedings by and against the Crown (Attachment of debts, etc.) |
| RSC 0.77, r.17(1) | Proceedings by and against the Crown (Proceedings relating to postal packets) |
| RSC 0.77, r.18(1) | Proceedings by and against the Crown (Applications under sections 17 and 29 of Crown Proceedings Act) |
| RSC 0.79, r.8(2) | Criminal Proceedings (Estreat of recognizances) |
| RSC 0.79, r.9(2) | Criminal Proceedings (Bail) |
| RSC 0.79, r.10(2) | Criminal Proceedings (Issue of witness summons, etc.) |
| RSC 0.79, r.11(1) | Criminal Proceedings (Application for warrant to arrest witness) |
| RSC 0.81, r.10(1) | Partners (Applications for orders charging partner's interest in partnership property) |
| RSC 0.82, r.8(2) | Defamation claims (Fulfilment of offer of amends under section 4 of the Defamation Act 1952) |
| RSC 0.88, r.3 | Mortgage claims (Commencement of claim)[1] |
| RSC 0.92, r.5(2) | Lodgment, Investment etc. of Funds in Court: Chancery Division (Applications with respect to funds in court) |
| RSC 0.93, r.5(2) | Applications and Appeals to High Court under Various Acts: Chancery Division (Applications under section 2(3) of the Public Order Act 1936) |
| RSC 0.93, r.6(2) | Applications and Appeals to High Court under Various Acts: Chancery Division (Application under the Variation of Trusts Act 1958) |
| RSC 0.93, r.18(2) | Applications and Appeals to High Court under Various Acts: Chancery Division (Proceedings under section 86 of the Civil Aviation Act 1982) |
| RSC 0.93, r.20(2) | Applications and Appeals to High Court under Various Acts: Chancery Division (Proceedings under section 50 of the Administration of Justice Act 1985) |
| RSC 0.93, r.21 | Applications and Appeals to High Court under Various Acts: Chancery Division (Proceedings under section 48 of the Administration of Justice Act 1985) |
| RSC 0.93, r.23(2)(a) | Applications and Appeals to High Court under Various Acts: Chancery Division (Proceedings under the Banking Act 1987: applications under sections 26(3), 71(3) and (5) and 77(3) and (5)). |
| RSC 0.94, r.5 | Applications and Appeals to High Court under Various Acts: Queen's Bench Division (Exercise of jurisdiction under Representation of the People Acts) |

[1] This type of claim may also be brought by the Part 8 procedure in Section B.

Table 1—*continued*

| | |
|---|---|
| RSC 0.95, r.2(1) | Bills of Sale Acts 1878 and 1882 and the Industrial and Provident Societies Act 1967 (Entry of satisfaction) |
| RSC 0.95, r.3 | Bills of Sale Acts 1878 and 1882 and the Industrial and Provident Societies Act 1967 (Restraining removal on sale of goods seized) |
| RSC 0.96, r.1 | The Mines (Working Facilities and Support) Act 1966 etc. (Assignment to Chancery Division) |
| RSC 0.96, r.3 | The Mines (Working Facilities and Support) Act 1966 etc. (Issue of claim form) |
| RSC 0.97, r.2 | The Landlord and Tenant Acts 1927, 1954 and 1987 (Assignment of proceedings to Chancery Division etc.) |
| RSC 0.97, r.5 | The Landlord and Tenant Acts 1927, 1954 and 1987 (Proceedings under Part I of the Act of 1927) |
| RSC 0.97, r.6(1) | The Landlord and Tenant Acts 1927, 1954 and 1987 (Application for new tenancy under section 24 of the Act of 1954) |
| RSC 0.97, r.6A(1) | The Landlord and Tenant Acts 1927, 1954 and 1987 (Application to authorise agreement) |
| RSC 0.97, r.9A(1)(b) | The Landlord and Tenant Acts 1927, 1954 and 1987 (Application to determine interim rent) |
| RSC 0.97, r.14 | The Landlord and Tenant Acts 1927, 1954 and 1987 (Application under section 19 of the Act of 1987) |
| RSC 0.97, r.15(3) | The Landlord and Tenant Acts 1927, 1954 and 1987 (Application for order under section 24 of the Act of 1987) |
| RSC 0.97, r.16(3) | The Landlord and Tenant Acts 1927, 1954 and 1987 (Application for acquisition order under section 29 of the Act of 1987) |
| RSC 0.99, r.3(1) | Inheritance (Provision for Family and Dependants) Act 1975 (Application for Financial Provision) (High Court and County Court Cases) |
| RSC 0.106, r.3(2) | Proceedings Relating to Solicitors: The Solicitors Act 1974 (Power to order solicitor to deliver cash account etc.) |
| RSC 0.106, r.6(2) | Proceedings Relating to Solicitors: The Solicitors Act 1974 (Applications under schedule 1 to the Act) |
| RSC 0.106, r.8(1) | Proceedings Relating to Solicitors: The Solicitors Act 1974 (Interim order restricting payment out of banking account) |
| RSC 0.109, r.1(3) | Administration Act 1960 (Applications under Act) |
| RSC 0.113, r.1 | Summary proceedings for possession of land (Proceedings to be brought by claim form) |

# CPR Part 19

## III Group Litigation

### Definition

D–023 19.10 A Group Litigation Order ("GLO") means an order made under rule 19.11 to provide for the case management of claims which give rise to common or related issues of fact or law (the "GLO issues").

### Group Litigation Order

D–024 19.11

(1) The court may make a GLO where there are or are likely to be a number of claims giving rise to the GLO issues.

(The practice direction provides the procedure for applying for a GLO)

(2) A GLO must —

(a) contain directions about the establishment of a register (the "group register") on which the claims managed under the GLO will be entered;
(b) specify the GLO issues which will identify the claims to be managed as a group under the GLO; and
(c) specify the court (the "management court") which will manage the claims on the group register.

(3) A GLO may —

(a) in relation to claims which raise one or more of the GLO issues —
(i) direct their transfer to the management court;
(ii) order their stay (GL) until further order; and
(iii) direct their entry on the group register;
(b) direct that from a specified date claims which raise one or more of the GLO issues should be started in the management court and entered on the group register; and
(c) give directions for publicising the GLO.

### Effect of the GLO

D–025 19.12

(1) Where a judgment or order is given or made in a claim on the group register in relation to one or more GLO issues —

(a) that judgment or order is binding on the parties to all other claims that are on the group register at the time the judgment is given or the order is made unless the court orders otherwise; and
(b) the court may give directions as to the extent to which that judgment or order is binding on the parties to any claim which is subsequently entered on the group register.

(2) Unless paragraph (3) applies, any party who is adversely affected by a judgment or order which is binding on him may seek permission to appeal the order.
(3) A party to a claim which was entered on the group register after a judgment or order which is binding on him was given or made may not —

(a) apply for the judgment or order to be set aside (GL), varied or stayed (GL); or

(b) appeal the judgment or order,

but may apply to the court for an order that the judgment or order is not binding on him.

(4) Unless the court orders otherwise, disclosure of any document relating to the GLO issues by a party to a claim on the group register is disclosure of that document to all parties to claims —

(a) on the group register; and
(b) which are subsequently entered on the group register.

**Case Management**

**19.13** **D–026**

Directions given by the management court may include directions —

(a) varying the GLO issues;
(b) providing for one or more claims on the group register to proceed as test claims;
(c) appointing the solicitor of one or more parties to be the lead solicitor for the claimants or defendants;
(d) specifying the details to be included in a statement of case in order to show that the criteria for entry of the claim on the group register have been met;
(e) specifying a date after which no claim may be added to the group register unless the court gives permission; and
(f) for the entry of any particular claim which meets one or more of the GLO issues on the group register.

(Part 3 contains general provisions about the case management powers of the court)

**Removal from the Register**

**19.14** **D–027**

(1) A party to a claim entered on the group register may apply to the management court for the claim to be removed from the register.
(2) If the management court orders the claim to be removed from the register it may give directions about the future management of the claim.

**Test Claims**

**19.15** **D–028**

(1) Where a direction has been given for a claim on the group register to proceed as a test claim and that claim is settled, the management court may order that another claim on the group register be substituted as the test claim.
(2) Where an order is made under paragraph (1), any order made in the test claim before the date of substitution is binding on the substituted claim unless the court orders otherwise.

## Practice Direction Supplementing Part 19

**Costs**

**16.1** CPR 48 contains rules about costs where a GLO has been made. **D–029**

**16.2** Where the court has made an order about costs in relation to any application or hearing which involved both —

(1) one or more of the GLO issues; and
(2) an issue or issues relevant only to individual claims;

and the court has not directed the proportion of the costs that is to relate to common costs and the proportion that is to relate to individual costs in accordance with rule 48.6A(5), the costs judge will make a decision as to the relevant proportions at or before the commencement of the detailed assessment of costs.

## CPR Part 25

### Security for costs

D–030 25.12

(1) A defendant to any claim may apply under this Section of this Part for security for his costs of the proceedings.
(Part 3 provides for the court to order payment of sums into court in other circumstances. Rule 20.3 provides for this Section of this Part to apply to Part 20 claims)
(2) An application for security for costs must be supported by written evidence.
(3) Where the court makes an order for security for costs, it will —
  (a) determine the amount of security; and
  (b) direct —
    (i) the manner in which; and
    (ii) the time within which
  the security must be given.

**Conditions to be Satisfied**

D–031 25.13

(1) The court may make an order for security for costs under rule 25.12 if —
  (a) it is satisfied, having regard to all the circumstances of the case, that it is just to make such an order; and
  (b) (i) one or more of the conditions in paragraph (2) applies, or
    (ii) an enactment permits the court to require security for costs.
(2) The conditions are —
  (a) the claimant is an individual —
    (i) who is ordinarily resident out of the jurisdiction; and
    (ii) is not a person against whom a claim can be enforced under the Brussels Conventions of the Lugano Convention, as defined by section 1(1) of the Civil Jurisdiction and Judgments Act 1982[43];
  (b) the claimant is a company or other incorporated body —
    (i) which is ordinarily resident out of the jurisdiction; and
    (ii) is not a body against whom a claim can be enforced under the Brussels Conventions or the Lugano Convention;
  (c) the claimant is a company or other body (whether incorporated inside or outside Great Britain) and there is reason to believe that it will be unable to pay the defendant's costs if ordered to do so;
  (d) the claimant has changed his address since the claim was commenced with a view to evading the consequences of the litigation;
  (e) the claimant failed to give his address in the claim form, or gave an incorrect address in that form;
  (f) the claimant is acting as a nominal claimant, other than as a representative claimant under Part 19, and there is reason to believe that he will be unable to pay the defendant's costs if ordered to do so;

(g) the claimant has taken steps in relation to his assets that would make it difficult to enforce an order for costs against him.

(Rule 3.4 allows the court to strike out a statement of case and Part 24 for it to give summary judgment)

**Security for costs other than from the claimant**

**25.14** **D–032**

(1) The defendant may seek an order against someone other than the claimant, and the court may make an order for security for costs against that person if —

  (a) it is satisfied, having regard to all the circumstances of the case, that it is just to make such an order; and
  (b) one or more of the conditions in paragraph (2) applies.

(2) The conditions are that the person —

  (a) has assigned the right to the claim to the claimant with a view to avoiding the possibility of a costs order being made against him; or
  (b) has contributed or agreed to contribute to the claimant's costs in return for a share of any money or property which the claimant may recover in the proceedings; and

is a person against whom a costs order may be made.
(Rule 48.2 makes provision for costs orders against non-parties)

**Security for costs of an appeal**

**25.15** **D–033**

(1) The court may order security for costs of an appeal against —

  (a) an appellant;
  (b) a respondent who also appeals,

on the same grounds as it may order security for costs against a claimant under this Part.

(2) The court may also make an order under paragraph (1) where the appellant, or the respondent who also appeals, is a limited company and there is reason to believe it will be unable to pay the costs of the other parties to the appeal should its appeal be unsuccessful.

# APPENDIX E

**Delete E–002 substitute**

**Definitions and application**

**43.2** E–002

(1) In Parts 44 to 48, unless the context otherwise requires—

(a) "'costs" includes fees, charges, disbursements, expenses, remuneration, reimbursement allowed to a litigant in person under rule 48.6, any additional liability incurred under a funding arrangement and any fee or reward charged by a lay representative for acting on behalf of a party in proceedings allocated to the small claims track;

(b) "costs judge" means a taxing master of the Supreme Court;

(c) "costs officer" means—

(i) a costs judge;

(ii) a district judge; and

(iii) an authorised court officer;

(d) "authorised court officer" means any officer of—

(i) a county court;

(ii) a district registry;

(iii) the Principal Registry of the Family Division; or

(iv) the Supreme Court Costs Office,

whom the Lord Chancellor has authorised to assess costs.

(e) "fund" includes any estate or property held for the benefit of any person or class of person and any fund to which a trustee or personal representative is entitled in his capacity as such;

(f) "receiving party" means a party entitled to be paid costs;

(g) "paying party" means a party liable to pay costs;

(h) "assisted person" means an assisted person within the statutory provisions relating to legal aid;

(i) "LSC funded client" means an individual who receives services funded by the Legal Services Commission as part of the Community Legal Service within the meaning of Part I of the Access to Justice Act 1999;

(j) "fixed costs" means the amounts which are to be allowed in respect of solicitors' charges in the circumstances set out in Part 45.

(k) "funding arrangement" means an arrangement where a person has —

(i) entered into a conditional fee agreement or a collective conditional fee agreement which provides for a success fee within the meaning of section 58(2) of the Courts and Legal Services Act 1990[6];

[6] 1990 c. 41. Section 58 was substituted by section 27 of the Access to Justice Act 1999 with effect from 1st April 2000 (the Access to Justice Act 1999 (Commencement No. 3, Transitional Provisions and Savings) Order 2000, S.I. 2000/774 and the Access to Justice Act 1999 (Transitional Provisions) Order 2000, S.I. 2000/900).

(ii) taken out an insurance policy to which section 29 of the Access to Justice Act 1999 (recovery of insurance premiums by way of costs) applies; or

(iii) made an agreement with a membership organisation to meet his legal costs;

(l) "percentage increase" means the percentage by which the amount of a legal representative's fee can be increased in accordance with a conditional fee agreement which provides for a success fee;

(m) "insurance premium" means a sum of money paid or payable for insurance against the risk of incurring a costs liability in the proceedings, taken out after the event that is the subject matter of the claim;

(n) "membership organisation" means a body prescribed for the purposes of section 30 of the Access to Justice Act 1999 (recovery where body undertakes to meet costs liabilities); and

(o) "additional liability" means the percentage increase, the insurance premium, or the additional amount in respect of provision made by a membership organisation, as the case may be.

(The Conditional Fee Agreements Regulations 2000[7], the Collective Conditional Fee Agreements Regulations 2000[8] and the Access to Justice (Membership Organisations) Regulations 2000[9] contain further provisions about conditional fee agreements and arrangements to meet costs liabilities)

(2) The costs to which Parts 44 to 48 apply include—

(a) the following costs where those costs may be assessed by the court—
   (i) costs of proceedings before an arbitrator or umpire;
   (ii) costs of proceedings before a tribunal or other statutory body; and
   (iii) costs payable by a client to his solicitor; and

(b) costs which are payable by one party to another party under the terms of a contract, where the court makes an order for an assessment of those costs.

**Costs orders relating to funding arrangements**

E–007 **44.3A**

(1) The court will not assess any additional liability until the conclusion of the proceedings, or the part of the proceedings, to which the funding arrangement relates.

("Funding arrangement" and "additional liability" are defined in rule 43.2)

(2) At the conclusion of the proceedings, or the part of the proceedings, to which the funding arrangement relates the court may —

(a) make a summary assessment of all the costs, including any additional liability;

(b) make an order for detailed assessment of the additional liability but make a summary assessment of the other costs; or

(c) make an order for detailed assessment of all the costs.

(Part 47 sets out the procedure for the detailed assessment of costs)

**Limits on recovery under funding arrangements**

**44.3B**

(1) A party may not recover as an additional liability —

(a) any proportion of the percentage increase relating to the cost to the legal representative of the postponement of the payment of his fees and expenses;

(b) any provision made by a membership organisation which exceeds the likely cost to that party of the premium of an insurance policy against the risk of incurring a liability to pay the costs of other parties to the proceedings;
(c) any additional liability for any period in the proceedings during which he failed to provide information about a funding arrangement in accordance with a rule, practice direction or court order;
(d) any percentage increase where a party has failed to comply with —
 (i) a requirement in the costs practice direction; or
 (ii) a court order,
to disclose in any assessment proceedings the reasons for setting the percentage increase at the level stated in the conditional fee agreement.

(2) his rule does not apply in an assessment under rule 48.9 (assessment of a solicitor's bill to his client).

(Rule 3.9 sets out the circumstances the court will consider on an application for relief from a sanction for failure to comply with any rule, practice direction or court order)

**Delete paragraph E-008 and substitute:**

**Basis of assessment**

**44.4** **E–008**

(1) Where the court is to assess the amount of costs (whether by summary or detailed assessment) it will assess those costs—

(a) on the standard basis; or
(b) on the indemnity basis,

but the court will not in either case allow costs which have been unreasonably incurred or are unreasonable in amount.

(Rule 48.3 sets out how the court decides the amount of costs payable under a contract)

(2) Where the amount of costs is to be assessed on the standard basis, the court will—

(a) only allow costs which are proportionate to the matters in issue; and
(b) resolve any doubt which it may have as to whether costs were reasonably incurred or reasonable and proportionate in amount in favour of the paying party.

(Factors which the court may take into account are set out in rule 44.5)

(3) Where the amount of costs is to be assessed on the indemnity basis, the court will resolve any doubt which it may have as to whether costs were reasonably incurred or were reasonable in amount in favour of the receiving party.
(4) Where—

(a) the court makes an order about costs without indicating the basis on which the costs are to be assessed; or
(b) the court makes an order for costs to be assessed on a basis other than the standard basis or the indemnity basis,

the costs will be assessed on the standard basis.
(6) Where the amount of a solicitor's remuneration in respect of non-contentious business is regulated by any general orders made under the

Solicitors Act 1974[66], the amount of the costs to be allowed in respect o any such business which falls to be assessed by the court will be decided ir accordance with those general orders rather than this rule and rule 44.5.

**Delete paragraph E-012 and substitute:**

**Time for complying with an order for costs**

E–012 **44.8**

A party must comply with an order for the payment of costs within 14 days of—

(a) the date of the judgment or order if it states the amount of those costs; or
(b) if the amount of those costs (or part of them) is decided later in accordance with Part 47, the date of the certificate which states the amount.
(c) in either case, such later date as the court may specify.

(Part 47 sets out the procedure for detailed assessment of costs)

**Insert after 44.12 in paragraph E-016:**

**Costs-only proceedings**

E–016 **44.12A**

(1) This rule sets out a procedure which may be followed where —

(a) the parties to a dispute have reached an agreement on all issues (including which party is to pay the costs) which is made or confirmed in writing; but
(b) they have failed to agree the amount of those costs; and
(c) no proceedings have been started.

(2) Either party to the agreement may start proceedings under this rule by issuing a claim form in accordance with Part 8.
(3) The claim form must contain or be accompanied by the agreement or confirmation.
(4) In proceedings to which this rule applies the court —

(a) may
  (i) make an order for costs; or
  (ii) dismiss the claim; and
(b) must dismiss the claim if it is opposed.

(5) Rule 48.3 (amount of costs where costs are payable pursuant to a contract) does not apply to claims started under the procedure in this rule. (Rule 7.2 provides that proceedings are started when the court issues a claim form at the request of the claimant)

(Rule 8.1(6) provides that a practice direction may modify the Part 8 procedure)

[66] 1974 c. 47.

**Delete paragraph E-017 and substitute:**

**Special situations**

**44.13**

(1) Where the court makes an order which does not mention costs -

(a) the general rule is that no party is entitled to costs in relation to that order; but

(b) this does not affect any entitlement of a party to recover costs out of a fund held by him as trustee or personal representative, or pursuant to any lease, mortgage or other security.

(2) The court hearing an appeal may, unless it dismisses the appeal, make orders about the costs of the proceedings giving rise to the appeal as well as the costs of the appeal.

(3) Where proceedings are transferred from one court to another, the court to which they are transferred may deal with all the costs, including the costs before the transfer.

(4) Paragraph 3 is subject to any order of the court which ordered the transfer.

**Delete paragraph E-018 and substitute:**

**Court's powers in relation to misconduct**

**44.14** **E–018**

(1) The court may make an order under this rule where—

(a) a party or his legal representative fails to conduct detailed assessment proceedings in accordance with Part 47 or any direction of the court; or

(b) it appears to the court that the conduct of a party or his legal representative, before or during the proceedings which gave rise to the assessment proceedings, was unreasonable or improper.

(2) Where paragraph (1) applies, the court may—

(a) disallow all or part of the costs which are being assessed; or

(b) order the party at fault or his legal representative to pay costs which he has caused any other party to incur.

(3) Where—

(a) the court makes an order under paragraph (2) against a legally represented party; and

(b) the party is not present when the order is made,

the party's solicitor must notify his client in writing of the order no later than 7 days after the solicitor receives notice of the order.

(Other rules about costs can be found—

(a) in Schedule 1, in the following RSC - O.45 (court may order act to be done at the expense of disobedient party); O.47 (writ of fieri facias to enforce payment of costs); and

(b) in Schedule 2, in the following CCR - O.27 (attachment of earnings - judgment creditor's entitlement to costs); O.28 (costs on judgment summons); O.30 (garnishee proceedings - judgment creditor's entitlement to costs); O.49 (costs incurred in making a payment in under section 63 of the Trustee Act 1925 to be assessed by the detailed procedure)).

**Providing information about funding arrangements**

E–018/1 44.15

(1) A party who seeks to recover an additional liability must provide information about the funding arrangement to the court and to other parties as required by a rule, practice direction or court order.
(2) Where the funding arrangement has changed, and the information a party has previously provided in accordance with paragraph (1) is no longer accurate, that party must file notice of the change and serve it on all other parties within 7 days.
(3) Where paragraph (2) applies, and a party has already filed —

(a) an allocation questionnaire; or
(b) a listing questionnaire,

he must file and serve a new estimate of costs with the notice.

(The costs practice direction sets out —

- the information to be provided when a party issues or responds to a claim form, files an allocation questionaire, a listing questionnaire, and a claim for costs;
- the meaning of estimate of costs and the information required in it)
(Rule 44.3B sets out situations where a party will not recover a sum representing any additional liability)

**Adjournment where legal representative seeks to challenge disallowance of any amount of percentage increase**

E–018/2 44.16

Where—

(a) the court disallows any amount of a legal representative's percentage increase in summary or detailed assessment proceedings; and
(b) the legal representative applies for an order that the disallowed amount should continue to be payable by his client,

the court may adjourn the hearing to allow the legally represented party to be notified of the order sought.

(Regulation 3(2)(b) of the Conditional Fee Agreements Regulations 2000 provides that a conditional fee agreement which provides for a success fee must state that any amount of a percentage increase disallowed on assessment ceases to be payable unless the court is satisfied that it should continue to be so payable. Regulation 5(2)(b) of the Collective Conditional Fee Agreements Regulations 2000 makes similar provision in relation to collective conditional fee agreements)

**Application of costs rules**

E–018/3 44.17

This Part and Part 45 (fixed costs), Part 46 (fast track trial costs), Part 47 (procedure for detailed assessment of costs and default provisions) and Part 48 (special cases), do not apply to the assessment of costs in proceedings to the extent that —

(a) section 11 of the Access to Justice Act 1999, and provisions made under that Act, or
(b) regulations made under the Legal Aid Act 1989[9],

[9] 1998 c. 34.

make different provision. (The costs practice direction sets out the procedure to be followed where a party was wholly or partially funded by the Legal Services Commission).

**Delete paragraph E-019 and substitute:**

**Scope of this part**

**45.1**

(1) This Part sets out the amounts which, unless the court orders otherwise, are to be allowed in respect of solicitors' charges in the cases to which this Part applies.
(The definitions contained in Part 43 are relevant to this Part)

(2) This part applies where-

(a) the only claim is a claim for a specified sum of money where the value of the claim exceeds £25 and—
 (i) judgment in default is obtained under rule 12.4(1);
 (ii) judgment on admission is obtained under rule 14.4(3);
 (iii) judgment on admission on part of the claim is obtained under rule 14.5(6);
 (iv) summary judgment is given under Part 24;
 (v) the court has made an order to strike out (GL) a defence under rule 3.4(2)(a) as disclosing no reasonable grounds for defending the claim; or
 (vi) rule 45.3 applies; or

(b) the only claim is a claim where the court gave a fixed date for the hearing when it issued the claim and judgment is given for the delivery of goods, and the value of the claim exceeds £25; or;

(c) a judgment creditor has taken steps under Parts 70 to 73 to enforce a judgment or order.
(The practice direction supplementing rule 7.9 sets out the types of case where a court may give a fixed date for a hearing when it issues a claim)

**Insert after 45.5 in paragraph E-023:**

**Fixed enforcement costs**

45.6 The table in this rule (Table 4) shows the amount to be allowed in respect of solicitors' costs in the circumstances mentioned. The amounts shown in Table 3 are to be allowed in addition, if applicable.

TABLE 4 *FIXED ENFORCEMENT COSTS*

| | |
|---|---|
| For an application under rule 70.5(4) that an award may be enforced as if payable under a court order, where the amount outstanding under the award: | |
| exceeds £25 but does not exceed £250 | £30.75 |
| exceeds £250 but does not exceed £600 | £41.00 |
| exceeds £600 but does not exceed £2,000 | £69.50 |
| exceeds £2,000 | £75.50 |

| | |
|---|---|
| On attendance to question a judgment debtor (or officer of a company or other corporation) who has been ordered to attend court under rule 71.2 where the questioning takes place before a court officer, including attendance by a responsible representative of the solicitor: | for each half-hour or part, £15.00 |
| | (When the questioning takes place before a judge, he may summarily assess any costs allowed.) |
| On the making of a final third party debt order under rule 72.8(6)(a) or an order for the payment to the judgment creditor of money in court under rule 72.10(1)(b): | |
| if the amount recovered is less than £150 | one-half of the amount recovered |
| otherwise | £98.50 |
| On the making of a final charging order under rule 73.8(2)(a): | £110.00 |
| | The court may also allow reasonable disbursements in respect of search fees and the registration of the order. |

**Delete paragraph E-026 and substitute:**

**Power to award more or less than the amount of fast track trial costs**

E–026 **46.3**

(1) This rule sets out when a court may award—

(a) an additional amount to the amount of fast track trial costs shown in the table in rule 46.2(1); and
(b) less than those amounts.

(2) If—

(a) in addition to the advocate, a party's legal representative attends the trial;
(b) the court considers that it was necessary for a legal representative to attend to assist the advocate; and
(c) the court awards fast track trial costs to that party,

the court may award an additional £250 in respect of the legal representative's attendance at the trial.

(Legal representative is defined in rule 2.3)

(2A)The court may in addition award a sum representing an additional liability.

(The requirements to provide information about a funding arrangement where a party wishes to recover any additional liability under a funding arrangement are set out in the costs practice direction)

("Additional liability" is defined in rule 43.2)

(3) If the court considers that it is necessary to direct a separate trial of an issue then the court may award an additional amount in respect of the separate trial but that amount is limited in accordance with paragraph (4) of this rule.
(4) The additional amount the court may award under paragraph 3 must not

exceed two-thirds of the amount payable for that claim, subject to a minimum award of £350.

(5) Where the party to whom fast track trial costs are to be awarded is a litigant in person, the court will award—

(a) if the litigant in person can prove financial loss, two-thirds of the amount that would otherwise be awarded; or
(b) if the litigant in person fails to prove financial loss, an amount in respect of the time spent reasonably doing the work at the rate specified in the costs practice direction.

(6) Where a defendant has made a counterclaim against the claimant, and—

(a) the claimant has succeeded on his claim; and
(b) the defendant has succeeded on his counterclaim,

the court will quantify the amount of the award of fast track trial costs to which—

(i) but for the counterclaim, the claimant would be entitled for succeeding on his claim; and
(ii) but for the claim, the defendant would be entitled for succeeding on his counterclaim,

and make one award of the difference, if any, to the party entitled to the higher award of costs.

(7) Where the court considers that the party to whom fast track trial costs are to be awarded has behaved unreasonably or improperly during the trial, it may award that party an amount less than would otherwise be payable for that claim, as it considers appropriate.
(8) Where the court considers that the party who is to pay the fast track trial costs has behaved improperly during the trial the court may award such additional amount to the other party as it considers appropriate.

**Delete paragraph E-035 and substitute:**

**Sanction for delay in commencing detailed assessment proceedings**

**47.8** **E–035**

(1) Where the receiving party fails to commence detailed assessment proceedings within the period specified—

(a) in rule 47.7; or
(b) by any direction of the court,

the paying party may apply for an order requiring the receiving party to commence detailed assessment proceedings within such time as the court may specify.

(2) On an application under paragraph (1), the court may direct that, unless the receiving party commences detailed assessment proceedings within the time specified by the court, all or part of the costs to which the receiving party would otherwise be entitled will be disallowed.
(3) If—

(a) the paying party has not made an application in accordance with paragraph (1); and
(b) the receiving party commences the proceedings later than the period specified in rule 47.7,

the court may disallow all or part of the interest otherwise payable to the receiving party under—

(i) section 17 of the Judgments Act 1838[71]; or
(ii) section 74 of the County Courts Act 1984[72],

but must not impose any other sanction except in accordance with rule 44.14 (powers in relation to misconduct).

(4) Where the costs to be assessed in a detailed assessment are payable out of the Community Legal Service Fund, this rule applies as if the receiving party were the solicitor to whom the costs are payable and the paying party were the Legal Services Commission.

**Delete paragraph E-037 and substitute:**

**Procedure where costs are agreed**

E–037 47.10

(1) the paying party and the receiving party agree the amount of costs, either party may apply for a costs certificate (either interim or final) in the amount agreed.

(Rule 47.15 and rule 47.16 contain further provisions about interim and final costs certificates respectively)

(2) An application for a certificate under paragraph (1) must be made to the court which would be the venue for detailed assessment proceedings under rule 47.4.

(a) where the right to detailed assessment arises from a judgement or court order —
  (i) to the court where the judgment or order was given or made, if the proceedings have not been transferred since then; or
  (ii) to the court to which the proceedings have been transferred; and
(b) in any other case, to the court which would be the venue for detailed assessment proceedings under rule 47.4.

**Delete paragraph E-040 and substitute:**

IV COSTS PAYABLE BY ONE PARTY TO ANOTHER—PROCEDURE WHERE POINTS OF DISPUTE ARE SERVED

**Optional reply**

E–040 47.13

(1) Where any party to the detailed assessment proceedings serves points of dispute, the receiving party may serve a reply on the other parties to the assessment proceedings.
(2) He may do so within 21 days after service on him of the points of dispute to which his reply relates.

(The costs practice direction sets out the meaning of reply)

**Delete paragraph E-044 and substitute:**

(71) 1838 c. 110. Section 17 was amended by S.I. 1998/2940.
(72) 1984 c. 28. Section 74 was amended by section 2 of the Private International Law (Miscellaneous Provisions) Act 1995 (c. 42).

## VI Detailed Assessment Procedure for Costs of an Assisted Person where Costs are Payable Out of the Legal Aid Fund

**etailed assessment procedure for costs of an assisted person where costs are ayable out of the legal aid fund**

**7.17** **E–044**

(1) here the court is to assess costs of an assisted person which are payable out of the legal aid fund, the assisted person's solicitor may commence detailed assessment proceedings by filing a request in the relevant practice form.
(2) A request under paragraph (1) must be filed within 3 months after the date when the right to detailed assessment arose.
(3) The solicitor must also serve a copy of the request for detailed assessment on the LSC funded client or the assisted person, if notice of that person's interest has been given to the court in accordance with Community Legal Service or legal aid regulations.
(4) Where the solicitor has certified that the assisted person wishes to attend an assessment hearing, the court will, on receipt of the request for assessment, fix a date for the assessment hearing.
(5) Where paragraph (3) does not apply, the court will, on receipt of the request for assessment provisionally assess the costs without the attendance of the solicitor, unless it considers that a hearing is necessary.
(6) After the court has provisionally assessed the bill, it will return the bill to the solicitor.
(7) The court will fix a date for an assessment hearing if the solicitor informs the court, within 14 days after he receives the provisionally assessed bill, that he wants the court to hold such a hearing.

**)etailed assessment procedure where costs are payable out of a fund other than he community legal service fund**

**ɫ7.17A** **E–044/1**

(1) Where the court is to assess costs which are payable out of a fund other than the Community Legal Service Fund, the receving party may commence detailed assessment proceedings by filing a request in the relevant practice form.
(2) A request under paragraph (1) must be filed within 3 months after the date when the right to detailed assessment arose.
(3) The court may direct that the party seeking assessment serve a copy of the request on any person who has a financial interest in the outcome of the assessment.
(4) The court will, on receipt of the request for assessment, provisionally assess the costs without the attendance of the receiving party, unless it considers that a hearing is necessary.
(5) After the court has provisionally assessed the bill, it will return the bill to the receiving party.
(6) The court will fix a date for an assessment hearing if the party informs the court, within 14 days after he receives the provisionally assessed bill, that he wants the court to hold such a hearing.

**Delete paragraph E-046 and substitute:**

**Offers to settle without prejudice save as to costs of the detailed assessment proceedings**

**47.19** **E–046**

(1) Where —

(a) a party (whether the paying party or the receiving party) makes a wr ten offer to settle the costs of the proceedings which gave rise to t assessment proceedings; and
(b) the offer is expressed to be without prejudice(GL) save as to the cos of the detailed assessment proceedings,

the court will take the offer into account in deciding who should pay t costs of those proceedings.

(2) The fact of the offer must not be communicated to the costs officer until t question of costs of the detailed assessment proceedings falls to be decide

(The costs practice direction provides that rule 47.19 does not apply where t receiving party is a LSC funded client or an assisted person)

**Delete paragraphs E–047 to E–053, substitute:**

VIII APPEALS FROM AUTHORISED COURT OFFICERS IN DETAILED ASSESSMENT PROCEEDINGS

**Right to appeal**

E–047 47.20

(1) Any party to detailed assessment proceedings may appeal against a decisic of an authorised court officer in those proceedings.
(2) For the purposes of this Section, a LSC funded client or an assisted persc is not a party to detailed assessment proceedings.

(Part 52 sets out general rules about appeals)

**Court to hear appeal**

E–048 47.21 An appeal against a decision of an authorised court officer is to a costs judg or a district judge of the High Court.

**Appeal procedure**

E–049 47.22

(1) The appellant must file an appeal notice within 14 days after the date c the decision he wishes to appeal against.
(2) On receipt of the appeal notice, the court will —

(a) serve a copy of the notice on the parties to the detailed assessmer proceedings; and
(b) give notice of the appeal hearing to those parties.

**Powers of the court on appeal**

E–050 47.23

On an appeal from an authorised court officer the court will —

(a) re-hear the proceedings which gave rise to the decision appeale against; and
(b) make any order and give any directions as it considers appropriate.

**Delete paragraph E-055 and substitute:**

**Costs orders in favour of or against non-parties**

E–055 48.2

(1) Where the court is considering whether to exercise its power under sectio

51 of the Supreme Court Act 1981[81] (costs are in the discretion of the court) to make a costs order in favour of or against a person who is not a party to proceedings—

(a) that person must be added as a party to the proceedings for the purposes of costs only; and
(b) he must be given a reasonable opportunity to attend a hearing at which the court will consider the matter further.

(2) This rule does not apply—

(a) where the court is considering whether to—
  (i) make an order against the Legal Services Commission;
  (ii) make a wasted costs order (as defined in 48.7); and
(b) in proceedings to which rule 48.1 applies (pre-commencement disclosure and orders for disclosure against a person who is not a party).

**Delete paragraph E-057 and substitute:**

**Limitations on court's power to award costs in favour of trustee or personal representative**

**48.4**

(1) This rule applies where—

(a) a person is or has been a party to any proceedings in the capacity of trustee or personal representative; and
(b) rule 48.3 does not apply.

(2) The general rule is that he is entitled to be paid the costs of those proceedings, insofar as they are not recovered from or paid by any other person, out of the relevant trust fund or estate.
(3) Where he is entitled to be paid any of those costs out of the fund or estate, those costs will be assessed on the indemnity basis.

**Insert after rule 48.6:**

**Costs where the court has made a Group Litigation Order**

**48.6A** **E–059/1**

(1) This rule applied where the court has made a Group Litigation Order ("GLO").
(2) In this rule—

(a) "individual costs" means costs incurred in relation to an individual claim on the group register;
(b) "common costs" means—
  (i) costs incurred in relation to the GLO issues;
  (ii) individual costs incurred in a claim while it is proceeding as a test claim, and
  (iii) costs incurred by the lead solicitor in administering the group litigation; and
(c) "group litigant" means a claimant or defendant, as the case may be, whose claim is entered on the group register.

(3) Unless the court orders otherwise, any order for common costs against

[81] 1981 c. 54. Section 51 was substituted by section 4(1) of the Courts and Legal Services Act 1990 (c. 41).

group litigants imposes on each group litigant several liability(GL) for an equal proportion of those common costs.

(4) The general rule is that where a group litigant is the paying party, he will in addition to any costs he is liable to pay to the receiving party, be liable for—

(a) the individual costs of his claim; and
(b) an equal proportion, together with all the other group litigants, of the common costs.

(5) Where the court makes an order about costs in relation to any application or hearing which involved—

(a) one or more GLO issues; and
(b) issues relevant only to individual claims,

the court will direct the proportion of the costs that is to relate to common costs and the proportion that is to relate to individual costs.

(6) Where common costs have been incurred before a claim is entered on the group register, the court may order the group litigant to be liable for a proportion of those costs.

(7) Where a claim is removed from the group register, the court may make an order for costs in that claim which includes a proportion of the common costs incurred up to the date on which the claim is removed from the group register. (Part 19 sets out rules about group litigation).

**Delete paragraphs E-060 to E-062 and substitute:**

II Costs Relating to Solicitors and other Legal Representatives

**Personal liability of legal representative for costs - wasted costs orders**

E–060 48.7

(1) This rule applies where the court is considering whether to make an order under section 51(6) of the Supreme Court Act 1981[83] (court's power to disallow or (as the case may be) order a legal representative to meet "wasted costs").

(2) The court must give the legal representative a reasonable opportunity to attend a hearing to give reasons why it should not make such an order.

(4) When the court makes a wasted costs order, it must specify the amount to be disallowed or paid.

(5) The court may direct that notice must be given to the legal representative's client, in such manner as the court may direct—

(a) of any proceedings under this rule; or
(b) of any order made under it against his legal representative.

(6) Before making a wasted costs order, the court may direct a costs judge or a district judge to inquire into the matter and report to the court.

(7) The court may refer the question of wasted costs to a costs judge or a district judge, instead of making a wasted costs order.

[83] 1981 c. 54. Section 51 was substituted by section 4(1) of the Courts and Legal Services Act 1990 (c. 41).

**asis of detailed assessment of solicitor and client costs**

3.8

(1) This rule applies to every assessment of a solicitor's bill to his client except a bill which is to be paid out of the Community Legal Service Fund under the Legal Aid Act 1988[8] or the Access to Justice Act 1999[9]; and

(1A) Section 74(3) of the Solicitors Act 1974(a) applies unless the solicitor and client have entered into a written agreement which expressly permits payment to the solicitor of an amount of costs greater than that which the client could have recovered from another party to the proceedings.

(2) Subject to paragraph (1A), costs are to be assessed on the indemnity basis but are to be presumed-

(a) to have been reasonably incurred if they were incurred with the express or implied approval of the client;

(b) to be reasonable in amount if their amount was expressly or impliedly approved by the client;

(c) to have been unreasonably incurred if—

(i) they are of an unusual nature or amount; and

(ii) the solicitor did not tell his client that as a result he might not recover all of them from the other party.

(3) Where the court is considering a percentage increase, whether on the application of the legal
representative under rule 44.16 or on the application of the client, the court will have regard to all the relevant factors as they reasonably appeared to the solicitor or counsel when the conditional fee agreement was entered into or varied.

(4) In paragraph (3), "conditional fee agreement" means an agreement enforceable under section 58 of the Courts and Legal Services Act 1990[10] at the date on which that agreement was entered into or varied.

**:onditional fees**

**)elete paragraph E-062.** **E–062**

**Renumber 48.10 as 48.9 in paragraph E-063.**

[8] 1988, c. 34.

[9] 1999, c. 22.

[10] 1990, c. 41. Section 58 was substituted by section 27 of the Access to Justice Act 1999 (c. 22) with effect from April 1, 2000 (the Access to Justice Act 1999 (Commencement No. 3, Transitional Provisions and Savings) Order 2000, S.I. 2000 No. 774, and the Access to Justice Act 1999 (Transitional Provisions) Order 2000, S.I. 2000 No. 900).

# APPENDIX F

**Delete Appendix F and replace with:**

# PRACTICE DIRECTION SUPPLEMENTING PARTS 43 TO 48 OF THE CIVIL PROCEDURE RULES

F–001



## Directions Relating To Part 44—General Rules About Costs

F–002

WISHES TO RECOVER FROM HIS CLIENT AN AGREED PERCENT-AGE INTEREST WHICH HAS BEEN DISALLOWED OR REDUCE ON ASSESSMENT. RULE 44.16.

- SECTION 21 APPLICATION OF COSTS RULES: RULE 44.17
- SECTION 22 ORDERS FOR COSTS TO WHICH THE ACCESS T JUSTICE ACT 1991 SECTION 11 APPLIES
- SECTION 23 DETERMINATION PROCEEDINGS AND SIMILAR PRO-CEEDINGS UNDER THE COMMUNITY LEGAL SERVICE (COST REGULATIONS 2000

## Directions Relating To Part 45—Fixed Costs

F–003

- SECTION 24 FIXED COSTS IN SMALL CLAIMS
- SECTION 25 FIXED COSTS ON THE ISSUE OF A DEFAULT COST CERTIFICATE

## Directions Relating to Part 46—Fast Track Trial Costs

F–004

- SECTION 26 SCOPE OF PART 46: RULE 46.1
- SECTION 27 POWER TO AWARD MORE OR LESS THAN TH AMOUNT OF FAST TRACK TRIAL COSTS: RULE 46.3

## Directions Relating to Part 47 —Procedure for Detailed Assessment of Costs and Default Provisions

F–005

- SECTION 28 TIME WHEN ASSESSMENT MAY BE CARRIED OU RULE 47.1
- SECTION 29 NO STAY OF DETAILED ASSESSMENT WHERE THER IS AN APPEAL: RULE 47.2
- SECTION 30 POWERS OF AN AUTHORISED COURT OFFICE RULE 47.3
- SECTION 31 VENUE FOR DETAILED ASSESSMENT PROCEEDING RULE 47.4
- SECTION 32 COMMENCEMENT OF DETAILED ASSESSMENT PRO-CEEDINGS: RULE 47.6
- SECTION 33 PERIOD FOR COMMENCING DETAILED ASSESSMEN PROCEEDINGS: RULE 47.7
- SECTION 34 SANCTION FOR DELAY IN COMMENCING DETAILE ASSESSMENT PROCEEDINGS: RULE 47.8
- SECTION 35 POINTS OF DISPUTE AND CONSEQUENCES OF NO SERVING: RULE 47.9
- SECTION 36 PROCEDURE WHERE COSTS ARE AGREED: RUL 47.10
- SECTION 37 DEFAULT COSTS CERTIFICATE: RULE 47.11
- SECTION 38 SETTING ASIDE DEFAULT COSTS CERTIFICATE: RUL 47.12
- SECTION 39 OPTIONAL REPLY: RULE 47.13
- SECTION 40 DETAILED ASSESSMENT HEARING: RULE 47.14
- SECTION 41 POWER TO ISSUE AN INTERIM CERTIFICATE: RUL 47.15
- SECTION 42 FINAL COSTS CERTIFICATE: RULE 47.16

- SECTION 43 DETAILED ASSESSMENT PROCEDURE WHERE COSTS ARE PAYABLE OUT OF THE COMMUNITY LEGAL SERVICE FUND: RULE 47.17
- SECTION 44 COSTS OF DETAILED ASSESSMENT PROCEEDINGS WHERE COSTS ARE PAYABLE OUT OF A FUND OTHER THAN THE COMMUNITY LEGAL SERVICE FUND: RULE 47.17A
- SECTION 45 LIABILITY FOR COSTS OF DETAILED ASSESSMENT PROCEEDINGS: RULE 47.18
- SECTION 46 OFFERS TO SETTLE WITHOUT PREJUDICE SAVE AS TO THE COSTS OF THE DETAILED ASSESSMENT PROCEEDINGS: RULE 47.19
- SECTION 47 APPEALS FROM AUTHORISED COURT OFFICERS IN DETAILED ASSESSMENT PROCEEDINGS: RIGHT TO APPEAL: RULE 47.20
- SECTION 48 PROCEDURE ON APPEAL FROM AUTHORISED COURT OFFICERS: RULE 47.22
- SECTION 49 COSTS PAYABLE BY THE LSC AT PRESCRIBED RATES

## Directions Relating To Part 48 Costs—Special Cases

F–006

- SECTION 50 AMOUNT OF COSTS WHERE COSTS ARE PAYABLE PURSUANT TO CONTRACT: RULE 48.3
- SECTION 51 COSTS WHERE MONEY IS PAYABLE BY OR TO A CHILD OR PATIENT: RULE 48.5
- SECTION 52 LITIGANTS IN PERSON: RULE 48.6
- SECTION 53 PERSONAL LIABILITY OF LEGAL REPRESENTATIVE FOR COSTS -WASTED COSTS ORDERS: RULE 48.7
- SECTION 54 BASIS OF DETAILED ASSESSMENT OF SOLICITOR AND CLIENT COSTS: RULE 48.8
- SECTION 55 CONDITIONAL FEES: RULE 48.9
- SECTION 56 PROCEDURE ON ASSESSMENT OF SOLICITOR AND CLIENT COSTS: RULE 48.10
- SECTION 57 TRANSITIONAL ARRANGEMENTS

## Schedule Of Costs Precedents

F–007

A: Model form of bill of costs (receiving party's solicitor and counsel on CFA terms)
B: Model form of bill of costs (detailed assessment of additional liability only)
C: Model form of bill of costs (payable by Defendant and the LSC)
D: Model form of bill of costs (alternative form, single column for amounts claimed, separate parts for costs payable by the LSC only)
E: Legal Aid/ LSC Schedule of Costs
F: Certificates for inclusion in bill of costs
G. Points of Dispute
H: Estimate of costs served on other parties
J: Solicitors Act 1974: Part 8 claim form under Part III of the Act
K: Solicitors Act 1974: order for delivery of bill
L: Solicitors Act 1974: order for detailed assessment (client)
M: Solicitors Act 1974: order for detailed assessment (solicitors)
P: Solicitors Act 1974: breakdown of costs

## SECTION 1 Introduction

F–008

1.1 This Practice Direction supplements Parts 43 to 48 of the Civil Procedure Rules. It applies to all proceedings to which those Parts apply.

*1.2 Paragraphs 57.1 to 57.9 of this Practice Direction deal with various transitional provisions affecting proceedings about costs.

1.3 Attention is drawn to the powers to make orders about costs conferred on the Supreme Court and any county court by Section 51 of the Supreme Court Act 1981.

*1.4 In these Directions:

"counsel" means a barrister or other person with a right of audience in relation to proceedings in the High Court or in the County Courts in which he is instructed to act.
"LSC" means Legal Services Commission.
"solicitor" means a solicitor of the Supreme Court or other person with a right of audience in relation to proceedings, who is conducting the claim or defence (as the case may be) on behalf of a party to the proceedings and where the context admits, includes a patent agent.

1.5 In respect of any document which is required by these Directions to be signed by a party or his legal representative the Practice Direction supplementing Part 22 will apply as if the document in question was a statement of truth. (The Practice Direction supplementing Part 22 makes provision for cases in which a party is a child, a patient or a company or other corporation and cases in which a document is signed on behalf of a partnership).

*1.6 This edition of the Costs Practice Direction comes into force as from 3rd July 2000. In this edition, the paragraphs have been renumbered from 1.1 to 57.9.An asterisk appears in the margin beside every paragraph in which an amendment has been made in this edition other than an amendment caused solely by the renumbering.

## SECTION 2 Scope of costs rules and definitions

*Rule 43.2 Definitions and Application*

F–009

*2.1 Where the court makes an order for costs and the receiving party has entered into a funding arrangement as defined in rule 43.2, the costs payable by the paying party include any additional liability (also defined in rule 43.2) unless the court orders otherwise.

*2.2 In the following paragraphs—

"funding arrangement", "percentage increase", "insurance premium", "membership organisation" and "additional liability" have the meanings given to them by rule 43.2 .
* A "conditional fee agreement" is an agreement with a person providing advocacy or litigation services which provides for his fees and expenses, or part of them, to be payable only in specified circumstances, whether or not it provides for a success fee as mentioned in section 58(2)(b) of the Courts and Legal Services Act 1990.
"base costs" means costs other than the amount of any additional liability.

*2.3 Rule 44.3A(1) provides that the court will not assess any additional liability until the conclusion of the proceedings or the part of the proceedings to which the funding arrangement relates. (As to the time when detailed assessment may be carried out see paragraph 27.1 below).

*2.4 For the purposes of the following paragraphs of this practice direction and rule 44.3A proceedings are concluded when the court has finally determined the matters in issue in the claim, whether or not there is an appeal. The making of an award of provisional damages under Part 41 will also be treated as a final determination of the matters in issue.

.5 The court may order or the parties may agree in writing that, although the proceedings are continuing, they will nevertheless be treated as concluded.

## CTION 3 Model forms for claims for costs

*ıle 43.3 Meaning of summary assessment*

.1 Rule 43.3 defines summary assessment. When carrying out a summary assessment of costs where there is an additional liability the court may assess the base costs alone, or the base costs and the additional liability. **F–010**

.2 Form N260 is a model form of Statement of Costs to be used for summary assessments.

. Further details about Statements of Costs are given in paragraph 13.6 below.

*ıle 43.4 Meaning of detailed assessment*

.4 Rule 43.4 defines detailed assessment. When carrying out a detailed assessment of costs where there is an additional liability the court will assess both the base costs and the additional liability, or, if the base costs have already been assessed, the additional liability alone. **F–011**

.5 Precedents A, B, C and D in the Schedule of Costs Precedents annexed to this Practice Direction are model forms of bills of costs to be used for detailed assessments.

.6 Further details about bills of costs are given in the next section of these Directions and in paragraphs 28.1 to 49.1, below.

.7 Precedents A, B, C and D in the Schedule of Costs Precedents and the next section of this Practice Direction all refer to a model form of bill of costs. The use of a model form is not compulsory, but is encouraged. A party wishing to rely upon a bill which departs from the model forms should include in the background information of the bill an explanation for that departure.

.8 In any order of the court (whether made before or after 26 April 1999) the word "taxation" will be taken to mean "detailed assessment" and the words "to be taxed" will be taken to mean "to be decided by detailed assessment" unless in either case the context otherwise requires.

## CTION 4 Form and contents of bills of costs

. A bill of costs may consist of such of the following sections as may be appropriate: — **F–012**

(1) title page;
(2) background information;
(3) items of costs claimed under the headings specified in paragraph 4.6;
(4) summary showing the total costs claimed on each page of the bill;
(5) schedules of time spent on non-routine attendances; and
(6) the certificates referred to in paragraph 4.15.

.2 Where it is necessary or convenient to do so, a bill of costs may be divided into two or more parts, each part containing sections (2), (3) and (4) above. A division into parts will be necessary or convenient in the following circumstances: —

(1) Where the receiving party acted in person during the course of the proceedings (whether or not he also had a legal representative at that time) the bill should be divided into different parts so as to distinguish between;

(a) the costs claimed for work done by the legal representative; and

(b) the costs claimed for work done by the receiving party in person.

(2) Where the receiving party was represented by different solicitors during t course of the proceedings, the bill should be divided into different parts as to distinguish between the costs payable in respect of each solicitor.

(3) Where the receiving party obtained legal aid or LSC funding in respect all or part of the proceedings the bill should be divided into separate par so as to distinguish between;

(a) costs claimed before legal aid or LSC funding was granted;
(b) costs claimed after legal aid or LSC funding was granted; and
(c) any costs claimed after legal aid or LSC funding ceased.

(4) Where value added tax (VAT) is claimed and there was a change in t rate of VAT during the course of the proceedings, the bill should be divid into separate parts so as to distinguish between;

(a) costs claimed at the old rate of VAT; and
(b) costs claimed at the new rate of VAT.

(5) Where the bill covers costs payable under an order or orders under whi there are different paying parties the bill should be divided into parts so to deal separately with the costs payable by each paying party.

(6) Where the bill covers costs payable under an order or orders, in respect which the receiving party wishes to claim interest from different dates, t bill should be divided to enable such interest to be calculated.

*4.3 Where a party claims costs against another party and also claims costs agair the LSC only for work done in the same period, the costs claimed against t LSC only can be claimed either in a separate part of the bill or in additior columns in the same part of the bill. Precedents C and D in the Schedule Costs Precedents annexed to this Practice Direction show how bills should drafted when costs are claimed against the LSC only.

*4.4 The title page of the bill of costs must set out: —

(1) the full title of the proceedings;
(2) the name of the party whose bill it is and a description of the docume showing the right to assessment (as to which see paragraph 40.4, below
(3) if VAT is included as part of the claim for costs, the VAT number of t legal representative or other person in respect of whom VAT is claimed;
(4) details of all legal aid certificates, LSC certificates and relevant amendme certificates in respect of which claims for costs are included in the bill.

4.5 The background information included in the bill of costs should set out: —

(1) a brief description of the proceedings up to the date of the notice of co mencement;

(2) A statement of the status of the solicitor or solicitor's employee in resp of whom costs are claimed and (if those costs are calculated on the ba of hourly rates) the hourly rates claimed for each such person.

It should be noted that "legal executive" means a Fellow of the Instit of Legal Executives.

Other clerks, who are fee earners of equivalent experience, may entitled to similar rates. It should be borne in mind that Fellows of t Institute of Legal Executives will have spent approximately 6 years in pr tice, and taken both general and specialist examinations. The Fellows ha therefore acquired considerable practical and academic experience. Cler without the equivalent experience of legal executives will normally treated as being the equivalent of trainee solicitors and para-legals.

(3) a brief explanation of any agreement or arrangement between the receivi party and his solicitors, which affects the costs claimed in the bill.

4.6 The bill of costs may consist of items under such of the following heads as may be appropriate:—

(1) attendances on the court and counsel up to the date of the notice of commencement;
(2) attendances on and communications with the receiving party;
(3) attendances on and communications with witnesses including any expert witness;
(4) attendances to inspect any property or place for the purposes of the proceedings;
(5) attendances on and communications with other persons, including offices of public records;
(6) communications with the court and with counsel;
(7) work done on documents: preparing and considering documentation, including documentation relating to pre-action protocols where appropriate, work done in connection with arithmetical calculations of compensation and/or interest and time spent collating documents;
(8) work done in connection with negotiations with a view to settlement if not already covered in the heads listed above;
(9) attendances on and communications with London and other agents and work done by them;
(10) other work done which was of or incidental to the proceedings and which is not already covered in the heads listed above.

4.7 In respect of each of the heads of costs:—

(1) "communications" means letters out and telephone calls;
(2) communications, which are not routine communications, must be set out in chronological order;
(3) routine communications should be set out as a single item at the end of each head;

4.8 Routine communications are letters out, e mails out and telephone calls which because of their simplicity should not be regarded as letters or e mails of substance or telephone calls which properly amount to an attendance.

4.9 Each item claimed in the bill of costs must be consecutively numbered.

4.10 In each part of the bill of costs which claims items under head (1) (attendances on court and counsel) a note should be made of:

(1) all relevant events, including events which do not constitute chargeable items;
(2) any orders for costs which the court made (whether or not a claim is made in respect of those costs in this bill of costs).

4.11 The numbered items of costs may be set out on paper divided into columns.Precedents A, B, C and D in the Schedule of Costs Precedents annexed to this Practice Direction illustrate various model forms of bills of costs.

4.12 In respect of heads (2) to (10) in paragraph 4.6 above, if the number of attendances and communications other than routine communications is twenty or more, the claim for the costs of those items in that section of the bill of costs should be for the total only and should refer to a schedule in which the full record of dates and details is set out. If the bill of costs contains more than one schedule each schedule should be numbered consecutively.

4.13 The bill of costs must not contain any claims in respect of costs or court fees which relate solely to the detailed assessment proceedings other than costs claimed for preparing and checking the bill.

4.14 The summary must show the total profit costs and disbursements claimed separately from the total VAT claimed. Where the bill of costs is divided into parts the summary must also give totals for each part. If each page the bill gives a page total the summary must also set out the page totals f each page.

*4.15 The bill of costs must contain such of the certificates, the texts of which a set out in Precedent F of the Schedule of Costs Precedents annexed to th Practice Direction, as are appropriate.

*4.16 The following provisions relate to work done by solicitors:

(1) Routine letters out and routine telephone calls will in general be allow on a unit basis of 6 minutes each, the charge being calculated by referen to the appropriate hourly rate. The unit charge for letters out will inclu perusing and considering the relevant letters in and no separate char should be made for in-coming letters.

(2) E-mails received by solicitors will not normally be allowed. The court ma in its discretion, allow an actual time charge for preparation of e-mails se by solicitors, which properly amount to attendances provided that the tir taken has been recorded. The court may also, in its discretion, allow a su in respect of routine e-mails sent to the client or others on a unit basis 6 minutes each, the charge being calculated by reference to the appropria hourly rate.

(3) Local travelling expenses incurred by solicitors will not be allowed. T definition of "local" is a matter for the discretion of the court. While absolute rule can be laid down, as a matter of guidance, "local" will, general, be taken to mean within a radius of 10 miles from the cou dealing with the case at the relevant time. Where travelling and waiti time is claimed, this should be allowed at the rate agreed with the clie unless this is more than the hourly rate on the assessment.

(4) The cost of postage, couriers, out-going telephone calls, fax and telex mes ages will in general not be allowed but the court may exceptionally in discretion allow such expenses in unusual circumstances or where the co is unusually heavy.

(5) The cost of making copies of documents will not in general be allowed b the court may exceptionally in its discretion make an allowance for copyi in unusual circumstances or where the documents copied are unusual numerous in relation to the nature of the case. Where this discretion invoked the number of copies made, their purpose and the costs claim for them must be set out in the bill.

(6) Agency charges as between a principal solicitor and his agent will be de with on the principle that such charges, where appropriate, form part the principal solicitor's charges. Where these charges relate to head (1) paragraph 4.6 (attendances at court and on counsel) they should included in their chronological order in that head. In other cases th should be included in head (9) (attendances on London and other agent.

*4.17

(1) Where a claim is made for a percentage increase in addition to an hour rate or base fee, the amount of the increase must be shown separatel either in the appropriate arithmetic column or in the narrative colum (For an example see Precedent A or Precedent B.)

(2) Where a claim is made against the LSC only and includes enhanceme and where a claim is made in family proceedings and includes a claim f uplift or general care and conduct, the amount of enhancement uplift a general care and conduct must be shown, in respect of each item up which it is claimed, as a separate amount either in the appropriate arit metic column or in the narrative column. (For an example, see Precede C.)

"Enhancement" means the increase in prescribed rates which may allowed by a costs officer in accordance with the Legal Aid in Civil Proceedings (Remuneration) Regulations 1994 or the Legal Aid in Family Proceedings Regulations 1991.

**Costs of preparing the bill**

4.18 A claim may be made for the reasonable costs of preparing and checking the bill of costs. **F–013**

**SECTION 5 Special provisions relating to VAT**

5.1 This section deals with claims for value added tax (VAT) which are made in respect of costs being dealt with by way of summary assessment or detailed assessment. **F–014**

**VAT Registration Number**

5.2 The number allocated by HM Customs and Excise to every person registered under the Value Added Tax Act 1983 except a Government Department) must appear in a prominent place at the head of every statement, bill of costs, fee sheet, account or voucher on which VAT is being included as part of a claim for costs. **F–015**

**Entitlement to VAT on Costs**

5.3 VAT should not be included in a claim for costs if the receiving party is able to recover the VAT as input tax. Where the receiving party is able to obtain credit from HM Customs and Excise for a proportion of the VAT as input tax, only that proportion which is not eligible for credit should be included in the claim for costs. **F–016**

5.4 The receiving party has responsibility for ensuring that VAT is claimed only when the receiving party is unable to recover the VAT or a proportion thereof as input tax.

*5.5 Where there is a dispute as to whether VAT is properly claimed the receiving party must provide a certificate signed by the solicitors or the auditors of the receiving party substantially in the form illustrated in Precedent F in the Schedule of Costs Precedents annexed to this Practice Direction. Where the receiving party is a litigant in person who is claiming VAT, reference should be made by him to HM Customs and Excise and wherever possible a Statement to similar effect produced at the hearing at which the costs are assessed.

5.6 Where there is a dispute as to whether any service in respect of which a charge is proposed to be made in the bill is zero rated or exempt, reference should be made to HM Customs and Excise and wherever possible the view of HM Customs and Excise obtained and made known at the hearing at which the costs are assessed. Such application should be made by the receiving party. In the case of a bill from a solicitor to his own client, such application should be made by the client.

**Form of bill of costs where VAT rate changes**

5.7 Where there is a change in the rate of VAT, suppliers of goods and services are entitled by ss.88 (1) and (2) of the VAT Act 1994 in most circumstances to elect whether the new or the old rate of VAT should apply to a supply where the basic and actual tax points span a period during which there has been a change in VAT rates. **F–017**

5.8 It will be assumed, unless a contrary indication is given in writing, that an election to take advantage of the provisions mentioned in paragraph 5.7 above and to charge VAT at the lower rate has been made. In any case in which an election to charge at the lower rate is not made, such a decision must b justified to the court assessing the costs.

### Apportionment

F–018 5.9 All bills of costs, fees and disbursements on which VAT is included must b divided into separate parts so as to show work done before, on and after th date or dates from which any change in the rate of VAT takes effect. Where however, a lump sum charge is made for work which spans a period durin which there has been a change in VAT rates, and paragraphs 5.7 and 5. above do not apply, reference should be made to paragraphs 8 and 9 o Appendix F of Customs' Notice 700 (or any revised edition of that notice), copy of which should be in the possession of every registered trader. If neces sary, the lump sum should be apportioned. The totals of profit costs an disbursements in each part must be carried separately to the summary.

5.10 Should there be a change in the rate between the conclusion of a detaile assessment and the issue of the final costs certificate, any interested party ma apply for the detailed assessment to be varied so as to take account of an increase or reduction in the amount of tax payable. Once the final costs certi ficate has been issued, no variation under this paragraph will be permitted.

### Disbursements

F–019 5.11 Petty (or general) disbursements such as postage, fares etc which are normall treated as part of a solicitor's overheads and included in his profit costs shoul be charged with VAT even though they bear no tax when the solicitor incur them. The cost of travel by public transport on a specific journey for a particu lar client where it forms part of the service rendered by a solicitor to his clien and is charged in his bill of costs, attracts VAT.

5.12 Reference is made to the criteria set out in the VAT Guide (Customs an Excise Notice 700 - 1st August 1991 edition paragraph 83, or any revise edition of that Notice), as to expenses which are not subject to VAT. Charge for the cost of travel by public transport, postage, telephone calls and tele graphic transfers where these form part of the service rendered by the solicito to his client are examples of charges which do not satisfy these criteria an are thus liable to VAT at the standard rate.

### Legal Aid/LSC Funding

F–020 *5.13 VAT will be payable in respect of every supply made pursuant to a Lega Aid/ LSC Certificate provided only that the person making the supply is a taxable person and that the assisted person/ LSC funded client is not residen outside the European Union. Where the assisted person/ LSC funded clien is registered for VAT and the legal services paid for by the LSC are in connec tion with that person's business, the VAT on those services will be payabl by the LSC only.

*5.14 Any summary of costs payable by the LSC must be drawn so as to show the total VAT on Counsel's fees as a separate item from the VAT on other disbursements and the VAT on profit costs.

### Tax invoice

F–021 5.15 A bill of costs filed for detailed assessment is always retained by the Court. Accordingly if a solicitor waives his solicitor and client costs and accepts the costs certified by the court as payable by the unsuccessful party in settlement, it will be necessary for a short statement as to the amount of the certified costs and the VAT thereon to be prepared for use as the tax invoice.

**Vouchers**

5.16 Where receipted accounts for disbursements made by the solicitor or his client are retained as tax invoices a photostat copy of any such receipted account may be produced and will be accepted as sufficient evidence of payment when disbursements are vouched. F–022

**Certificates**

*5.17 The total VAT allowed will be shown in the final costs certificate as a separate item. In a certificate of costs payable by the LSC the VAT on Counsel's fees will be shown separately from the remaining VAT. F–023

**Litigants acting in person**

*5.18 Where a litigant acts in litigation on his own behalf he is not treated for the purposes of VAT as having supplied services and therefore no VAT is chargeable in respect of work done by that litigant (even where, for example, that litigant is a solicitor or other legal representative). F–024

5.19 Consequently in the circumstances described in the preceding paragraph, a bill of costs presented for agreement or assessment should not claim any VAT which will not be allowed on assessment.

**Government Departments**

5.20 On an assessment between parties, where costs are being paid to a Government Department in respect of services rendered by its legal staff, VAT should not be added. F–025

**SECTION 6 Estimates of costs**

6.1* This section sets out certain steps which parties and their legal representatives must take in order to keep the parties informed about their potential liability in respect of costs and in order to assist the court to decide what, if any, order to make about costs and about case management. F–026

*6.2

(1) In this section an "estimate of costs" means—

(a) an estimate of base costs (including disbursements) already incurred; and

(b) an estimate of base costs (including disbursements) to be incurred,

which a party intends to seek to recover from any other party under an order for costs if he is successful in the case. ("Base costs" are defined in paragraphs 2.2 of this Practice Direction.)

(2) A party who intends to recover an additional liability (defined in rule 43.2) need not reveal the amount of that liability in the estimate.

6.3 The court may at any stage in a case order any party to file an estimate of base costs and to serve copies of the estimate on all other parties. The court may direct that the estimate be prepared in such a way as to demonstrate the likely effects of giving or not giving a particular case management direction which the court is considering, for example a direction for a split trial or for the trial of a preliminary issue. The court may specify a time limit for filing and serving the estimate. However, if no time limit is specified the estimate should be filed and served within 28 days of the date of the order.

*6.4

(1) When a party to a claim which is outside the financial scope of the small claims track, files an allocation questionnaire, he must also file an estimate of base costs and serve a copy of it on every other party, unless the court

otherwise directs. The legal representative must in addition serve an estimate upon the party he represents.

(2) Where a party to a claim which is being dealt with on the fast track or the multi track, or under Part 8, files a listing questionnaire, he must also file an estimate of base costs and serve a copy of it on every other party, unless the court otherwise directs. Where a party is represented, the legal representative must in addition serve an estimate on the party he represents.

(3) This paragraph does not apply to litigants in person.

*6.5 An estimate of base costs should be substantially in the form illustrated in Precedent H in the Schedule of Costs Precedents annexed to the Practice Direction.

*6.6 On an assessment of the costs of a party the court may have regard to any estimate previously filed by that party, or by any other party in the same proceedings. Such an estimate may be taken into account as a factor among others, when assessing the reasonableness of any costs claimed.

# Directions Relating To Part 44

*General rules about costs*

**SECTION 7 Solicitor's duty to notify client: rule 44.2**

F–027

*7.1 For the purposes of rule 44.2 "client" includes a party for whom a solicitor is acting and any other person (for example, an insurer, a trade union or the LSC) who has instructed the solicitor to act or who is liable to pay his fees.

7.2 Where a solicitor notifies a client of an order under that rule, he must also explain why the order came to be made.

7.3 Although rule 44.2 does not specify any sanction for breach of the rule the court may, either in the order for costs itself or in a subsequent order, require the solicitor to produce to the court evidence showing that he took reasonable steps to comply with the rule.

**SECTION 8 Court's discretion and circumstances to be taken into account when exercising its discretion as to costs: rule 44.3**

F–028

8.1 Attention is drawn to the factors set out in this rule which may lead the court to depart from the general rule stated in rule 44.3(2) and to make a different order about costs.

8.2 In a probate claim where a defendant has in his defence given notice that he requires the will to be proved in solemn form (see paragraph 8.3 of the Contentious Probate Practice Direction Supplementing Part 49), the court will not make an order for costs against the defendant unless it appears that there was no reasonable ground for opposing the will. The term "probate claim" is defined in paragraph 1.2 of the Contentious Probate Practice Direction.

*8.3

(1) The court may make an order about costs at any stage in a case.

(2) In particular the court may make an order about costs when it deals with any application, makes any order or holds any hearing and that order about costs may relate to the costs of that application, order or hearing.

(3) * Rule 44.3A(1) provides that the court will not assess any additional liability until the conclusion of the proceedings or the part of the proceedings to which the funding arrangement relates. (Paragraphs 2.4 and 2.5 above explain when proceedings are concluded. As to the time when detailed assessment may be carried out see paragraphs 28.1, below.)

8.4 In deciding what order to make about costs the court is required to have regard to all the circumstances including any payment into court or admissible offer to settle made by a party which is drawn to the court's attention (whether or not it is made in accordance with Part 36). Where a claimant has made a Part 36 offer and fails to obtain a judgment which is more advantageous than that offer, that circumstance alone will not lead to a reduction in the costs awarded to the claimant under this rule.

8.5 There are certain costs orders which the court will commonly make in proceedings before trial. The following table sets out the general effect of these orders. The table is not an exhaustive list of the orders which the court may make.

F–029

| Term | Effect |
|---|---|
| • Costs<br>• Costs in any event | The party in whose favour the order is made is entitled to the costs in respect of the part of the proceedings to which the order relates, whatever other costs orders are made in the proceedings. |
| • Costs in the case<br>• Costs in the application | The party in whose favour the court makes an order for costs at the end of the proceedings is entitled to his costs of the part of the proceedings to which the order relates. |
| • Costs reserved | The decision about costs is deferred to a later occasion, but if no later order is made the costs will be costs in the case. |
| • Claimant's/ Defendant's costs in the case/ application | If the party in whose favour the costs order is made is awarded costs at the end of the proceedings, that party is entitled to his costs of the part of the proceedings to which the order relates. If any other party is awarded costs at the end of the proceedings, the party in whose favour the final costs order is made is not liable to pay the costs of any other party in respect of the part of the proceedings to which the order relates. |
| • Costs thrown away | Where, for example, a judgment or order is set aside, the party in whose favour the costs order is made is entitled to the costs which have been incurred as a consequence. This includes the costs of —<br>a) preparing for and attending any hearing at which the judgment or order which has been set aside was made;<br>b) preparing for and attending any hearing to set aside the judgment or order in question;<br>c) preparing for and attending any hearing at which the court orders the proceedings or the part in question to be adjourned;<br>d)any steps taken to enforce a judgment or order which has subsequently been set aside. |
| • Costs of and caused by | Where, for example, the court makes this order on an application to amend a statement of case, the party in whose favour the costs order is made is entitled to the costs of preparing for and attending the application and the costs of any consequential amendment to his own statement of case. |
| • Costs here and below | The party in whose favour the costs order is made is entitled not only to his costs in respect of the proceedings in which the court makes the order but also to his costs of the proceedings in any lower court. In the case of an appeal |

| | |
|---|---|
| | from a Divisional Court the party is not entitled to any costs incurred in any court below the Divisional Court. |
| • No order as to costs<br>• Each party to pay his own costs | Each party is to bear his own costs of the part of the proceedings to which the order relates whatever costs order the court makes at the end of the proceedings. |

8.6 Where, under rule 44.3(8), the court orders an amount to be paid before costs are assessed—

(1) the order will state that amount, and
(2) if no other date for payment is specified in the order rule 44.8 (Time for complying with an order for costs) will apply.

**Fees of counsel**

F–030 *8.7

(1) This paragraph applies where the court orders the detailed assessment of the costs of a hearing at which one or more counsel appeared for a party.
(2) Where an order for costs states the opinion of the court as to whether or not the hearing was fit for the attendance of one or more counsel, a costs officer conducting a detailed assessment of costs to which that order relates will have regard to the opinion stated.
(3) The court will generally express an opinion only where:

(a) the paying party asks it to do so;
(b) more than one counsel appeared for a party or,
(c) the court wishes to record its opinion that the case was not fit for the attendance of counsel.

**Fees payable to conveyancing counsel appointed by the court to assist it**

F–031 *8.8

(1) Where the court refers any matter to the conveyancing counsel of the court the fees payable to counsel in respect of the work done or to be done will be assessed by the court in accordance with rule 44.3.
(2) An appeal from a decision of the court in respect of the fees of such counsel will be dealt with under the general rules as to appeals set out in Part 52. If the appeal is against the decision of an authorised court officer, it will be dealt with in accordance with rules 47.20 to 47.23.

**SECTION 9 Costs orders relating to funding arrangements:** Rule 44.3A

F–032 *9.1 Under an order for payment of "costs" the costs payable will include an additional liability incurred under a funding arrangement.

*9.2

(1) If before the conclusion of the proceedings the court carries out a summary assessment of the base costs it may identify separately the amount allowed in respect of: solicitors' charges; counsels' fees; other disbursements; and any value added tax (VAT). (Sections 13 and 14 of this Practice Direction deal with summary assessment.)
(2) If an order for the base costs of a previous application or hearing did

not identify separately the amounts allowed for solicitor's charges, counsel's fees and other disbursements, a court which later makes an assessment of an additional liability may apportion the base costs previously ordered.

**SECTION 10 Limits on recovery under funding arrangements:** Rule 44.3B

F-033

*10.1 In a case to which rule 44.3B(1)(c) or (d) applies the party in default may apply for relief from the sanction. He should do so as quickly as possible after he becomes aware of the default. An application, supported by evidence, should be made under Part 23 to a costs judge or district judge of the court which is dealing with the case. (Attention is drawn to rules 3.8 and 3.9 which deal with sanctions and relief from sanctions).

*10.2 Where the amount of any percentage increase recoverable by counsel may be affected by the outcome of the application, the solicitor issuing the application must serve on counsel a copy of the application notice and notice of the hearing as soon as practicable and in any event at least 2 days before the hearing. Counsel may make written submissions or may attend and make oral submissions at the hearing. (Paragraph 1.4 contains definitions of the terms "counsel" and "solicitor".)

**SECTION 11 Factors to be taken into account in deciding the amount of costs:** Rule 44.5

F-034

11.1 In applying the test of proportionality the court will have regard to rule 1.1(2)(c). The relationship between the total of the costs incurred and the financial value of the claim may not be a reliable guide. A fixed percentage cannot be applied in all cases to the value of the claim in order to ascertain whether or not the costs are proportionate.

11.2 In any proceedings there will be costs which will inevitably be incurred and which are necessary for the successful conduct of the case. Solicitors are not required to conduct litigation at rates which are uneconomic. Thus in a modest claim the proportion of costs is likely to be higher than in a large claim, and may even equal or possibly exceed the amount in dispute.

11.3 Where a trial takes place, the time taken by the court in dealing with a particular issue may not be an accurate guide to the amount of time properly spent by the legal or other representatives in preparation for the trial of that issue.

*11.4 Where a party has entered into a funding arrangement the costs claimed may, subject to rule 44.3B include an additional liability.

*11.5 In deciding whether the costs claimed are reasonable and (on a standard basis assessment) proportionate, the court will consider the amount of any additional liability separately from the base costs.

*11.6 In deciding whether the base costs are reasonable and (if relevant) proportionate the court will consider the factors set out in rule 44.5.

*11.7 Subject to paragraph 17.8(2), when the court is considering the factors to be taken into account in assessing an additional liability, it will have regard to the facts and circumstances as they reasonably appeared to the solicitor or counsel when the funding arrangement was entered into and at the time of any variation of the arrangement.

*11.8

(1) In deciding whether a percentage increase is reasonable relevant factors to be taken into account may include:—

(a) the risk that the circumstances in which the costs, fees or expenses would be payable might or might not occur;

(b) the legal representative's liability for any disbursements;
(c) what other methods of financing the costs were available to the receiving party.

(2) The court has the power, when considering whether a percentage increase is reasonable, to allow different percentages for different items of costs or for different periods during which costs were incurred.

*11.9A percentage increase will not be reduced simply on the ground that, when added to base costs which are reasonable (where relevant) proportionate, the total appears disproportionate.

*11.10 In deciding whether the cost of insurance cover is reasonable, relevant factors to be taken into account include:

(1) where the insurance cover is not purchased in support of a conditional fee agreement with a success fee, how its cost compares with the likely cost of funding the case with a conditional fee agreement with a success fee and supporting insurance cover;
(2) the level and extent of the cover provided;
(3) the availability of any pre-existing insurance cover;
(4) whether any part of the premium would be rebated in the event of early settlement;
(5) the amount of commission payable to the receiving party or his legal representatives or other agents.

*11.11 Where the court is considering a provision made by a membership organisation, rule 44.3B(1) (b) provides that any such provision which exceeds the likely cost to the receiving party of the premium of an insurance policy against the risk of incurring a liability to pay the costs of other parties to the proceedings is not recoverable. In such circumstances the court will, when assessing the additional liability, have regard to the factors set out in paragraph 11.10 above, in addition to the factors set out in rule 44.5.

**SECTION 12 Procedure for assessing costs: Rule 44.7**

F–035

12.1 Where the court does not order fixed costs (or no fixed costs are provided for) the amount of costs payable will be assessed by the court. This rule allows the court making an order about costs either

(a) to make a summary assessment of the amount of the costs, or
(b) to order the amount to be decided in accordance with Part 47 (a detailed assessment).

12.2 An order for costs will be treated as an order for the amount of costs to be decided by a detailed assessment unless the order otherwise provides.

12.3 Whenever the court awards costs to be assessed by way of detailed assessment it should consider whether to exercise the power in rule 44.3(8) (Courts Discretion as to Costs) to order the paying party to pay such sum of money as it thinks just on account of those costs.

**SECTION 13 Summary assessment: general provisions**

F–036

13.1 Whenever a court makes an order about costs which does not provide for fixed costs to be paid the court should consider whether to make a summary assessment of costs.

*13.2 The general rule is that the court should make a summary assessment of the costs:

(1) at the conclusion of the trial of a case which has been dealt with on the

fast track, in which case the order will deal with the costs of the whole claim, and

(2) at the conclusion of any other hearing, which has lasted not more than one day, in which case the order will deal with the costs of the application or matter to which the hearing related. If this hearing disposes of the claim, the order may deal with the costs of the whole claim;

(3) in hearings in the Court of Appeal to which Paragraph 14 of the Practice Direction supplementing Part 52 (Appeals) applies;

unless there is good reason not to do so e.g. where the paying party shows substantial grounds for disputing the sum claimed for costs that cannot be dealt with summarily or there is insufficient time to carry out a summary assessment.

13.3 The general rule in paragraph 13.2 does not apply to a mortgagee's costs incurred in mortgage possession proceedings or other proceedings relating to a mortgage unless the mortgagee asks the court to make an order for his costs to be paid by another party. Paragraphs 50.3 and 50.4 deal in more detail with costs relating to mortgages.

13.4 Where an application has been made and the parties to the application agree an order by consent without any party attending, the parties should agree a figure for costs to be inserted in the consent order or agree that there should be no order for costs. If the parties cannot agree the costs position, attendance on the appointment will be necessary but, unless good reason can be shown for the failure to deal with costs as set out above, no costs will be allowed for that attendance.

*13.5

(1) It is the duty of the parties and their legal representatives to assist the judge in making a summary assessment of costs in any case to which paragraph 13.2 above applies, in accordance with the following paragraphs.

(2) Each party who intends to claim costs must prepare a written statement of the costs he intends to claim showing separately in the form of a schedule:

(a) the number of hours to be claimed,
(b) the hourly rate to be claimed,
(c) the grade of fee earner;
(d) the amount and nature of any disbursement to be claimed, other than counsel's fee for appearing at the hearing,
(e) the amount of solicitor's costs to be claimed for attending or appearing at the hearing,
(f) the fees of counsel to be claimed in respect of the hearing, and
(g) any value added tax (VAT) to be claimed on these amounts.

*(3) The statement of costs should follow as closely as possible Form N260 and must be signed by the party or his legal representative. Where a litigant is an assisted person or is a LSC funded client or is represented by a solicitor in the litigant's employment the statement of costs need not include the certificate appended at the end of Form N260.

(4) The statement of costs must be filed at court and copies of it must be served on any party against whom an order for payment of those costs is intended to be sought. The statement of costs should be filed and the copies of it should be served as soon as possible and in any event not less than 24 hours before the date fixed for the hearing.

(5) *Where the litigant is or may be entitled to claim an additional liability the statement filed and served need not reveal the amount of that liability.

13.6 The failure by a party, without reasonable excuse, to comply with the foregoing paragraphs will be taken into account by the court in deciding what order to make about the costs of the claim, hearing or application, and about the costs of any further hearing or detailed assessment hearing that may be necessary as a result of that failure.

*13.7 If the court makes a summary assessment of costs at the conclusion of proceedings the court will specify separately

(1) the base costs, and if appropriate, the additional liability allowed as solicitor's charges, counsel's fees, other disbursements and any VAT; and
(2) the amount which is awarded under Part 46 (Fast Track Trial Costs).

*13.8 The court awarding costs cannot make an order for a summary assessment of costs by a costs officer. If a summary assessment of costs is appropriate but the court awarding costs is unable to do so on the day, the court must give directions as to a further hearing before the same judge.

13.9* The court will not make a summary assessment of the costs of a receiving party who is an assisted person or LSC funded client.

13.10* A summary assessment of costs payable by an assisted person or LSC funded client is not by itself a determination of that person's liability to pay those costs (as to which see rule 44.17 and paragraphs 21.1 to 23.17 of this Practice Direction).

*13.11

(1) The court will not make a summary assessment of the costs of a receiving party who is a child or patient within the meaning of Part 21 unless the solicitor acting for the child or patient has waived the right to further costs (see paragraph 51.1 below).
(2) The court may make a summary assessment of costs payable by a child or patient.

13.12*

(1) Attention is drawn to rule 44.3A which prevents the court from making a summary assessment of an additional liability before the conclusion of the proceedings or the part of the proceedings to which the funding arrangement relates. Where this applies, the court should nonetheless make a summary assessment of the base costs of the hearing or application unless there is a good reason not to do so.
(2) Where the court makes a summary assessment of the base costs all statements of costs and costs estimates put before the judge will be retained on the court file.

13.13 The court will not give its approval to disproportionate and unreasonable costs. Accordingly:

(a) When the amount of the costs to be paid has been agreed between the parties the order for costs must state that the order is by consent.
(b) If the judge is to make an order which is not by consent, the judge will, so far as possible, ensure that the final figure is not disproportionate and/or unreasonable having regard to Part 1 of the CPR. The judge will retain this responsibility notwithstanding the absence of challenge to individual items in the make-up of the figure sought. The fact that the paying party is not disputing the amount of costs can however be taken as some indication that the amount is proportionate and reasonable. The judge will therefore intervene only if satisfied that the costs are so disproportionate that it is right to do so.

## SECTION 14 Summary assessment where costs claimed include an additional liability

### Orders made before the conclusion of the proceedings

F–037

*14.1 The existence of a conditional fee agreement or other funding arrangement within the meaning of rule 43.2 is not by itself a sufficient reason for not carrying out a summary assessment.

*14.2 Where a legal representative acting for the receiving party has entered into a conditional fee agreement the court may summarily assess all the costs (other than any additional liability).

*14.3 Where costs have been summarily assessed an order for payment will not be made unless the court has been satisfied that in respect of the costs claimed, the receiving party is at the time liable to pay to his legal representative an amount equal to or greater than the costs claimed. A statement in the form of the certificate appended at the end of Form N260 may be sufficient proof of liability. The giving of information under rule 44.15 (where that rule applies) is not sufficient.

*14.4 The court may direct that any costs, for which the receiving party may not in the event be liable, shall be paid into court to await the outcome of the case, or shall not be enforceable until further order, or it may postpone the receiving party's right to receive payment in some other way.

### Orders made at the conclusion of the proceedings

F–038

*14.5 Where there has been a trial of one or more issues separately from other issues, the court will not normally order detailed assessment of the additional liability until all issues have been tried unless the parties agree.

*14.6 Rule 44.3A(2) sets out the ways in which the court may deal with the assessment of the costs where there is a funding arrangement. Where the court makes a summary assessment of the base costs:

(1) The order may state separately the base costs allowed as (a)solicitor's charges, (b) counsel's fees, (c) any other disbursements and (d) any VAT;

(2) the statements of costs upon which the judge based his summary assessment will be retained on the court file.

*14.7 Where the court makes a summary assessment of an additional liability at the conclusion of proceedings, that assessment must relate to the whole of the proceedings; this will include any additional liability relating to base costs allowed by the court when making a summary assessment on a previous application or hearing.

*14.8 Paragraph 13.13 applies where the parties are agreed about the total amount to be paid by way of costs, or are agreed about the amount of the base costs that will be paid. Where they disagree about the additional liability the court may summarily assess that liability or make an order for a detailed assessment.

*14.9 In order to facilitate the court in making a summary assessment of any additional liability at the conclusion of the proceedings the party seeking such costs must prepare and have available for the court a bundle of documents which must include—

(1) a copy of every notice of funding arrangement (Form N251) which has been filed by him;

(2) a copy of every estimate and statement of costs filed by him;

(3) a copy of the risk assessment prepared at the time any relevant funding arrangement was entered into and on the basis of which the amount of the additional liability was fixed.

**SECTION 15 Costs on the small claims track and fast track:** Rule 44.9

F–039 15.1

(1) Before a claim is allocated to one of those tracks the court is not restricted by any of the special rules that apply to that track.

(2) Where a claim has been allocated to one of those tracks, the special rules which relate to that track will apply to work done before as well as after allocation save to the extent (if any) that an order for costs in respect of that work was made before allocation.

(3) (i) This paragraph applies where a claim, issued for a sum in excess of the normal financial scope of the small claims track, is allocated to that track only because an admission of part of the claim by the defendant reduces the amount in dispute to a sum within the normal scope of that track.

See also paragraph 7.4 of the practice direction supplementing CPR Part 26)

(ii) On entering judgment for the admitted part before allocation of the balance of the claim the court may allow costs in respect of the proceedings down to that date.

**SECTION 16 Costs following allocation and re-allocation:** Rule 44.11

F–040 16.1 This paragraph applies where the court is about to make an order to reallocate a claim from the small claims track to another track.

16.2 Before making the order to re-allocate the claim, the court must decide whether any party is to pay costs to any other party down to the date of the order to re-allocate in accordance with the rules about costs contained in Part 27 (The Small Claims Track).

16.3 If it decides to make such an order about costs, the court will make a summary assessment of those costs in accordance with that Part.

**SECTION 17 Costs —only proceedings:** Rule 44.12A

F–041 *17.1 A claim form under this rule should be issued in the court which would have been the appropriate office in accordance with rule 47.4 had proceedings been brought in relation to the substantive claim. A claim form under this rule should not be issued in the High Court unless the dispute to which the agreement relates was of such a value or type that had proceedings been begun they would have been commenced in the High Court.

*17. A claim form which is to be issued in the High Court at the Royal Courts of Justice will be issued in the Supreme Court Costs Office.

*17.3 Attention is drawn to rule 8.2 (in particular to paragraph (b)(ii)) and to rule 44.12A(3). The claim form must:

(1) identify the claim or dispute to which the agreement to pay costs relates;
(2) state the date and terms of the agreement on which the claimant relies;
(3) set out or have attached to it a draft of the order which the claimant seeks;
(4) state the amount of the costs claimed; and,
(5) state whether the costs are claimed on the standard or indemnity basis. If no basis is specified the costs will be treated as being claimed on the standard basis.

*17.4 The evidence to be filed and served with the claim form under Rule 8.5 must include copies of the documents on which the claimant relies to prove the defendant's agreement to pay costs.

*17.5 A costs judge or a district judge has jurisdiction to hear and decide any issue which may arise in a claim issued under this rule irrespective of the amount of the costs claimed or of the value of the claim to which the agreement to pay costs relates. A costs officer may make an order by consent under paragraph17.7, or an order dismissing a claim under paragraph 17.9 below.

*17.6 When the time for filing the defendant's acknowledgement of service has expired, the claimant may by letter request the court to make an order in the terms of his claim, unless the defendant has filed an acknowledgement of service stating that he intends to contest the claim or to seek a different order.

*17.7 Rule 40.6 applies where an order is to be made by consent. An order may be made by consent in terms which differ from those set out in the claim form.

*17.8

(1) An order for costs made under this rule will be treated as an order for the amount of costs to be decided by a detailed assessment to which Part 47 and the practice directions relating to it apply. Rule 44.4(4) (determination of basis of assessment) also applies to the order.

(2) In cases in which an additional liability is claimed, the costs judge or district judge should have regard to the time when and the extent to which the claim has been settled and to the fact that the claim has been settled without the need to commence proceedings.

*17.9 A claim will be treated as opposed for the purposes of rule 44.12A(4)(b) if the defendant files an acknowledgement of service stating that he intends to contest the proceedings or to seek a different remedy. An order dismissing it will be made as soon as such an acknowledgement is filed. The dismissal of a claim under rule 44.12A(4) does not prevent the claimant from issuing another claim form under Part 7 or Part 8 based on the agreement or alleged agreement to which the proceedings under this rule related.

*17.10

(1) Rule 8.9 (which provides that claims issued under Part 8 shall be treated as allocated to the multi-track) shall not apply to claims issued under this rule. A claim issued under this rule may be dealt with without being allocated to a track.

(2) Rule 8.1(3) and Part 24 do not apply to proceedings brought under rule 44.12A.

*17.11 Nothing in this rule prevents a person from issuing a claim form under Part 7 or Part 8 to sue on an agreement made in settlement of a dispute where that agreement makes provision for costs, nor from claiming in that case an order for costs or a specified sum in respect of costs.

**SECTION 18 Court's powers in relation to misconduct:** Rule 44.14

F–042

18.1 Before making an order under rule 44.14 the court must give the party or legal representative in question a reasonable opportunity to attend a hearing to give reasons why it should not make such an order.

18.2 Conduct before or during the proceedings which gave rise to the assessment which is unreasonable or improper includes steps which are calculated to prevent or inhibit the court from furthering the overriding objective.

18.3 Although rule 44.14(3) does not specify any sanction for breach of the obligation imposed by the rule the court may, either in the order under paragraph (2) or in a subsequent order, require the solicitor to produce to the court evidence that he took reasonable steps to comply with the obligation.

## SECTION 19 Providing information about funding arrangements: Rule 44.15

F–043 *19.1

(1) A party who wishes to claim an additional liability in respect of a funding arrangement must give any other party information about that claim if he is to recover the additional liability. There is no requirement to specify the amount of the additional liability separately nor to state how it is calculated until it falls to be assessed. That principle is reflected in rules 44.3A and 44.15, in the following paragraphs and in Sections 6, 13, 14 and 31 of this Practice Direction. Section 6 deals with estimates of costs, Sections 13 and 14 deal with summary assessment and Section 31 deals with detailed assessment.

(2) In the following paragraphs a party who has entered into a funding arrangement is treated as a person who intends to recover a sum representing an additional liability by way of costs.

(3) Attention is drawn to paragraph 57.9 of this Practice Direction which sets out time limits for the provision of information where a funding arrangement is entered into between 31 March and 2 July 2000 and proceedings relevant to that arrangement are commenced before 3 July 2000.

### Method of giving information

F–044 *19.2

(1) In this paragraph, "claim form" includes petition and application notice, and the notice of funding to be filed or served is a notice containing the information set out in Form N251.

(2) (a) A claimant who has entered into a funding arrangement before starting the proceedings to which it relates must provide information to the court by filing the notice when he issues the claim form.

(b) He must provide information to every other party by serving the notice. If he serves the claim form himself he must serve the notice with the claim form. If the court is to serve the claim form, the court will also serve the notice if the claimant provides it with sufficient copies for service.

(3) A defendant who has entered into a funding arrangement before filing any document

(a) must provide information to the court by filing notice with his first document. A "first document" may be an acknowledgement of service, a defence, or any other document, such as an application to set aside a default judgment.

(b) must provide information to every party by serving notice. If he serves his first document himself he must serve the notice with that document. If the court is to serve his first document the court will also serve the notice if the defendant provides it with sufficient copies for service.

(4) In all other circumstances a party must file and serve notice within 7 days of entering into the funding arrangement concerned.

(5) There is no requirement in this Practice Direction for the provision of information about funding arrangements before the commencement of proceedings. Such provision is however recommended and may be required by a pre-action protocol.

### Notice of change of information

F–045 *19.3

(1) Rule 44.15 imposes a duty on a party to give notice of change if the

information he has previously provided is no longer accurate. To comply he must file and serve notice containing the information set out in Form N251. Rule 44.15(3) may impose other duties in relation to new estimates of costs.

(2) Further notification need not be provided where a party has already given notice:

(a) that he has entered into a conditional fee agreement with a legal representative and during the currency of that agreement either of them enters into another such agreement with an additional legal representative; or

(b) of some insurance cover, unless that cover is cancelled or unless new cover is taken out with a different insurer.

(3) Part 6 applies to the service of notices.

(4) The notice must be signed by the party or by his legal representative.

**nformation which must be provided**

19.4 F–046

(1) Unless the court otherwise orders, a party who is required to supply information about a funding arrangement must state whether he has—

entered into a conditional fee agreement which provides for a success fee within the meaning of section 58(2) of the Courts and Legal Services Act 1990;

taken out an insurance policy to which section 29 of the Access to Justice Act 1999 applies;

made an arrangement with a body which is prescribed for the purpose of section 30 of that Act;

or more than one of these.

(2) Where the funding arrangement is a conditional fee agreement, the party must state the date of the agreement and identify the claim or claims to which it relates (including Part 20 claims if any).

(3) Where the funding arrangement is an insurance policy the party must state the name of the insurer, the date of the policy and must identify the claim or claims to which it relates (including Part 20 claims if any).

(4) Where the funding arrangement is by way of an arrangement with a relevant body the party must state the name of the body and set out the date and terms of the undertaking it has given and must identify the claim or claims to which it relates (including Part 20 claims if any).

(5) Where a party has entered into more than one funding arrangement in respect of a claim, for example a conditional fee agreement and an insurance policy, a single notice containing the information set out in Form N251 may contain the required information about both or all of them

*19.5 Where the court makes a Group Litigation Order, the court may give directions as to the extent to which individual parties should provide information in accordance with rule 44.15. (Part 19 deals with Group Litigation Orders.)

**ECTION 20 Procedure where legal representative wishes to recover from his client an agreed percentage increase which has been disallowed or reduced on assessment:** Rule 44.16

*20.1 Attention is drawn to Regulation 3(2)(b) of the Conditional Fee Agreements Regulations 2000, which provides that any amount of an agreed percentage increase, which is disallowed on assessment, ceases to be payable under that F–047

agreement unless the court is satisfied that it should continue to be so payable. Rule 44.16 allows the court to adjourn a hearing at which the legal representative acting for the receiving party applies for an order that a disallowed amount should continue to be payable under the agreement.

*20.2 In the following paragraphs "counsel" means counsel who has acted in the case under a conditional fee agreement which provides for a success fee. A reference to counsel includes a reference to any person who appeared as an advocate in the case and who is not a partner or employee of the solicitor or firm which is conducting the claim or defence (as the case may be) on behalf of the receiving party.

**Procedure following Summary Assessment**

F–048 *20.3

(1) If the court disallows any amount of a legal representative's percentage increase, the court will, unless sub-paragraph (2) applies, give directions to enable an application to be made by the legal representative for the disallowed amount to be payable by his client, including, if appropriate, a direction that the application will be determined by a costs judge or district judge of the court dealing with the case.

(2) The court that has made the summary assessment may then and there decide the issue whether the disallowed amount should continue to be payable, if:

(a) the receiving party and all parties to the relevant agreement consent to the court doing so;
(b) the receiving party (or, if corporate, an officer) is present in court; and
(c) the court is satisfied that the issue can be fairly decided then and there.

**Procedure following Detailed Assessment**

F–049 *20.4

(1) Where detailed assessment proceedings have been commenced, and the paying party serves points of dispute (as to which see Section 34 of this Practice Direction), which show that he is seeking a reduction in any percentage increase charged by counsel on his fees, the solicitor acting for the receiving party must within 3 days of service deliver to counsel a copy of the relevant points of dispute and the bill of costs or the relevant parts of the bill.

(2) Counsel must within 10 days thereafter inform the solicitor in writing whether or not he will accept the reduction sought or some other reduction. Counsel may state any points he wishes to have made in a reply to the points of dispute, and the solicitor must serve them on the paying party as or as part of a reply.

(3) Counsel who fails to inform the solicitor within the time limits set out above will be taken to accept the reduction unless the court otherwise orders.

*20.5 Where the paying party serves points of dispute seeking a reduction in any percentage increase charged by a legal representative acting for the receiving party, and that legal representative intends, if necessary, to apply for an order that any amount of the percentage disallowed as against the paying party shall continue to be payable by his client, the solicitor acting for the receiving party must, within 14 days of service of the points of dispute, give to his client a clear written explanation of the nature of the relevant point of dispute and the effect it will have if it is upheld in whole or in part by the court, and of the client's right to attend any subsequent hearings at court when the matter is raised.

*20.6 Where the solicitor acting for a receiving party files a request for a detailed assessment hearing it must if appropriate, be accompanied by a certificate signed by him stating:

(1) that the amount of the percentage increase in respect of counsel's fees or solicitor's charges is disputed;
(2) whether an application will be made for an order that any amount of that increase which is disallowed should continue to be payable by his client;
(3) that he has given his client an explanation in accordance with paragraph 20.5; and,
(4) whether his client wishes to attend court when the amount of any relevant percentage increase may be decided.

*20.7
(1) The solicitor acting for the receiving party must within 7 days of receiving from the court notice of the date of the assessment hearing, notify his client, and if appropriate, counsel in writing of the date, time and place of the hearing.
(2) Counsel may attend or be represented at the detailed assessment hearing and may make oral or written submissions.

*20.8
(1) At the detailed assessment hearing, the court will deal with the assessment of the costs payable by one party to another, including the amount of the percentage increase, and give a certificate accordingly.
(2) The court may decide the issue whether the disallowed amount should continue to be payable under the relevant conditional fee agreement without an adjournment if:
   (a) the receiving party and all parties to the relevant agreement consent to the court deciding the issue without an adjournment,
   (b) the receiving party (or, if corporate, an officer or employee who has authority to consent on behalf of the receiving party) is present in court, and
   (c) the court is satisfied that the issue can be fairly decided without an adjournment.

(3) In any other case the court will give directions and fix a date for the hearing of the application.

## SECTION 21 Application of costs rules: Rule 44.17

F–050

*21.1 Rule 44.17(b) excludes the costs rules to the extent that regulations under the Legal Aid Act 1988 make different provision. The primary examples of such regulations are the regulations providing prescribed rates (with or without enhancement).
*21.2 Rule 44.17(a) also excludes the procedure for the detailed assessment of costs in cases to which Section 11 of the Access to Justice Act 1999 applies, whether it applies in whole or in part. In these excluded cases the procedure for determination of costs is set out in Section 22 of this Practice Direction.
*21.3 Section 11 of the Access to Justice Act 1999 provides special protection against liability for costs for litigants who receive funding by the LSC (Legal Services Commission) as part of the Community Legal Service. Any costs ordered to be paid by a LSC funded client must not exceed the amount which is reasonable for him to pay having regard to all the circumstances including:

(a) the financial resources of all the parties to the proceedings, and
(b) their conduct in connection with the dispute to which the proceedings relate.

*21.4 In this Practice Direction
"cost protection" means the limit on costs awarded against a LSC funded client set out in Section 11(1) of the Access to Justice Act 1999.
"partner" has the meaning given by the Community Legal Service (Costs) Regulations 2000.

F–051 *21.5 Whether or not cost protection applies depends upon the "level of service" for which funding was provided by the LSC in accordance with the Funding Code approved under section 9 of the Access to Justice Act 1999. The levels of service referred to are:
**(1) Legal Help**—advice and assistance about a legal problem, not including representation or advocacy in proceedings.
**(2) Help at Court**—advocacy at a specific hearing, where the advocate is not formally representing the client in the proceedings.
**(3) Family Mediation.**
**(4) Legal Representation**—representation in actual or contemplated proceedings. Legal Representation can take the form of **Investigative Help** (limited to investigating the merits of a potential claim) or **Full Representation.**
**(5) Approved Family Help**—this can take the form of **Help with Mediation** (legal advice in support of the family mediation process) or **General Family Help** (help negotiating a settlement to a family dispute without recourse to adversarial litigation).
**(6) Support Funding**—partial funding in expensive cases that are primarily being funded privately, under or with a view to a conditional fee agreement. Support Funding can take the form of **Investigative Support** (equivalent to *Investigative Help*) or **Litigation Support** (equivalent to *Full Representation*).

*21.6 Levels of service (4) (5) and (6) are provided under a certificate (similar to a legal aid certificate). The certificate will state which level of service is covered.Where there are proceedings, a copy of the certificate will be lodged with the court.

*21.7 Cost protection does not apply where:

(1) The LSC funded client receives Help at Court;
(2) the LSC funded client receives Litigation Support (but see further, paragraph 21.8);
(3) the LSC funded client receives Investigative Support (except where the proceedings for which Investigative Support was given are not pursued after the certificate is discharged). Investigative Support will not normally cover the issue of proceedings (except for disclosure), but cost protection may be relevant if the defendant seeks an assessment of pre-action costs;
(4) the LSC funded client receives Legal Help only i.e. where the solicitor is advising, but not representing a litigant in person. However, where the LSC funded client receives Legal Help e.g. to write a letter before action, but later receives Legal Representation or Approved Family Help in respect of the same dispute, cost protection does apply to all costs incurred by the receiving party in the funded proceedings or prospective proceedings.

*21.8 Where cost protection does not apply, the court may award costs in the normal way. In the case of Litigation Support, costs that are not covered by the LSC funded client's insurance are usually payable by the LSC rather than the funded client, and the court should order accordingly (see Regulation. 6 of the Community Legal Service (Cost Protection) Regulations 2000).

*21.9 Where work is done before the issue of a certificate, cost protection does not apply to those costs, except where:

(1) pre-action Legal Help is given and the LSC funded client subsequently receives Legal Representation or Approved Family Help in the same dispute; or
(2) where urgent work is undertaken immediately before the grant of an emergency certificate when no emergency application could be made as the LSC's offices were closed, provided that the solicitor seeks an emergency certificate at the first available opportunity and the certificate is granted.

*21.10 If a LSC funded client's certificate is revoked, costs protection does not apply to work done before or after revocation.

*21.11 If a LSC funded client's certificate is discharged, costs protection only applies to costs incurred before the date on which funded services ceased to be provided under the certificate. This may be a date before the date on which the certificate is formally discharged by the LSC (Burridge v Stafford: Khan v Ali [2000] 1 WLR 927, [1999] 4 All ER 660 C.A.).

*Assessing a LSC Funded Client's Resources*

*21.12 The first £100,000 of the value of the LSC funded client's interest in the main or only home is disregarded when assessing his or her financial resources for the purposes of S.11 and cannot be the subject of any enforcement process by the receiving party. The receiving party cannot apply for an order to sell the LSC funded client's home, but could secure the debt against any value exceeding £100,000 by way of a charging order.

*21.13 The court may only take into account the value of the LSC funded client's clothes, household furniture, tools and implements of trade to the extent that it considers that having regard to the quantity or value of the items, the circumstances are exceptional.

*21.14 The LSC funded client's resources include the resources of his partner, unless the partner has a contrary interest in the dispute in respect of which funded services are provided.

*Party acting in a Representative, Fiduciary or Official Capacity*

*21.15 F–052

(1) Where a LSC funded client is acting in a representative, fiduciary or official capacity, the court shall not take the personal resources of the party into account for the purposes of either a Section 11 order or costs against the Commission, but shall have regard to the value of any property or estate or the amount of any fund out of which the party is entitled to be indemnified, and may also have regard to the resources of any persons who are beneficially interested in the property, estate or fund.
(2) The purpose of this provision is to ensure that any liability is determined with reference to the value of the property or fund being used to pay for the litigation, and the financial position of those who may benefit from or rely on it.

*Costs against the LSC*

F–053 *21.16 Regulation 5 of the Community Legal Service (Cost Protection) Regulations 2000 governs when costs can be awarded against the LSC. This provision only applies where cost protection applies and the costs ordered to be paid by the LSC funded client do not fully meet the costs that would have been ordered to be paid by him if cost protection did not apply.

*21.17 In this Section and the following two Sections of this Practice Direction "non-funded party" means a party to proceedings who has not received LSC funded services in relation to these proceedings under a legal aid certificate or a certificate issued under the LSC Funding Code other than a certificate which has been revoked.

*21.18 The following criteria set out in Regulation 5 must be satisfied before the LSC can be ordered to pay the whole or any part of the costs incurred by a non-funded party:

(1) the proceedings are finally decided in favour of a non-funded party;
(2) the non-funded party provides written notice of intention to seek an order against the LSC within three months of the making of the section 11(1) costs order;
(3) the court is satisfied that it is just and equitable in the circumstances that provision for the costs should be made out of public funds; and
(4) where costs are incurred in a court of first instance, the following additional criteria must also be met:

 (i) the proceedings were instituted by the LSC funded client; and
 (ii) the non-funded party will suffer severe financial hardship unless the order is made.

"Section 11(1) costs order" is defined in paragraph 22.1, below).

*21.19 In determining whether conditions (3) and (4) are satisfied, the court shall take into account the resources of the non-funded party and his partner, unless the partner has a contrary interest.

*Effect of Appeals*

F–054 *21.20

(1) An order for costs can only be made against the LSC when the proceedings (including any appeal) are finally decided. Therefore, where a court of first instance decides in favour of a non-funded party and an appeal lies, any order made against the LSC shall not take effect unless:

 (a) where permission to appeal is required, the time limit for permission to appeal expires, without permission being granted;
 (b) where permission to appeal is granted or is not required, the time limit for appeal expires without an appeal being brought.

(2) Accordingly, if the LSC funded client appeals, any earlier order against the LSC can never take effect. If the appeal is unsuccessful, an application can be made to the appeal court for a fresh order.

**SECTION 22 Orders for costs to which section 11 of the Access to Justice Act 1999 applies**

F–055 *22.1 In this Practice Direction:

"order for costs to be determined" means an order for costs to which Section

11 of the Access to Justice Act 1999 applies under which the amount of costs payable by the LSC funded client is to be determined by a costs judge or district judge under Section 23 of this Practice Direction.

"order specifying the costs payable" means an order for costs to which Section 11 of the Act applies and which specifies the amount which the LSC funded client is to pay.

"full costs" means, where an order to which Section 11 of the Act applies is made against a LSC funded client, the amount of costs which that person would, had cost protection not applied, have been ordered to pay.

"determination proceedings" means proceedings to which paragraphs 22.1 to 22.10 apply.

"Section 11(1) costs order" means an order for costs to be determined or an order specifying the costs payable other than an order specifying the costs payable which was made in determination proceedings.

"statement of resources" means

(1) a statement, verified by a statement of truth, made by a party to proceedings setting out:
   (a) his income and capital and financial commitments during the previous year and, if applicable, those of his partner;
   (b) his estimated future financial resources and expectations and, if applicable, those of his partner ("partner" is defined in paragraph 21.4, above);
   (c) a declaration that he and, if applicable, his partner, has not deliberately foregone or deprived himself of any resources or expectations;
   (d) particulars of any application for funding made by him in connection with the proceedings; and,
   (e) any other facts relevant to the determination of his resources; or

(2) a statement, verified by a statement of truth, made by a client receiving funded services, setting out the information provided by the client under Regulation 6 of the Community Legal Service (Financial) Regulations 2000, and stating that there has been no significant change in the client's financial circumstances since the date on which the information was provided or, as the case may be, details of any such change.
"Regional Director" means any Regional Director appointed by the LSC and any member of his staff authorised to act on his behalf.

22.2 Regulations 8 to 13 of the Community Legal Service (Costs) Regulations 2000 set out the procedure for seeking costs against a funded client and the LSC. The effect of these Regulations is set out in this section and the next section of this Practice Direction.

22.3 As from 5 June 2000, Regulations 9 to13 of the Community Legal Service (Costs) Regulations 2000 also apply to certificates issued under the Legal Aid Act 1988 where costs against the assisted person fall to be assessed under Regulation 124 of the Civil Legal Aid (General) Regulations 1989. In this section and the next section of this Practice Direction the expression "LSC funded client" includes an assisted person (defined in rule 43.2).

22.4 Regulation 8 of the Community Legal Service (Costs) Regulations 2000 provides that a party intending to seek an order for costs against a LSC funded client may at any time file and serve on the LSC funded client a statement of resources. If that statement is served 7 or more days before a date fixed for a hearing at which an order for costs may be made, the LSC funded client must also make a statement of resources and produce it at the hearing.

22.5 If the court decides to make an order for costs against a LSC funded client to whom cost protection applies it may either:

(1) make an order for costs to be determined, or

(2) make an order specifying the costs payable.

*22.6 If the court makes an order for costs to be determined it may also

(1) state the amount of full costs, or
(2) make findings of facts, e.g., concerning the conduct of all the parties whic are to be taken into account by the court in the subsequent determinatic proceedings.

*22.7 The court will not make an order specifying the costs payable unless:

(1) it considers that it has sufficient information before it to decide wh amount is a reasonable amount for the LSC funded client to pay in accor ance with Section 11 of the Act, and
(2) either
   (a) the order also states the amount of full costs, or
   (b) the court considers that it has sufficient information before it to decic what amount is a reasonable amount for the LSC funded client to pa in accordance with Section 11 of the Act and is satisfied that, if it we to determine the full costs at that time, they would exceed the amoun specified in the order.

*22.8 Where an order specifying the costs payable is made and the LSC funde client does not have cost protection in respect of all of the costs awarded i that order, the order must identify the sum payable (if any) in respect c which the LSC funded client has cost protection and the sum payable ( any) in respect of which he does not have cost protection.

*22.9 The court cannot make an order under Regulations 8 to 13 of the Commu ity Legal Service (Costs) Regulations 2000 except in proceedings to whic the next section of this Practice Direction applies.

**SECTION 23 Determination proceedings and similar proceedings under the Community Legal Service (Costs) Regulations 2000**

F–056

*23.1 This section of this Practice Direction deals with

(1) proceedings subsequent to the making of an order for costs to be dete mined,
(2) variations in the amount stated in an order specifying the amount of cost payable and
(3) the late determination of costs under an order for costs to be determined

*23.2 In this section of this Practice Direction "appropriate court office" means:

(1) the district registry or county court in which the case was being dealt wit when the Section 11(1) order was made, or to which it has subsequentl been transferred; or
(2) in all other cases, the Supreme Court Costs Office.

*23.3

(1) A receiving party seeking an order specifying costs payable by an LS funded client and/or by the LSC may within 3 months of an order for cost to be determined, file in the appropriate court office an application in Forn N244 accompanied by
   (a) the receiving party's bill of costs (unless the full costs have alread been determined);
   (b) the receiving party's statement of resources; and
   (c) if the receiving party intends to seek costs against the LSC, writte notice to that effect.
(2) If the LSC funded client's liability has already been determined and is les

than the full costs, the application will be for costs against the LSC only. If the LSC funded client's liability has not yet been determined, the receiving party must indicate if costs will be sought against the LSC if the funded client's liability is determined as less than the full costs.

(The LSC funded client's certificate will contain the addresses of the LSC funded client, his solicitor, and the relevant Regional Office of the LSC.)

23.4 The receiving party must file the above documents in the appropriate court office and (where relevant) serve copies on the LSC funded client and the Regional Director. Failure to file a request within the 3 months time limit specified in Regulation 10(2) is an absolute bar to the making of a costs order against the LSC.

23.5 On being served with the application, the LSC funded client must respond by filing a statement of resources and serving a copy of it on the receiving party (and the Regional Director where relevant) within 21 days. The LSC funded client may also file and serve written points disputing the bill within the same time limit. (Under rule 3.1 the court may extend or shorten this time limit.)

23.6 If the LSC funded client fails to file a statement of resources without good reason, the court will determine his liability (and the amount of full costs if relevant) and need not hold an oral hearing for such determination.

23.7 When the LSC funded client files a statement or the 21 day period for doing so expires, the court will fix a hearing date and give the relevant parties at least 14 days notice. The court may fix a hearing without waiting for the expiry of the 21 day period if the application is made only against the LSC.

23.8 Determination proceedings will be listed for hearing before a costs judge or district judge.

23.9 Where the LSC funded client does not have cost protection in respect of all of the costs awarded, the order made by the costs judge or district judge must in addition to specifying the costs payable, identify the full costs in respect of which cost protection applies and the full costs in respect of which cost protection does not apply.

23.10 The Regional Director may appear at any hearing at which a costs order may be made against the LSC. Instead of appearing, he may file a written statement at court and serve a copy on the receiving party. The written statement should be filed and a copy served, not less than 7 days before the hearing.

*Variation of an order specifying the costs payable*

23.11 F–057

(1) This paragraph applies where the amount stated in an order specifying the costs payable plus the amount ordered to be paid by the LSC is less than the full costs to which cost protection applies.

(2) The receiving party may apply to the court for a variation of the amount which the LSC funded client is required to pay on the ground that there has been a significant change in the client's circumstances since the date of the order.

23.12 On an application under paragraph 23.11, where the order specifying the costs payable does not state the full costs

(1) the receiving party must file with his application the receiving party's statement of resources and bill of costs and copies of these documents should be served with the application.

(2) The LSC funded client must respond to the application by making a stat ment of resources which must be filed at court and served on the receivi party within 21 days thereafter. The LSC funded client may also file ar serve written points disputing the bill within the same time limit.

(3) The court will, when determining the application assess the full costs ide tifying any part of them to which cost protection does apply and any pa of them to which cost protection does not apply.

*23.13 On an application under paragraph 23.11 the order specifying the cos payable may be varied as the court thinks fit. That variation must n increase:

(1) the amount of any costs ordered to be paid by the LSC, and
(2) the amount payable by the LSC funded client,

to a sum which is greater than the amount of the full costs plus the cos of the application.

*23.14

(1) Where an order for costs to be determined has been made but the receivin party has not applied, within the three month time limit under paragrap 23.2, the receiving party may apply on any of the following grounds for determination of the amount which the funded client is required to pay:

(a) there has been a significant change in the funded client's circumstanc since the date of the order for costs to be determined; or
(b) material additional information about the funded client's financi resources is available which could not with reasonable diligence hav been obtained by the receiving party at the relevant time; or
(c) there were other good reasons for the failure by the receiving party t make an application within the time limit.

(2) An application for costs payable by the LSC cannot be made under th paragraph.

*23.15

(1) Where the receiving party has received funded services in relation to th proceedings, the LSC may make an application under paragraphs 23.1 and 23.14 above.

(2) In respect of an application under paragraph 23.11 made by the LSC, th LSC must file and serve copies of the documents described in paragrap 23.12(1)

*23.16 An application under paragraph 23.11, 23.14 and 23.15 must be com menced before the expiration of 6 years from the date on which the cou made the order specifying the costs payable, or (as the case may be) th order for costs to be determined.

*23.17 Applications under paragraphs 23.11, 23.14 and 23.15 should be made i the appropriate court office and should be made in Form N244 to be liste for a hearing before a costs judge or district judge.

# Directions Relating to Part 45

*Fixed Costs*

**ECTION 24 Fixed costs in small claims**

4.1 Under Rule 27.14 the costs which can be awarded to a claimant in a small claims track case include the fixed costs payable under Part 45 attributable to issuing the claim. F–058

4.2 Those fixed costs shall be the sum of

(a) the fixed commencement costs calculated in accordance with Table 1 of Rule 45.2 and;

(b) the appropriate court fee or fees paid by the claimant.

**ECTION 25 Fixed costs on the issue of a default costs certificate**

5.1 Unless paragraph 24.2 applies or unless the court orders otherwise, the fixed costs to be included in a default costs certificate are £80 plus a sum equal to any appropriate court fee payable on the issue of the certificate. F–059

5.2 The fixed costs included in a certificate must not exceed the maximum sum specified for costs and court fee in the notice of commencement.

# Directions Relating to Part 46

*Fast track trial costs*

**ECTION 26 Scope of Part 46:** Rule 46.1

6.1 Part 46 applies to the costs of an advocate for preparing for and appearing at the trial of a claim in the fast track. F–060

6.2 It applies only where, at the date of the trial, the claim is allocated to the fast track. It does not apply in any other case, irrespective of the final value of the claim.

6.3 In particular it does not apply to:

(a) the hearing of a claim which is allocated to the small claims track with the consent of the parties given under rule 26.7(3); or

(b) a disposal hearing at which the amount to be paid under a judgment or order is decided by the court (see paragraph 12.8 of the Practice Direction which supplements Part 26 (Case Management - Preliminary Stage)).

**:ases which settle before trial**

6.4 Attention is drawn to rule 44.10 (limitation on amount court may award where a claim allocated to the fast track settles before trial). F–061

**ECTION 27 Power to award more or less than the amount of fast track trial osts:** Rule 46.3

27.1 Rule 44.15 (providing information about funding arrangements) sets out the requirement to provide information about funding arrangements to the court F–062 and other parties. Section 19 of this Practice Direction sets out the inform tion to be provided and when this is to be done.

*27.2 Section 11, of this Practice Direction explains how the court will approa the question of what sum to allow in respect of additional liability.

*27.3 The court has the power, when considering whether a percentage increase reasonable, to allow different percentages for different items of costs or f different periods during which costs were incurred.

## Directions Relating to Part 47

*Procedure for detailed assessment of costs and default provisions*

**SECTION 28 Time when assessment may be carried out:** Rule 47.1

**F–063** *28.1

(1) For the purposes of rule 47.1, proceedings are concluded when the cou has finally determined the matters in issue in the claim, whether or n there is an appeal.
(2) For the purposes of this rule, the making of an award of provisional da ages under Part 41 will be treated as a final determination of the matte in issue.
(3) The court may order or the parties may agree in writing that, althou the proceedings are continuing, they will nevertheless be treated as co cluded.

(4) (a) A party who is served with a notice of commencement (see paragra 32.3 below) may apply to a costs judge or a district judge to determi whether the party who served it is entitled to commence detail assessment proceedings.
(b) On hearing such an application the orders which the court may ma include: an order allowing the detailed assessment proceedings to co tinue, or an order setting aside the notice of commencement.

(5) A costs judge or a district judge may make an order allowing detail assessment proceedings to be commenced where there is no realistic pr spect of the claim continuing.

**SECTION 29 No stay of detailed assessment where there is an appeal:** Rule 47.

**F–064** 29.1

(1) Rule 47.2 provides that detailed assessment is not stayed pending an appe unless the court so orders.
(2) An application to stay the detailed assessment of costs pending an appe may be made to the court whose order is being appealed or to the cou who will hear the appeal.

**SECTION 30 Powers of an authorised court officer:** Rule 47.3

**F–065** *30.1

(1) The court officers authorised by the Lord Chancellor to assess costs in t Supreme Court Costs Office and the Principal Registry of the Family Div sion are authorised to deal with claims for costs not exceeding £17,5

(excluding VAT) in the case of senior executive officers and £35,000 (excluding VAT) in the case of principal officers.

(2) In calculating whether or not a bill of costs is within the authorised amounts, the figure to be taken into account is the total claim for costs including any additional liability.

(3) Where the receiving party, paying party and any other party to the detailed assessment proceedings who has served points of dispute are agreed that the assessment should not be made by an authorised court officer, the receiving party should so inform the court when requesting a hearing date. The court will then list the hearing before a costs judge or a district judge.

(4) In any other case a party who objects to the assessment being made by an authorised court officer must make an application to the costs judge or district judge under Part 23 (General Rules about Applications for Court Orders) setting out the reasons for the objection and if sufficient reason is shown the court will direct that the bill be assessed by a costs judge or district judge.

## ECTION 31 Venue for detailed assessment proceedings: Rule 47.4

31.1 For the purposes of rule 47.4(1) the "appropriate office" means **F–066**

(1) the district registry or county court in which the case was being dealt with when the judgment or order was made or the event occurred which gave rise to the right to assessment, or to which it has subsequently been transferred; or

(2) in all other cases, the Supreme Court Costs Office.

1.2

(1) A direction under rule 47.4(2) or (3) specifying a particular court, registry or office as the appropriate office may be given on application or on the court's own initiative.

(2) Before making such a direction on its own initiative the court will give the parties the opportunity to make representations.

(3) Unless the Supreme Court Costs Office is the appropriate office for the purposes of Rule 47.4(1) an order directing that an assessment is to take place at the Supreme Court Costs Office will be made only if it is appropriate to do so having regard to the size of the bill of costs, the difficulty of the issues involved, the likely length of the hearing, the cost to the parties and any other relevant matter.

## ECTION 32 Commencement of detailed assessment proceedings: Rule 47.6

2.1 * Precedents A, B, C and D in the Schedule of Costs Precedents annexed to this Practice Direction are model forms of bills of costs for detailed assessment. Further information about bills of costs is set out in Section 4. **F–067**

32.2 A detailed assessment may be in respect of:

(1) base costs, where a claim for additional liability has not been made or has been agreed;

(2) a claim for additional liability only, base costs having been summarily assessed or agreed; or

(3) both base costs and additional liability.

32.3 If the detailed assessment is in respect of costs without any additional liability, the receiving party must serve on the paying party and all the other relevant persons the following documents:

(a) a notice of commencement;
(b) a copy of the bill of costs;
(c) copies of the fee notes of counsel and of any expert in respect of fe
claimed in the bill;
(d) written evidence as to any other disbursement which is claimed and whi
exceeds £250;
(e) a statement giving the name and address for service of any person upo
whom the receiving party intends to serve the notice of commenc
ment.

*32.4 If the detailed assessment is in respect of an additional liability only, t
receiving party must serve on the paying party and all other relevant perso
the following documents:
(a) a notice of commencement;
(b) a copy of the bill of costs;
(c) the relevant details of the additional liability;
(d) a statement giving the name and address of any person upon whom t
receiving party intends to serve the notice of commencement.

*32.5 The relevant details of an additional liability are as follows:

(1) In the case of a conditional fee agreement with a success fee:

(a) a statement showing the amount of costs which have been summari
assessed or agreed, and the percentage increase which has be
claimed in respect of those costs;
(b) a statement of the reasons for the percentage increase given in accor
ance with Regulation 3 of the Conditional Fee Agreement Regulatio
2000.

(2) If the additional liability is an insurance premium: a copy of the insuran
certificate showing whether the policy covers the receiving party's ow
costs; his opponents costs; or his own costs and his opponent's costs; an
the maximum extent of that cover, and the amount of the premium pa
or payable.
(3) If the receiving party claims an additional amount under Section 30 of t
Access of Justice Act 1999: a statement setting out the basis upon whi
the receiving party's liability for the additional amount is calculated.

*32.6 Attention is drawn to the fact that the additional amount recoverable purs
ant to section 30 of the Access to Justice Act 1999 in respect of a membe
ship organisation must not exceed the likely cost of the premium of an insu
ance policy against the risk of incurring a liability to pay the costs of oth
parties to the proceedings as provided by the Access to Justice (Membersh
Organisation) Regulations 2000 Regulation 4.

*32.7 If a detailed assessment is in respect of both base costs and an addition
liability, the receiving party must serve on the paying party and all oth
relevant persons the documents listed in paragraph 32.3 and the doc
ments giving relevant details of an additional liability listed in paragra
32.5.

*32.8

(1) The Notice of Commencement should be in Form N252.
(2) Before it is served, it must be completed to show as separate items;

(a) the total amount of the costs claimed in the bill;
(b) the extra sum which will be payable by way of fixed costs and co
fees if a default costs certificate is obtained.

32.9

(1) This paragraph applies where the notice of commencement is to be served outside England and Wales.
(2) The date to be inserted in the notice of commencement for the paying party to send points of dispute is a date (not less than 21 days from the date of service of the notice) which must be calculated by reference to Part 6 Section III as if the notice were a claim form and as if the date to be inserted was the date for the filing of a defence.

32.10

(1) For the purposes of rule 47.6(2) a "relevant person" means:

(a) any person who has taken part in the proceedings which gave rise to the assessment and who is directly liable under an order for costs made against him;
(b) any person who has given to the receiving party notice in writing that he has a financial interest in the outcome of the assessment and wishes to be a party accordingly;
(c) any other person whom the court orders to be treated as such.

(2) Where a party is unsure whether a person is or is not a relevant person, that party may apply to the appropriate office for directions.
(3) The court will generally not make an order that the person in respect of whom the application is made will be treated as a relevant person, unless within a specified time he applies to the court to be joined as a party to the assessment proceedings in accordance with Part 19 (Parties and Group Litigation).

32.11

(1) This paragraph applies in cases in which the bill of costs is capable of being copied onto a computer disk.
(2) If, before the detailed assessment hearing, a paying party requests a disk copy of a bill to which this paragraph applies, the receiving party must supply him with a copy free of charge not more than 7 days after the date on which he received the request.

**SECTION 33 Period for commencing detailed assessment proceedings:** Rule 47.7

33.1 The parties may agree under rule 2.11 (Time limits may be varied by parties) to extend or shorten the time specified by rule 47.7 for commencing the detailed assessment proceedings. **F–068**
33.2 A party may apply to the appropriate office for an order under rule 3.1(2)(a) to extend or shorten that time.
33.3 Attention is drawn to rule 47.6(1). The detailed assessment proceedings are commenced by service of the documents referred to.
33.4 Permission to commence assessment proceedings out of time is not required.

**SECTION 34 Sanction for delay in commencing detailed assessment proceedings:** Rule 47.8

34.1 **F–069**

(1) An application for an order under rule 47.8 must be made in writing and be issued in the appropriate office.

(2) The application notice must be served at least 7 days before th
hearing.

SECTION 35 **Points of dispute and consequences of not serving:** Rule 47.9

F–070

35.1 The parties may agree under rule 2.11 (Time limits may be varied by parties to extend or shorten the time specified by rule 47.9 for service of points o dispute. A party may apply to the appropriate office for an order under rul 3.1(2)(a) to extend or shorten that time.

*35.2 Points of dispute should be short and to the point and should follow a closely as possible Precedent G of the Schedule of Costs Precedents annexe to this Practice Direction.

35.3 Points of dispute must—

(1) identify each item in the bill of costs which is disputed,
(2) in each case, state concisely the nature and grounds of dispute,
(3) where practicable suggest a figure to be allowed for each item in respect o which a reduction is sought, and
(4) be signed by the party serving them or his solicitor.

*35.4

(1) The normal period for serving points of dispute is 21 days after the dat of service of the notice of commencement.
(2) Where a notice of commencement is served on a party outside England an Wales the period within which that party should serve points of dispute i to be calculated by reference to Part 6 Section III as if the notice of com mencement was a claim form and as if the period for serving points o dispute were the period for filing a defence.

35.5 A party who serves points of dispute on the receiving party must at the sam time serve a copy on every other party to the detailed assessment proceedings whose name and address for service appears on the statement served by th receiving party in accordance with paragraph 32.3 or 32.4 above.

35.6

(1) This paragraph applies in cases in which Points of Dispute are capable o being copied onto a computer disk.
(2) If, within 14 days of the receipt of the Points of Dispute, the receiving part requests a disk copy of them, the paying party must supply him with a cop free of charge not more than 7 days after the date on which he received th request.

*35.7

(1) Where the receiving party claims an additional liability, a party who serve points of dispute on the receiving party may include a request for informa tion about other methods of financing costs which were available to th receiving party.
(2) Part 18 (further information) and the Practice Direction Supplementin that part apply to such a request.

SECTION 36 **Procedure where costs are agreed:** Rule 47.10

F–071

36.1 Where the parties have agreed terms as to the issue of a costs certificate (eithe interim or final) they should apply under rule 40.6 (Consent judgments an orders) for an order that a certificate be issued in terms set out in the applica tion. Such an application may be dealt with by a court officer, who may issu the certificate.

*36.2 Where in the course of proceedings the receiving party claims that the paying party has agreed to pay costs but that he will neither pay those costs nor join in a consent application under paragraph 36.1, the receiving party may apply under Part 23 (General Rules about Applications for Court Orders) for a certificate either interim or final to be issued.

36.3 An application under paragraph 36.2 must be supported by evidence and will be heard by a costs judge or a district judge. The respondent to the application must file and serve any evidence he relies on at least two days before the hearing date.

36.4 Nothing in rule 47.10 prevents parties who seek a judgment or order by consent from including in the draft a term that a party shall pay to another party a specified sum in respect of costs.

36.5

(1) The receiving party may discontinue the detailed assessment proceedings in accordance with Part 38 (Discontinuance).
(2) Where the receiving party discontinues the detailed assessment proceedings before a detailed assessment hearing has been requested, the paying party may apply to the appropriate office for an order about the costs of the detailed assessment proceedings.
(3) Where a detailed assessment hearing has been requested the receiving party may not discontinue unless the court gives permission.
(4) A bill of costs may be withdrawn by consent whether or not a detailed assessment hearing has been requested.

## SECTION 37 Default costs certificate: Rule 47.11

37.1 A request for the issue of a default costs certificate must be made in Form N254 and must be signed by the receiving party or his solicitor. F–072

37.2 The request must be filed at the appropriate office.

37.3 A default costs certificate will be in Form N255.

37.4 Attention is drawn to Rules 40.3 (Drawing up and Filing of Judgments and Orders) and 40.4 (Service of Judgments and Orders) which apply to the preparation and service of a default costs certificate. The receiving party will be treated as having permission to draw up a default costs certificate by virtue of this Practice Direction.

*37.5 The issue of a default costs certificate does not prohibit, govern or affect any detailed assessment of the same costs which are payable out of the Community Legal Service Fund.

37.6 An application for an order staying enforcement of a default costs certificate may be made either—

(1) to a costs judge or district judge of the court office which issued the certificate; or
(2) to the court (if different) which has general jurisdiction to enforce the certificate.

37.7 Proceedings for enforcement of default costs certificates may not be issued in the Supreme Court Costs Office.

37.8* The fixed costs payable in respect of solicitor's charges on the issue of the default costs certificate are £80.

## SECTION 38 Setting aside default costs certificate: Rule 47.12

38.1 F–073

(1) A court officer may set aside a default costs certificate at the request of the receiving party under rule 47.12(3).

(2) A costs judge or a district judge will make any other order or give an directions under this rule.

*38.2

(1) An application for an order under rule 47.12(2) to set aside or vary default costs certificate must be supported by evidence.
(2) In deciding whether to set aside or vary a certificate under rule 47.12(2 the matters to which the court must have regard include whether the part seeking the order made the application promptly.
(3) As a general rule a default costs certificate will be set aside under rul 47.12(2) only if the applicant shows a good reason for the court to do s and if he files with his application a copy of the bill and a copy of th default costs certificate, and a draft of the points of dispute he proposes t serve if his application is granted.

38.3

(1) Attention is drawn to rule 3.1(3) (which enables the court when makin an order to make it subject to conditions) and to rule 44.3(8) (whic enables the court to order a party whom it has ordered to pay costs to pa an amount on account before the costs are assessed).
(2) A costs judge or a district judge may exercise the power of the court t make an order under rule 44.3(8) although he did not make the orde about costs which led to the issue of the default costs certificate.

38.4 If a default costs certificate is set aside the court will give directions for th management of the detailed assessment proceedings.

**SECTION 39 Optional reply:** Rule 47.13

F–074 39.1

(1) Where the receiving party wishes to serve a reply, he must also serve copy on every other party to the detailed assessment proceedings. The tim for doing so is within 21 days after service of the points of dispute.
(2) A reply means:—

(i) a separate document prepared by the receiving party; or
(ii) his written comments added to the points of dispute.

(3) A reply must be signed by the party serving it or his solicitor.

**SECTION 40 Detailed assessment hearing:** Rule 47.14

F–075 40.1 The time for requesting a detailed assessment hearing is within 3 months c the expiry of the period for commencing detailed assessment proceedings.

*40.2 The request for a detailed assessment hearing must be in Form N258. Th request must be accompanied by:

(a) a copy of the notice of commencement of detailed assessment proceeding
(b) a copy of the bill of costs;
(c) the document giving the right to detailed assessment (see paragraph 40. below);
(d) a copy of the points of dispute, annotated as necessary in order to shov which items have been agreed and their value and to show which item remain in dispute and their value;

(e) as many copies of the points of dispute so annotated as there are persons who have served points of dispute;
(f) a copy of any replies served;
(g) a copy of all orders made by the court relating to the costs which are to be assessed;
(h) copies of the fee notes and other written evidence as served on the paying party in accordance with paragraph 32.3 above;
(i) where there is a dispute as to the receiving party's liability to pay costs to the solicitors who acted for the receiving party, any agreement, letter or other written information provided by the solicitor to his client explaining how the solicitor's charges are to be calculated;
(j) a statement signed by the receiving party or his solicitor giving the name, address for service, reference and telephone number and fax number, if any, of—

(i) the receiving party;
(ii) the paying party;
(iii) any other person who has served points of dispute or who has given notice to the receiving party under paragraph 32.10(1)(b) above;

and giving an estimate of the length of time the detailed assessment hearing will take;
(k) where the application for a detailed assessment hearing is made by a party other than the receiving party, such of the documents set out in this paragraph as are in the possession of that party;
(l) where the court is to assess the costs of an assisted person or LSC funded client—

(i) the legal aid certificate, LSC certificate and relevant amendment certificates, any authorities and any certificates of discharge or revocation.
(ii) a certificate, in Precedent F(3) of the Schedule of Costs Precedents;
(iii) if the assisted person has a financial interest in the detailed assessment hearing and wishes to attend, the postal address of that person to which the court will send notice of any hearing;
(iv) if the rates payable out of the LSC fund are prescribed rates, a schedule to the bill of costs setting out all the items in the bill which are claimed against other parties calculated at the legal aid prescribed rates with or without any claim for enhancement: (further information as to this schedule is set out in Section 48 of this Practice Direction);
(v) a copy of any default costs certificate in respect of costs claimed in the bill of costs.

40.3

(1) This paragraph applies to any document described in paragraph 40.2(i) above which the receiving party has filed in the appropriate office. The document must be the latest relevant version and in any event have been filed not more than 2 years before filing the request for a detailed assessment hearing.
(2) In respect of any documents to which this paragraph applies, the receiving party may, instead of filing a copy of it, specify in the request for a detailed assessment hearing the case number under which a copy of the document was previously filed.

40.4 "The document giving the right to detailed assessment" means such one or more of the following documents as are appropriate to the detailed assessment proceedings:

(a) a copy of the judgment or order of the court giving the right to detailed assessment;

(b) a copy of the notice served under rule 3.7 (sanctions for non-payment c certain fees) where a claim is struck out under that rule;
(c) a copy of the notice of acceptance where an offer to settle is accepted unde Part 36 (Offers to settle and payments into court);
(d) a copy of the notice of discontinuance in a case which is discontinued unde Part 38 (Discontinuance);
(e) a copy of the award made on an arbitration under any Act or pursuant t an agreement, where no court has made an order for the enforcement c the award;
(f) a copy of the order, award or determination of a statutorily constitute tribunal or body;
(g) in a case under the Sheriffs Act 1887, the sheriff's bill of fees and charge unless a court order giving the right to detailed assessment has been made
(h) a notice of revocation or discharge under Regulation 82 of the Civil Lega Aid (General) Regulations 1989.
(j) In the county courts certain Acts and Regulations provide for cost incurred in proceedings under those Acts and Regulations to be assessed i the county court if so ordered on application. Where such an applicatio is made, a copy of the order.

40.5 On receipt of the request for a detailed assessment hearing the court will fi a date for the hearing, or, if the costs officer so decides, will give direction or fix a date for a preliminary appointment.

40.6

(1) The court will give at least 14 days notice of the time and place of th detailed assessment hearing to every person named in the statemen referred to in paragraph 40.2(j) above.
(2) The court will when giving notice, give each person who has served point of dispute a copy of the points of dispute annotated by the receiving part in compliance with paragraph 40.2(d) above.
(3) Attention is drawn to rule 47.14(6)&(7): apart from the receiving party only those who have served points of dispute may be heard on the detaile assessment unless the court gives permission, and only items specified i the points of dispute may be raised unless the court gives permission.

*40.7

(1) If the receiving party does not file a request for a detailed assessment hear ing within the prescribed time, the paying party may apply to the court t fix a time within which the receiving party must do so. The sanction, fo failure to commence detailed assessment proceedings within the time speci fied by the court, is that all or part of the costs may be disallowed (see rul 47.8(2)).
(2) Where the receiving party commences detailed assessment proceedings afte the time specified in the rules but before the paying party has made a application to the court to specify a time, the only sanction which the cour may impose is to disallow all or part of the interest which would otherwis be payable for the period of delay, unless the court exercises its power under rule 44.14 (court's powers in relation to misconduct).

40.8 If either party wishes to make an application in the detailed assessment pro ceedings the provisions of Part 23 (General Rules about Applications fo Court Orders) apply.

40.9

(1) This paragraph deals with the procedure to be adopted where a date ha been given by the court for a detailed assessment hearing and

(a) the detailed assessment proceedings are settled; or
(b) a party to the detailed assessment proceedings wishes to apply to vary the date which the court has fixed; or
(c) the parties to the detailed assessment proceedings agree about changes they wish to make to any direction given for the management of the detailed assessment proceedings.

(2) If detailed assessment proceedings are settled, the receiving party must give notice of that fact to the court immediately, preferably by fax.
(3) A party who wishes to apply to vary a direction must do so in accordance with Part 23 (General Rules about Applications for Court Orders).
(4) If the parties agree about changes they wish to make to any direction given for the management of the detailed assessment proceedings—

(a) they must apply to the court for an order by consent; and
(b) they must file a draft of the directions sought and an agreed statement of the reasons why the variation is sought; and
(c) the court may make an order in the agreed terms or in other terms without a hearing, but it may direct that a hearing is to be listed.

40.10

(1) If a party wishes to vary his bill of costs, points of dispute or a reply, an amended or supplementary document must be filed with the court and copies of it must be served on all other relevant parties.
(2) Permission is not required to vary a bill of costs, points of dispute or a reply but the court may disallow the variation or permit it only upon conditions, including conditions as to the payment of any costs caused or wasted by the variation.

40.11 Unless the court directs otherwise the receiving party must file with the court the papers in support of the bill not less than 7 days before the date for the detailed assessment hearing and not more than 14 days before that date.

40.12 The following provisions apply in respect of the papers to be filed in support of the bill;

(a) If the claim is for costs only without any additional liability the papers to be filed, and the order in which they are to be arranged are as follows:

(i) instructions and briefs to counsel arranged in chronological order together with all advices, opinions and drafts received and response to such instructions;
(ii) reports and opinions of medical and other experts;
(iii) any other relevant papers;
(iv) a full set of any relevant pleadings to the extent that they have not already been filed in court.
(v) correspondence, files and attendance notes;

(b) where the claim is in respect of an additional liability only, such of the papers listed at (a) above, as are relevant to the issues raised by the claim for additional liability;
(c) where the claim is for both base costs and an additional liability, the papers listed at (a) above, together with any papers relevant to the issues raised by the claim for additional liability.

40.13 The provisions set out in Section 20 of this Practice Direction apply where the court disallows any amount of a legal representative's percentage increase, and the legal representative applies for an order that the disallowed amount should continue to be payable by the client in accordance with Rule 44.16.

40.14 The court may direct the receiving party to produce any document which in the opinion of the court is necessary to enable it to reach its decision These documents will in the first instance be produced to the court, but the court may ask the receiving party to elect whether to disclose the particular document to the paying party in order to rely on the contents of the document, or whether to decline disclosure and instead rely on other evidence.

*40.15 Costs assessed at a detailed assessment at the conclusion of proceedings may include an assessment of any additional liability in respect of the costs of a previous application or hearing.

40.16 Once the detailed assessment hearing has ended it is the responsibility of the legal representative appearing for the receiving party or, as the case may be, the receiving party in person to remove the papers filed in support of the bill.

**SECTION 41 Power to issue an interim certificate:** Rule 47.15

F–076 41.1

(1) A party wishing to apply for an interim certificate may do so by making an application in accordance with Part 23 (General Rules about Applications for Court Orders).

(2) Attention is drawn to the fact that the court's power to issue an interim certificate arises only after the receiving party has filed a request for a detailed assessment hearing.

**SECTION 42 Final costs certificate:** Rule 47.16

F–077 42.1 At the detailed assessment hearing the court will indicate any disallowance or reduction in the sums claimed in the bill of costs by making an appropriate note on the bill.

*42.2 The receiving party must, in order to complete the bill after the detailed assessment hearing make clear the correct figures agreed or allowed in respect of each item and must re-calculate the summary of the bill appropriately.

42.3 The completed bill of costs must be filed with the court no later than 14 days after the detailed assessment hearing.

*42.4 At the same time as filing the completed bill of costs, the party whose bill is is must also produce receipted fee notes and receipted accounts in respect of all disbursements except those covered by a certificate in Precedent F(5) in the Schedule of Costs Precedents annexed to this Practice Direction.

42.5 No final costs certificate will be issued until all relevant court fees payable on the assessment of costs have been paid.

42.6 If the receiving party fails to file a completed bill in accordance with rule 47.16 the paying party may make an application under Part 23 (General Rules about Applications for Court Orders) seeking an appropriate order under rule 3.1 (The court's general powers of management).

42.7 A final costs certificate will show:

(a) the amount of any costs which have been agreed between the parties or which have been allowed on detailed assessment;

(b) where applicable the amount agreed or allowed in respect of VAT on the costs agreed or allowed.

This provision is subject to any contrary provision made by the statutory provisions relating to costs payable out of the Community Legal Service Fund.

42.8 A final costs certificate will include disbursements in respect of the fees of counsel only if receipted fee notes or accounts in respect of those disbursements have been produced to the court and only to the extent indicated by those receipts.

42.9 Where the certificate relates to costs payable between parties a separate certificate will be issued for each party entitled to costs.

42.10 Form N257 is a model form of interim costs certificate and Form N256 is a model form of final costs certificate.

42.11 An application for an order staying enforcement of an interim costs certificate or final costs certificate may be made either:

(1) to a costs judge or district judge of the court office which issued the certificate; or
(2) to the court (if different) which has general jurisdiction to enforce the certificate.

42.12 Proceedings for enforcement of interim costs certificates or final costs certificates may not be issued in the Supreme Court Costs Office.

## SECTION 43 Detailed assessment procedure where costs are payable out of the community legal service fund: Rule 47.17

F–078

43.1 The provisions of this section apply where the court is to assess costs which are payable only out of the community legal service fund. Paragraphs 39.1 to 40.16 and 49.1 to 49.8 apply in cases involving costs payable by another person as well as costs payable only out of the community legal service fund.

43.2 The time for requesting a detailed assessment under rule 47.17 is within 3 months after the date when the right to detailed assessment arose.

*43.3 The request for a detailed assessment of costs must be in Form N258A. The request must be accompanied by:

(a) a copy of the bill of costs;
(b) the document giving the right to detailed assessment (for further information as to this document, see paragraph 40.4 above);
(c) a copy of all orders made by the court relating to the costs which are to be assessed;
(d) copies of any fee notes of counsel and any expert in respect of fees claimed in the bill;
(e) written evidence as to any other disbursement which is claimed and which exceeds £250;
(f) the legal aid certificates, LSC certificates, any relevant amendment certificates, any authorities and any certificates of discharge or revocation;
(g) In the Supreme Court Costs Office the relevant papers in support of the bill as described in paragraph 40.12 above; in cases proceeding in District Registries and county courts this provision does not apply and the papers should only be lodged if requested by the costs officer.
(h) a statement signed by the solicitor giving his name, address for service, reference, telephone number, fax number and, if the assisted person has a financial interest in the detailed assessment and wishes to attend, giving the postal address of that person, to which the court will send notice of any hearing.

43.4 Rule 47.17 provides that the court will hold a detailed assessment hearing if the assisted person has a financial interest in the detailed assessment and wishes to attend. The court may also hold a detailed assessment hearing in any other case, instead of provisionally assessing a bill of costs, where it considers that a hearing is necessary. Before deciding whether a hearing is necessary under this rule, the court may require the solicitor whose bill it is, to provide further information relating to the bill.

43.5 Where the court has provisionally assessed a bill of costs it will send to the solicitor a notice, in Form N253 annexed to this practice direction, of the amount of costs which the court proposes to allow together with the bill itself. The legal representative should, if the provisional assessment is to be accepted, then complete the bill.

43.6 The court will fix a date for a detailed assessment hearing if the solicitor informs the court within 14 days after he receives the notice of the amount allowed on the provisional assessment that he wants the court to hold such a hearing.

43.7 The court will give at least 14 days notice of the time and place of the detailed assessment hearing to the solicitor and, if the assisted person has a financial interest in the detailed assessment and wishes to attend, to the assisted person.

43.8 If the solicitor whose bill it is, or any other party wishes to make an application in the detailed assessment proceedings, the provisions of Part 23 (General Rules about Applications for Court Orders) applies.

*43.9 It is the responsibility of the legal representative to complete the bill by entering in the bill the correct figures allowed in respect of each item, recalculating the summary of the bill appropriately and completing the Community Legal Service assessment certificate (Form EX80A).

**SECTION 44 Costs of detailed assessment proceedings where costs are payable out of a fund other than the community legal service fund:** Rule 47.17A

F–079

44.1* Rule 47.17A provides that the court will make a provisional assessment of a bill of costs payable out of a fund (other than the Community Legal Service Fund) unless it considers that a hearing is necessary. It also enables the court to direct under rule 47.17A(3) that the receiving party must serve a copy of the request for assessment and copies of the documents which accompany it, on any person who has a financial interest in the outcome of the assessment.

*44.2

(a) A person has a financial interest in the outcome of the assessment if the assessment will or may affect the amount of money or property to which he is or may become entitled out of the fund.

(b) Where an interest in the fund is itself held by a trustee for the benefit of some other person, that trustee will be treated as the person having such a financial interest.

(c) "Trustee" includes a personal representative, receiver or any other person acting in a fiduciary capacity.

*44.3 The request for a detailed assessment of costs out of the fund should be in Form N258B, be accompanied by the documents set out at paragraph 43.3(a) to (e) and (g) above and the following;

(a) a statement signed by the receiving party giving his name, address for service, reference, telephone number, fax number and,

(b) a statement of the postal address of any person who has a financial interest in the outcome of the assessment, to which the court may send notice of any hearing; and

(c) in respect of each person stated to have such an interest if such person is a child or patient, a statement to that effect.

*44.4 The court will decide, having regard to the amount of the bill, the size of the fund and the number of persons who have a financial interest, which of those persons should be served. The court may dispense with service on all or some of them.

*44.5 Where the court makes an order dispensing with service on all such persons it may proceed at once to make a provisional assessment, or, if it decides that a hearing is necessary, give appropriate directions. Before deciding whether a hearing is necessary under this rule, the court may require the receiving party to provide further information relating to the bill.

*44.6

(1) Where the court has provisionally assessed a bill of costs, it will send to the receiving party, a notice in Form N253 of the amount of costs which the court proposes to allow together with the bill itself. If the receiving party is legally represented the legal representative should, if the provisional assessment is to be accepted, then complete the bill.

(2) The court will fix a date for a detailed assessment hearing, if the receiving party informs the court within 14 days after he receives the notice in Form N253 of the amount allowed on the provisional assessment, that he wants the court to hold such a hearing.

*44.7 Where the court makes an order that a person who has a financial interest is to be served with a copy of the request for assessment, it may give directions about service and about the hearing.

*44.8 The court will give at least 14 days notice of the time and place of the detailed assessment hearing to the receiving party and, to any person who has a financial interest in the outcome of the assessment and has been served with a copy of the request for assessment.

*44.9 If the receiving party, or any other party or any person who has a financial interest in the outcome of assessment, wishes to make an application in the detailed assessment proceedings, the provisions of Part 23 (General Rules about Applications for Court Orders) applies.

*44.10 If the receiving party is legally represented the legal representative must in order to complete the bill after the assessment make clear the correct figures allowed in respect of each item and must recalculate the summary of the bill if appropriate.

**SECTION 45 Liability for costs of detailed assessment proceedings:** Rule 47.18

F–080

45.1 As a general rule the court will assess the receiving party's costs of the detailed assessment proceedings and add them to the bill of costs

45.2 If the costs of the detailed assessment proceedings are awarded to the paying party, the court will either assess those costs by summary assessment or make an order for them to be decided by detailed assessment

*45.3 No party should file or serve a statement of costs of the detailed assessment proceedings unless the court orders him to do so.

45.4 Attention is drawn to the fact that in deciding what order to make about the costs of detailed assessment proceedings the court must have regard to the conduct of all parties, the amount by which the bill of costs has been reduced and whether it was reasonable for a party to claim the costs of a particular item or to dispute that item.

**SECTION 46 Offers to settle without prejudice save as to the costs of the detailed assessment proceedings:** Rule 47.19

F–081

46.1 Rule 47.19 allows the court to take into account offers to settle, without prejudice save as to the costs of detailed assessment proceedings, when deciding who is liable for the costs of those proceedings. The rule does not specify a time within which such an offer should be made. An offer made by the paying party should usually be made within 14 days after service of the notice of commencement on that party. If the offer is made by the receiving party, it should normally be made within 14 days after the service of points of dispute by the paying party. Offers made after these periods are likely to be given less weight by the court in deciding what order as to costs to make unless there is good reason for the offer not being made until the later time.

*46.2 Where an offer to settle is made it should specify whether or not it is intended to be inclusive of the cost of preparation of the bill, interest and value added tax (VAT). The offer may include or exclude some or all of these items but the position must be made clear on the face of the offer so that the offeree is clear about the terms of the offer when it is being considered. Unless the offer states otherwise, the offer will be treated as being inclusive of all these items.

46.3 Where an offer to settle is accepted, an application may be made for a certificate in agreed terms, or the bill of costs may be withdrawn, in accordance with rule 47.10 (Procedure where costs are agreed).

46.4 Where the receiving party is an assisted person or an LSC funded client, an offer to settle without prejudice save as to the costs of the detailed assessment proceedings will not have the consequences specified under rule 47.19 unless the court so orders.

**SECTION 47 Appeals from authorised court officers in detailed assessment proceedings: right to appeal:** Rule 47.20

F–082

*47.1 This Section and the next Section of this Practice Direction relate only to appeals from authorised court officers in detailed assessment proceedings. All other appeals arising out of detailed assessment proceedings (and arising out of summary assessments) are dealt with in accordance with Part 52 and the Practice Direction which supplements that Part. The destination of appeals is dealt with in accordance with the Access to Justice Act 1999 (Destination of Appeals) Order 2000.

*47.2 In respect of appeals from authorised court officers, there is no requirement to obtain permission, or to seek written reasons.

**SECTION 48 Procedure on appeal from authorised court officers:** Rule 47.22

F–083

*48.1 The appellant must file a notice which should be in Form N161 (an appellant's notice).

*48.2 The appeal will be heard by a costs judge or a district judge of the High Court, and is a re-hearing.

*48.3 The appellant's notice should, if possible, be accompanied by a suitable record of the judgment appealed against. Where reasons given for the decision have been officially recorded by the court an approved transcript of that record should accompany the notice. Photocopies will not be accepted for this purpose. Where there is no official record the following documents will be acceptable:

(1) The officer's comments written on the bill.
(2) Advocates' notes of the reasons where the appellant is unrepresented.

When the appellant was unrepresented before the authorised court officer, it is the duty of any advocate for the respondent to make his own note of the reasons promptly available, free of charge to the appellant where there is no official record or if the court so directs. Where the appellant was represented before the authorised court officer, it is the duty of his/her own former advocate to make his/her notes available. The appellant should submit the note of the reasons to the costs judge or district judge hearing the appeal.

*48.4 The appellant may not be able to obtain a suitable record of the authorised court officer's decision within the time in which the appellant's notice must be filed. In such cases, the appellant's notice must still be completed to the best of the appellant's ability. It may however be amended subsequently with the permission of the costs judge or district judge hearing the appeal.

**SECTION 49 Costs payable by the LSC at prescribed rates:**

F–084

*49.1 This section applies to a bill of costs of an assisted person or LSC funded client which is payable by another person where the costs which can be claimed against the LSC are restricted to prescribed rates (with or without enhancement).

*49.2 Where this section applies, the solicitor of the assisted person or LSC funded client must file a legal aid/ LSC schedule in accordance with Paragraph 40.2(l) above. The schedule should follow as closely as possible Precedent E of the Schedule of Costs Precedents annexed to this Practice Direction.

49.3 The schedule must set out by reference to the item numbers in the bill of costs, all the costs claimed as payable by another person, but the arithmetic in the schedule should claim those items at prescribed rates only (with or without any claim for enhancement).

49.4 Where there has been a change in the prescribed rates during the period covered by the bill of costs, the schedule (as opposed to the bill) should be divided into separate parts, so as to deal separately with each change of rate. The schedule must also be divided so as to correspond with any divisions in the bill of costs.

49.5* If the bill of costs contains additional columns setting out costs claimed against the LSC only, the schedule may be set out in a separate document or, alternatively, may be included in the additional columns of the bill.

*49.6 The detailed assessment of the legal aid/ LSC schedule will take place immediately after the detailed assessment of the bill of costs.

*49.7 Attention is drawn to the possibility that, on occasions, the court may decide to conduct the detailed assessment of the legal aid/ LSC schedule separately from any detailed assessment of the bill of costs. This will occur, for example, where a default costs certificate is obtained as between the parties but that certificate is not set aside at the time of the detailed assessment pursuant to the Legal Aid Act 1988 or regulations thereunder.

*49.8 Where costs have been assessed at prescribed rates it is the responsibility of the legal representative to enter the correct figures allowed in respect of each item and to recalculate the summary of the legal aid/ LSC schedule.

# Directions Relating to Part 48

*Costs—special cases*

**SECTION 50 Amount of costs where costs are payable pursuant to contract:**
Rule 48.3

F–085

50.1 Where the court is assessing costs payable under a contract, it may make an order that all or part of the costs payable under the contract shall be disallowed if it is satisfied by the paying party that costs have been unreasonably incurred or are unreasonable in amount.

50.2 Rule 48.3 only applies if the court is assessing costs payable under a contract. It does not—

(1) require the court to make an assessment of such costs; or
(2) require a mortgagee to apply for an order for those costs that he has a contractual right to recover out of the mortgage funds.

50.3 The following principles apply to costs relating to a mortgage—

(1) An order for the payment of costs of proceedings by one party to another is always a discretionary order: section 51 of the Supreme Court Act 1981
(2) Where there is a contractual right to the costs the discretion should ordinarily be exercised so as to reflect that contractual right.
(3) The power of the court to disallow a mortgagee's costs sought to be added to the mortgage security is a power that does not derive from section 51, but from the power of the courts of equity to fix the terms on which redemption will be allowed.
(4) A decision by a court to refuse costs in whole or in part to a mortgagee litigant may be—

(a) a decision in the exercise of the section 51 discretion;
(b) a decision in the exercise of the power to fix the terms on which redemption will be allowed;
(c) a decision as to the extent of a mortgagee's contractual right to add his costs to the security; or
(d) a combination of two or more of these things.

The statements of case in the proceedings or the submissions made to the court may indicate which of the decisions has been made.

(5) A mortgagee is not to be deprived of a contractual or equitable right to add costs to the security merely by reason of an order for payment of costs made without reference to the mortgagee's contractual or equitable rights, and without any adjudication as to whether or not the mortgagee should be deprived of those costs.

50.4

(1) Where the contract entitles a mortgagee to—

(a) add the costs of litigation relating to the mortgage to the sum secured by it;
(b) require a mortgagor to pay those costs, or
(c) both,

the mortgagor may make an application for the court to direct that an account of the mortgagee's costs be taken.
(Rule 25.1(1)(n) provides that the court may direct that a party file an account)

(2) The mortgagor may then dispute an amount in the mortgagee's account on the basis that is has been unreasonably incurred or is unreasonable in amount.
(3) Where a mortgagor disputes an amount, the court may make an order that the disputed costs are assessed under rule 48.3

**SECTION 51 Costs where money is payable by or to a child or patient:** Rule 48.5

F–086 51.1 The circumstances in which the court need not order the assessment of costs under rule 48.5(3) are as follows:

(a) where there is no need to do so to protect the interests of the child or patient or his estate;

(b) where another party has agreed to pay a specified sum in respect of the costs of the child or patient and the solicitor acting for the child or patient has waived the right to claim further costs;
(c) where the court has decided the costs payable to the child or patient by way of summary assessment and the solicitor acting for the child or patient has waived the right to claim further costs;
(d) where an insurer or other person is liable to discharge the costs which the child or patient would otherwise be liable to pay to his solicitor and the court is satisfied that the insurer or other person is financially able to discharge those costs.

**SECTION 52 Litigants in person: Rule 48.6**

52.1 In order to qualify as an expert for the purpose of rule 48.6(3)(c) (expert assistance in connection with assessing the claim for costs), the person in question must be a **F–087**

(1) barrister,
(2) solicitor,
(3) Fellow of the Institute of Legal Executives,
(4) Fellow of the Association of Law Costs Draftsmen,
(5) law costs draftsman who is a member of the Academy of Experts,
(6) law costs draftsman who is a member of the Expert Witness Institute.

52.2 Where a litigant in person wishes to prove that he has suffered financial loss he should produce to the court any written evidence he relies on to support that claim, and serve a copy of that evidence on any party against whom he seeks costs at least 24 hours before the hearing at which the question may be decided.

52.3 Where a litigant in person commences detailed assessment proceedings under rule 47.6 he should serve copies of that written evidence with the notice of commencement.

52.4 The amount, which may be allowed to a litigant in person under rule 46.3(5)(b) and rule 48.6(4), is £9.25 per hour.

52.5 Attention is drawn to rule 48.6(6)(b). A solicitor who, instead of acting for himself, is represented in the proceedings by his firm or by himself in his firm name, is not, for the purpose of the Civil Procedure Rules, a litigant in person.

**SECTION 53 Personal liability of legal representative for costs—wasted costs orders: Rule 48.7**

53.1 Rule 48.7 deals with wasted costs orders against legal representatives. Such orders can be made at any stage in the proceedings up to and including the proceedings relating to the detailed assessment of costs. In general, applications for wasted costs are best left until after the end of the trial. **F–088**

53.2 The court may make a wasted costs order against a legal representative on its own initiative.

53.3 A party may apply for a wasted costs order—

(1) by filing an application notice in accordance with Part 23; or
(2) by making an application orally in the course of any hearing.

53.4 It is appropriate for the court to make a wasted costs order against a legal representative, only if—

(1) the legal representative has acted improperly, unreasonably or negligently;
(2) his conduct has caused a party to incur unnecessary costs, and
(3) it is just in all the circumstances to order him to compensate that party for the whole or part of those costs.

53.5 The court will give directions about the procedure that will be followed in each case in order to ensure that the issues are dealt with in a way which is fair and as simple and summary as the circumstances permit.

53.6 As a general rule the court will consider whether to make a wasted costs order in two stages—

(1) in the first stage, the court must be satisfied—

(a) that it has before it evidence or other material which, if unanswered, would be likely to lead to a wasted costs order being made; and

(b) the wasted costs proceedings are justified notwithstanding the likely costs involved.

(2) at the second stage (even if the court is satisfied under paragraph (1)) the court will consider, after giving the legal representative an opportunity to give reasons why the court should not make a wasted costs order, whether it is appropriate to make a wasted costs order in accordance with paragraph 53.4 above.

53.7 On an application for a wasted costs order under Part 23 the court may proceed to the second stage described in paragraph 53.6 without first adjourning the hearing if it is satisfied that the legal representative has already had a reasonable opportunity to give reasons why the court should not make a wasted costs order. In other cases the court will adjourn the hearing before proceeding to the second stage.

53.8 On an application for a wasted costs order under Part 23 the application notice and any evidence in support must identify—

(1) what the legal representative is alleged to have done or failed to do; and

(2) the costs that he may be ordered to pay or which are sought against him.

53.9 A wasted costs order is an order—

(1) that the legal representative pay a specified sum in respect of costs to a party; or

(2) for costs relating to a specified sum or items of work to be disallowed.

*53.10 Attention is drawn to rule 44.3A(1) and (2) which respectively prevent the court from assessing any additional liability until the conclusion of the proceedings (or the part of the proceedings) to which the funding arrangement relates, and set out the orders the court may make at the conclusion of the proceedings.

**SECTION 54 Basis of detailed assessment of solicitor and client costs:** Rule 48.8

F–089

54.1 A client and his solicitor may agree whatever terms they consider appropriate about the payment of the solicitor's charges for his services. If however, the costs are of an unusual nature (either in amount or in the type of costs incurred) those costs will be presumed to have been unreasonably incurred unless the solicitor satisfies the court that he informed the client that they were unusual and, where the costs relate to litigation, that he informed the client they might not be allowed on an assessment of costs between the parties. That information must have been given to the client before the costs were incurred.

54.2

(1) Costs as between a solicitor and client are assessed on the indemnity basis as defined by rule 44.4.

(2) Attention is drawn to the presumptions set out in rule 48.8(2). These presumptions may be rebutted by evidence to the contrary.

*54.3 Rule 48.10 and Section 56 of this Practice Direction deal with the procedure to be followed for obtaining the assessment of a solicitor's bill pursuant to an order under Part III of the Solicitors Act 1974.

54.4 If a party fails to comply with the requirements of rule 48.10 concerning the service of a breakdown of costs or points of dispute, any other party may apply to the court in which the detailed assessment hearing should take place for an order requiring compliance with rule 48.10. If the court makes such an order, it may—

(a) make it subject to conditions including a condition to pay a sum of money into court; and
(b) specify the consequence of failure to comply with the order or a condition.

**SECTION 55 Conditional fees:** Rule 48.9

*55.1 F–090

(1) Attention is drawn to rule 48.9(1) as amended by the Civil Procedure (Amendment No.3) Rules 2000 (SI 2000/1317) with effect from 3 July 2000. Rule 48.9 applies only where the solicitor and the client have entered into a conditional fee agreement as defined in section 58 of the Courts and Legal Services Act 1990 as it was in force before 1 April 2000. A client who has entered into a conditional fee agreement with a solicitor may apply for assessment of the base costs (which is carried out in accordance with rule 48.8(2) as if there were no conditional fee agreement) or for assessment of the percentage increase (success fee) or both.
(2) Where the court is to assess the percentage increase the court will have regard to all the relevant factors as they appeared to the solicitor or counsel when the conditional fee agreement was entered into.

55.2 Where the client applies to the court to reduce the percentage increase which the solicitor has charged the client under the conditional fee agreement, the client must set out in his application notice:

(a) the reasons why the percentage increase should be reduced; and
(b) what the percentage increase should be.

55.3 The factors relevant to assessing the percentage increase include—

(a) the risk that the circumstances in which the fees or expenses would be payable might not occur;
(b) the disadvantages relating to the absence of payment on account;
(c) whether the amount which might be payable under the conditional fee agreement is limited to a certain proportion of any damages recovered by the client;
(d) whether there is a conditional fee agreement between the solicitor and counsel;
(e) the solicitor's liability for any disbursements.

*55.4 When the court is considering the factors to be taken into account, it will have regard to the circumstances as they reasonably appeared to the solicitor or counsel when the conditional fee agreement was entered into.

**SECTION 56 Procedure on assessment of solicitor and client costs:** Rule 48.10

*56.1 The paragraphs in this section apply to orders made under Part III of the Solicitors Act 1974 for the assessment of costs. In these paragraphs "client" F–091 includes any person entitled to make an application under Part III of that Act.

*56.2 The procedure for obtaining an order under Part III of the Solicitors Act 1974 is by the alternative procedure for claims under Part 8. The provisions of RSC Order 106 appear, appropriately amended, in Schedule 1 to the CPR. Precedent J of the Schedule of Costs Precedents annexed to this Practice Direction is a model form of claim form. The application must be accompanied by the bill or bills in respect of which assessment is sought, and, if the claim concerns a conditional fee agreement, a copy of that agreement. If the original bill is not available a copy will suffice.

*56.3 Model forms of order, which the court may make, are set out in Precedents K, L and M of the Schedule of Costs Precedents annexed to this Practice Direction.

56.4 Attention is drawn to the time limits within which the required steps must be taken: i.e. the solicitor must serve a breakdown of costs within 28 days of the order for costs to be assessed, the client must serve points of dispute within 14 days after service on him of the breakdown, and any reply must be served within 14 days of service of the points of dispute.

56.5 The breakdown of costs referred to in rule 48.10 is a document which contains the following information:

(a) details of the work done under each of the bills sent for assessment; and

(b) in applications under Section 70 of the Solicitors Act 1974, an account showing money received by the solicitor to the credit of the client and sums paid out of that money on behalf of the client but not payments out which were made in satisfaction of the bill or of any items which are claimed in the bill.

*56.6 Precedent P of the Schedule of Costs Precedents annexed to this Practice Direction is a model form of breakdown of costs. A party who is required to serve a breakdown of costs must also serve—

(1) copies of the fee notes of counsel and of any expert in respect of fees claimed in the breakdown, and

(2) written evidence as to any other disbursement which is claimed in the breakdown and which exceeds £250.

56.7 The provisions relating to default costs certificates (rule 47.11) do not apply to cases to which rule 48.10 applies.

56.8 Points of dispute should, as far as practicable, be in the form complying with paragraphs 35.1 to 35.7.

56.9 The time for requesting a detailed assessment hearing is within 3 months after the date of the order for the costs to be assessed.

*56.10 The form of request for a hearing date must be in Form N258C. The request must be accompanied by copies of—

(a) the order sending the bill or bills for assessment;

(b) the bill or bills sent for assessment;

(c) the solicitor's breakdown of costs and any invoices or accounts served with that breakdown;

(d) a copy of the points of dispute, annotated as necessary in order to show which items have been agreed and their value and to show which items remain in dispute;

(e) as many copies of the points of dispute so annotated as there are other parties to the proceedings to whom the court should give details of the assessment hearing requested;

(f) a copy of any replies served;

(g) a statement signed by the party filing the request or his legal representative giving the names and addresses for service of all parties to the proceedings.

56.11 The request must include an estimate of the length of time the detailed assessment hearing will take.

56.12 On receipt of the request for a detailed assessment hearing the court will fix a date for the hearing or if the costs judge or district judge so decides, will give directions or fix a date for a preliminary appointment.

56.13

(1) The court will give at least 14 days notice of the time and place of the detailed assessment hearing to every person named in the statement referred to in paragraph 56.10(g) above.
(2) The court will when giving notice, give all parties other than the party who requested the hearing a copy of the points of dispute annotated by the party requesting the hearing in compliance with paragraph 56.10(e) above.
(3) Attention is drawn to rule 47.14(6) and (7): apart from the solicitor whose bill it is, only those parties who have served points of dispute may be heard on the detailed assessment unless the court gives permission, and only items specified in the points of dispute may be raised unless the court gives permission.

56.14

(1) If a party wishes to vary his breakdown of costs, points of dispute or reply, an amended or supplementary document must be filed with the court and copies of it must be served on all other relevant parties.
(2) Permission is not required to vary a breakdown of costs, points of dispute or a reply but the court may disallow the variation or permit it only upon conditions, including conditions as to the payment of any costs caused or wasted by the variation.

56.15 Unless the court directs otherwise the solicitor must file with the court the papers in support of the bill not less than 7 days before the date for the detailed assessment hearing and not more than 14 days before that date.

56.1 Once the detailed assessment hearing has ended it is the responsibility of the legal representative appearing for the solicitor or, as the case may be, the solicitor in person to remove the papers filed in support of the bill.

56.17

(1) Attention is drawn to rule 47.15 (power to issue an interim certificate).
(2) If, in the course of a detailed assessment hearing of a solicitor's bill to his client, it appears to the costs judge or district judge that in any event the solicitor will be liable in connection with that bill to pay money to the client, he may issue an interim certificate specifying an amount which in his opinion is payable by the solicitor to his client. Such a certificate will include an order to pay the sum it certifies unless the court orders otherwise.

*56.18

(1) Attention is drawn to rule 47.16 which requires the solicitor to file a completed bill within 14 days after the end of the detailed assessment hearing. The court may dispense with the requirement to file a completed bill.
(2) After the detailed assessment hearing is concluded the court will—

(a) complete the court copy of the bill so as to show the amount allowed;
(b) determine the result of the cash account;
(c) award the costs of the detailed assessment hearing in accordance with Section 70(8) of the Solicitors Act 1974; and
(d) issue a final costs certificate showing the amount due following the detailed assessment hearing.

56.19 A final costs certificate will include an order to pay the sum it certifies unless the court orders otherwise.

**SECTION 57 Transitional arrangements:**

F–092 57.1 In this section "the previous rules" means the Rules of the Supreme Court 1965 ("RSC") or County Court Rules 1981 ("CCR"), as appropriate.

**General Scheme of Transitional Arrangements concerning Costs Proceedings**

F–093 *57.2

(1) Paragraph 18 of the Practice Direction which supplements Part 51 (Transitional Arrangements) provides that the CPR govern any assessments of costs which take place on or after 26th April 1999 and states a presumption to be applied in respect of costs for work undertaken before 26th April 1999.

(2) The following paragraphs provide five further transitional arrangements:

(a) to provide an additional presumption to be applied when assessing costs which were awarded by an order made in a county court before 26th April 1999 which allowed costs "on Scale 1" to be determined in accordance with CCR Appendix A, or "on the lower scale" to be determined in accordance with CCR Appendix C.
(b) to preserve the effect of CCR Appendix B Part III, paragraph 2;
(c) to clarify the approach to be taken where a bill of costs was provisionally taxed before 26th April 1999 and the receiving party is unwilling to accept the result of the provisional taxation.
(d) to preserve the right to carry in objections or apply for a reconsideration in all taxation proceedings commenced before 26th April 1999.
(e) to deal with funding arrangements made before 3 July 2000.

**Scale 1 or lower scale costs**

F–094 57.3 Where an order was made in county court proceedings before 26th April 1999 under which the costs were allowed on Scale 1 or the lower scale, the general presumption is that no costs will be allowed under that order which would not have been allowed in a taxation before 26th April 1999.

**Fixed costs on the lower scale**

F–095 57.4 The amount to be allowed as fixed costs for making or opposing an application for a rehearing to set aside a judgment given before 26th April 1999 where the costs are on lower scale is £11.25.

**Bills provisionally taxed before 26th April 1999**

F–096 57.5 In respect of bills of costs provisionally taxed before 26th April 1999:

(1) The previous rules apply on the question who can request a hearing and the time limits for doing so; and
(2) The CPR govern any subsequent hearing in that case.

**Bills taxed before 26th April 1999**

F–097 57.6 Where a bill of costs was taxed before 26th April 1999, the previous rules govern the steps which can be taken to challenge that taxation.

### Other taxation proceedings

*57.7 F–098

(1) This paragraph applies to taxation proceedings which were commenced before 26th April 1999, were assigned for taxation to a Taxing Master or District Judge, and which were still pending on 26th April 1999.
(2) Any assessment of costs that takes place in cases to which this paragraph applies which is conducted on or after 26th April 1999, will be conducted in accordance with the CPR.
(3) In addition to the possibility of appeal under rules 47.20 to 47.23 and Part 52 any party to a detailed assessment who is dissatisfied with any decision on a detailed assessment made by a costs judge or district judge may apply to that costs judge or district judge for a review of the decision.The review shall, for procedural purposes, be treated as if it were an appeal from an authorised court officer.
(4) The right of review provided by paragraph (3) above, will not apply in cases in which, at least 28 days before the date of the assessment hearing, all parties were served with notice that the rights of appeal in respect of that hearing would be governed by Part 47 Section VIII (Appeals from Authorised Court Officers in Detailed Assessment Proceedings) and Part 52 (Appeals).
(5) An order for the service of notice under sub-paragraph (4) above may be made on the application of any party to the detailed assessment proceedings or may be made by the court of its own initiative.

### Transitional provisions concerning the Access to Justice Act 1999 sections 28 to 31

*57.8 F–099

(1) Sections 28 to 31 of the Access to Justice Act 1999, the Conditional Fee Agreements Regulations 2000, the Access to Justice (Membership Organisations) Regulations 2000, and the Access to Justice Act 1999 (Transitional Provisions) Order 2000 came into force on 1 April 2000. The Civil Procedure (Amendment No.3) Rules come into force on 3 July 2000.
(2) The Access to Justice Act 1999 (Transitional Provisions) Order 2000 provides that no conditional fee agreement or other arrangement about costs entered into before 1 April 2000 can be a funding arrangement, as defined in rule 43.2 The order also has the effect that where an conditional fee agreement or other funding arrangement has been entered into before 1 April 2000 and a second or subsequent funding arrangement is entered into on or after 1 April 2000, the second or subsequent funding arrangement does not give rise to an additional liability which is recoverable from a paying party.

*57.9

(1) Rule 39 of the Civil Procedure (Amendment No 3) Rules 2000 applies where between 1 April and 2 July 2000 (including both dates)—

    a funding arrangement is entered into, and
    proceedings are started in respect of a claim which is the subject of that agreement.

(2) Attention is drawn to the need to act promptly so as to comply with the requirements of the Rules and the Practice Directions by 31 July 2000 (i.e. within the 28 days from 3 July 2000 permitted by Rule 39) if that compliance is to be treated as compliance with the relevant provision. Attention is

drawn in particular to Rule 44.15 (Providing Information about Funding Arrangements) and Section 19 of this Practice Direction.

(3) Nothing in the legislation referred to above makes provision for a party who has entered into a funding arrangement to recover from another party any amount of an additional liability which relates to anything done or any costs incurred before the arrangement was entered into.

# APPENDIX G

Delete Appendix G and substitute

## SCHEDULE OF COSTS PRECEDENTS

A: Model form of bill of costs (receiving party's solicitor and counsel on CFA terms)
B: Model form of bill of costs (detailed assessment of additional liability only)
C: Model form of bill of costs (payable by Defendant and the LSC)
D: Model form of bill of costs (alternative form, single column for amounts claimed, separate parts for costs payable by the LSC only)
E: Legal Aid/ LSC Schedule of Costs
F: Certificates for inclusion in bill of costs
G. Points of Dispute
H: Estimate of costs served on other parties
J: Solicitors Act 1974: Part 8 claim form under Part III of the Act
K: Solicitors Act 1974: order for delivery of bill
L: Solicitors Act 1974: order for detailed assessment (client)
M: Solicitors Act 1974: order for detailed assessment (solicitors)
P: Solicitors Act 1974: breakdown of costs

SCHEDULE OF COSTS PRECEDENTS
PRECEDENT A

IN THE HIGH COURT OF JUSTICE 2000 - B - 999

QUEEN'S BENCH DIVISION

BRIGHTON DISTRICT REGISTRY

BETWEEN

AB Claimant

- and -

CD Defendant

**CLAIMANT'S BILL OF COSTS TO BE ASSESSED PURSUANT TO THE ORDER DATED 26th JULY 2000**

V.A.T. No. 33 4404 90

In these proceedings the claimant sought compensation for personal injuries and other losses suffered in a road accident which occurred on Friday 1st January 1999 near the junction between Bolingbroke Lane and Regency Road, Brighton, East Sussex. The claimant had been travelling as a front seat passenger in a car driven by the defendant. The claimant suffered severe injuries when, because of the defendant's negligence, the car left the road and collided with a brick wall.

The defendant was later convicted of various offences arising out of the accident including careless driving and driving under the influence of drink or drugs.

In the civil action the defendant alleged that immediately before the car journey began the claimant had known that the defendant was under the influence of alcohol and therefore consented to the risk of injury or was contributorily negligent as to it. It was also alleged that, immediately before the accident occurred, the claimant wrongfully took control of the steering wheel so causing the accident to occur.

The claimant first instructed solicitors, E F & Co, in this matter in July 2000. The claim form was issued in October 2000 and in February 2001 the proceedings were listed for a two day trial commencing 25th July 2001. At the trial the defendant was found liable but the compensation was reduced by 25% to take account of contributory negligence by the claimant. The claimant was awarded a total of £78,256.83 plus £1,207.16 interest plus costs.

The claimant instructed E F & Co under a conditional fee agreement dated 8th July 2000 which specifies the following base fees and success fees.

Partner - £180 per hour plus VAT
Assistant Solicitor - £140 per hour plus VAT
Other fee earners - £85 per hour plus VAT
Success fees exclusive of disbursement funding costs: 40%
Success fee in respect of disbursement funding costs: 7.5% (not claimed in this bill)

Except where the contrary is stated the proceedings were conducted on behalf of the claimant by an assistant solicitor, admitted November 1999.

E F & Co instructed Counsel (Miss GH, called 1992) under a conditional fee agreement dated 5th June 2001 which specifies a success fee of 75% and base fees, payable in various circumstances, of which the following are relevant

Fees for interim hearing whose estimated duration is up to 2 hours: £600
Brief for trial whose estimated duration is 2 days: £2,000
Fee for second and subsequent days: £650 per day

| Item No. | Description of work done | | V.A.T. | Disburse -ments | Profi Costs |
|---|---|---|---|---|---|
| | 8th July 2000 - EF & Co instructed | | | | |
| | 22nd July 2000 - AEI with Eastbird Legal Protection Ltd | | | | |
| 1 | Premium for policy | | — | £ 120.00 | |
| | 7th October 2000 - Claim issued | | | | |
| 2 | Issue fee | | — | £ 400.00 | |
| | 21st October 2000 - Particulars of claim served | | | | |
| | 25th November 2000 - Time for service of defence extended by agreement to 14th January 2001 | | | | |
| 3 | Fee on allocation | | — | £ 80.00 | |
| | 20th January 2001 - case allocated to multi-track | | | | |
| | 9th February 2001 - Case management conference at which costs were awarded to the claimant and the base costs were summarily assessed at £400 (paid on 24th February 2001) | | | | — |
| | 23rd February 2001 - Claimant's list of documents | | | | |
| | 12th April 2001 - Payment into court of £25,126.33 | | | | |
| | 13th April 2001 - Filing listing questionnaire | | | | |
| 4 | Fee on listing | | — | £ 400.00 | |
| | 28th June 2001 - Pre trial review: costs in case | | | | |
| | Engaged 1.5 hours | £210.00 | | | |
| | Travel and waiting 2.00 hours | £280.00 | | | |
| 5 | Total solicitor's base fee for attending | | | | £ 490.0 |
| 6 | Counsel's base fee for pre trial review (Miss GH) | | | £ 600.00 | |
| | 25th July 2001 - Attending first day of trial: adjourned part heard | | | | |
| | Engaged in Court 5.00 hours | £700.00 | | | |
| | Engaged in conference 0.75 hours | £105.00 | | | |
| | Travel and waiting 1.5 hours | £210.00 | | | |
| 7 | Total solicitor's base fee for attending | | | | £1,015.0 |
| 8 | Counsel's base fee for trial (Miss GH) | | | £2,000.00 | |
| 9 | Fee of expert witness (Dr. IJ) | | — | £ 850.00 | |
| 10 | Expenses of witnesses of fact | | — | £ 84.00 | |
| | 26th July 2001 - Attending second day of trial when judgment was given for the claimant in the sum of £78,256.53 plus £1207.16 interest plus costs | | | | |
| | Engaged in Court 3.00 hours | £420.00 | | | |
| | Engaged in conference 1.5 hours | £210.00 | | | |
| | Travel and waiting 1.5 hours | £210.00 | | | |
| 11 | Total solicitor's base fee for attending | | | | £ 840.0 |
| 12 | Counsel's base fee for second day (Miss GH) | | | £ 650.00 | |
| | To Summary | | £ — | £5,184.00 | £2,345.0 |

| Item No. | Description of work done | V.A.T. | Disburse -ments | Profit Costs |
|---|---|---|---|---|
| | **Claimant** | | | |
| 13 | 8th July 2000 - First instructions: 0.75 hours by Partner: base fee | | | £ 135.00 |
| | Other timed attendances in person and by telephone - See Schedule 1 | | | |
| 14 | Total base fee for Schedule 1 - 7.5 hours | | | £1,050.00 |
| 15 | Routine letters out and telephone calls - 29 (17 + 12) total base fee | | | £ 406.00 |
| | **Witnesses of Fact** | | | |
| | Timed attendances in person, by letter out and by telephone - See Schedule 2 | | | |
| 16 | Total base fee for Schedule 2 - 5.2 hours | | | £ 728.00 |
| 17 | Routine letters out, e mails and telephone calls - 8 (4 + 2 + 2 )total base fee | | | £ 112.00 |
| 18 | Paid travelling on 9th October 2000 | £ 4.02 | £ 22.96 | |
| | **Medical expert (Dr. IJ)** | | | |
| 19 | 11th September 2000 - long letter out 0.33 hours: base fee | | | £ 46.20 |
| 20 | 30th January 2001 - long letter out 0.25 hours base fee | | | £ 35.00 |
| 21 | 23rd May 2001 - telephone call 0.2 hours base fee | | | £ 28.00 |
| 22 | Routine letters out and telephone calls - 10 (6 + 4) total base fee | | | £ 140.00 |
| 23 | Dr. IJ's fee for report | — | £ 350.00 | |
| | **Defendant and his solicitor** | | | |
| 24 | 8th July 2000 - timed letter sent 0.5 hours: base fee | | | £ 70.00 |
| 25 | 19th February 2001 - telephone call 0.25 hours: base fee | | | £ 35.00 |
| 26 | Routine letters out and telephone calls - 24 (18 + 6) total base fee | | | £ 336.00 |
| | **Communications with the court** | | | |
| 27 | Routine letters out and telephone calls - 9 (8 + 1) total base fee | | | £ 126.00 |
| | **Communications with Counsel** | | | |
| 28 | Routine letters out, e mails and telephone calls - 19 (4 + 7 + 8) total base fee | | | £ 266.00 |
| | **Work done on documents** | | | |
| | Timed attendances - See Schedule 3 | | | |
| 29 | Total base fees for Schedule 3 - 0.75 hours at £180, 44.5 hours at £140, 12 hours at £85 | | | £7,385.00 |
| | **Work done on negotiations** | | | |
| | 23rd March 2001 - meeting at offices of Solicitors for the Defendant | | | |
| | Engaged - 1.5 hours £210.00 | | | |
| | Travel and waiting - 1.25 hours £175.00 | | | |
| 30 | Total base fee for meeting | | | £ 385.00 |
| | **Other work done** | | | |
| | Preparing and checking bill | | | |
| | Engaged: Solicitor - 1 hour £140.00 | | | |
| | Engaged: Costs Draftsman - 4 hours £340.00 | | | |
| 31 | Total base fee on other work done | | | £ 480.00 |
| | To Summary | £ 4.02 | £ 372.96 | £11,763.20 |

| Item No. | Description of work done | V.A.T. | Disburse -ments | Profit Costs |
|---|---|---|---|---|
| 32 | Success fee on solicitor's base fee on interim orders which were summarily assessed (40% of £400) plus VAT at 17.5% | £ 28.00 | | £ 160. |
| 33 | VAT on solicitor's other base fees (17.5% of £14,108.20) | £2,468.94 | | |
| 34 | Success fee on solicitor's other base fees (40% of £14,108.20) plus VAT at 17.5% | £ 987.58 | | £5,643.2 |
| 35 | VAT on Counsel's base fees (17.5% of £3,250)" | £ 568.75 | | |
| 36 | Success fee on Counsel's base fee (75% of £3,250) plus VAT at 17.5%" | £ 426.57 | £2,437.50 | |
| | To Summary | £4,479.84 | £2,437.50 | £5,803.2 |
| | **SUMMARY** | | | |
| | Page 3 | £ — | £5,184.00 | £2,345.0 |
| | Page 4 | £ 4.02 | £ 372.96 | £11,763.2 |
| | Page 5 | £4,479.84 | £2,437.50 | £5,803.2 |
| | Totals: | £4,483.86 | £7,994.46 | £19,911.4 |
| | Grand total: | | | £32,389.8 |

SCHEDULE OF COSTS PRECEDENTS
PRECEDENT B

IN THE HIGH COURT OF JUSTICE 2000 - B - 9999

QUEEN'S BENCH DIVISION

BRIGHTON DISTRICT REGISTRY

BETWEEN

AB Claimant

- and -

CD Defendant

**CLAIMANT'S BILL OF COSTS TO BE ASSESSED PURSUANT TO THE ORDER DATED 26th JULY 2001**

V.A.T. No. 33 4404 90

In these proceedings the claimant sought compensation for personal injuries and other losses suffered in a road accident which occurred on Friday 1st January 1999 near the junction between Bolingbroke Lane and Regency Road, Brighton, East Sussex. The claimant had been travelling as a front seat passenger in a car driven by the defendant. The claimant suffered severe injuries when, because of the defendant's negligence, the car left the road and collided with a brick wall.

The defendant was later convicted of various offences arising out of the accident including careless driving and driving under the influence of drink or drugs.

In the civil action the defendant alleged that immediately before the car journey began the claimant had known that the defendant was under the influence of alcohol and therefore consented to the risk of injury or was contributorily negligent as to it. It was also alleged that, immediately before the accident occurred, the claimant wrongfully took control of the steering wheel so causing the accident to occur.

The claimant first instructed solicitors, E F & Co, in this matter in July 2000. The claim form was issued in October 1999 and in February 2000 the proceedings were listed for a two day trial commencing 25th July 2001. At the trial the defendant was found liable but the compensation was reduced by 25% to take account of contributory negligence by the claimant. The claimant was awarded a total of £78,256.83 plus £1,207.16 interest plus costs, and the base costs were summarily assessed

The claimant instructed E F & Co under a conditional fee agreement dated 8th July 2000 which specifies the following base fees and success fees.

Partner - £180 per hour plus VAT
Assistant Solicitor - £140 per hour plus VAT
Other fee earners - £85 per hour plus VAT
Success fees exclusive of disbursement funding costs: 40%
Success fee in respect of disbursement funding costs: 7.5% (not claimed in this bill)

Except where the contrary is stated the proceedings were conducted on behalf of the claimant by an assistant solicitor, admitted November 1999.

E F & Co instructed Counsel (Miss GH, called 1992) under a conditional fee agreement dated 5th June 2001 which specifies a success fee of 75% and base fees, payable in various circumstances, of which the following are relevant.

Fees for interim hearing whose estimated duration is up to 2 hours: £600
Brief for trial whose estimated duration is 2 days: £2,000
Fee for second and subsequent days: £650 per day

| Item No. | Description of work done | V.A.T. | Disburse -ments | Profit Costs |
|---|---|---|---|---|
| | 8th July 2000 - EF & Co instructed | | | |
| | 22nd July 2000 - AEI with Eastbird Legal Protection Ltd | | | |
| 1 | Premium for policy | — | £ 120.00 | |
| | 9th February 2001 - Case management conference at which costs were awarded to the Claimant and the base costs were summarily assessed at £400 | | | |
| 2 | Success fee on costs of case management conference (40% of £400) plus VAT | £ 28.00 | | £ 160.00 |
| | 28th June 2001 - Pre trial review: costs in the case (base costs included base costs at trial) | | | |
| | 25th July 2001 - First day of trial | | | |
| | 26th July 2001 - Second day of trial at which judgment was given for the claimant as follows:<br>Compensation: £78,256.83<br>Interest thereon: £1,207.16<br>Base costs to trial<br>Solicitor's fees: £12,500.00 plus £2187.50 VAT thereon<br>Counsel's fees: £3,200.00 plus £560.00 VAT thereon<br>Other disbursements: £2,300.00 plus £4.02 VAT thereon | | | |
| 3 | Success fee on solicitor's base costs awarded at trial (40% of £12,500) plus VAT | £ 875.00 | | £5,000.00 |
| 4 | Success fee on Counsel's base costs awarded at trial (75% of £3,200) plus VAT | £ 420.00 | £2,400.00 | |
| | **Other work done**<br>Preparing and checking bill<br>Engaged: Solicitor - 0.25 hours £ 35.00<br>Engaged: Costs draftsman - 1.75 hours £ 148.75 | | | |
| 5 | Total base fee for other work done plus VAT | £ 32.16 | | £ 183.75 |
| 6 | Success fee for other work done (40% of £183.75) plus VAT | £ 12.87 | | £ 73.50 |
| | Totals: | £1,368.03 | £2,520.00 | £5,417.25 |
| | Profit Costs | | | £5,417.25 |
| | Disbursements | | | £2,520.00 |
| | VAT | | | £1,368.03 |
| | Grand total: | | | £9,305.28 |

SCHEDULE OF COSTS PRECEDENTS
PRECEDENT C

IN THE HIGH COURT OF JUSTICE 1999 - B - 9999

QUEEN'S BENCH DIVISION

BRIGHTON DISTRICT REGISTRY

BETWEEN

AB Claimant

~ and ~

CD Defendant

**CLAIMANT'S BILL OF COSTS TO BE ASSESSED PURSUANT TO THE ORDER DATED 26th JULY 2000 AND IN ACCORDANCE WITH REGULATION 107A OF THE CIVIL LEGAL AID (GENERAL) REGULATIONS 1989**

Legal Aid Certificate No. 01. 01. 99. 32552X issued on 9th September 1999.

V.A.T. No. 33 4404 90

In these proceedings the claimant sought compensation for personal injuries and other losses suffered in a road accident which occurred on Friday 1st January 1999 near the junction between Bolingbroke Lane and Regency Road, Brighton, East Sussex. The claimant had been travelling as a front seat passenger in a car driven by the defendant. The claimant suffered severe injuries when, because of the defendant's negligence, the car left the road and collided with a brick wall.

The defendant was later convicted of various offences arising out of the accident including careless driving and driving under the influence of drink or drugs.

In the civil action the defendant alleged that immediately before the car journey began the claimant had known that the defendant was under the influence of alcohol and therefore consented to the risk of injury or was contributorily negligent as to it. It was also alleged that, immediately before the accident occurred, the claimant wrongfully took control of the steering wheel so causing the accident to occur.

The claimant first instructed solicitors, E F & Co, in this matter in July 1999. The claim form was issued in October 1999 and in February 2000 the proceedings were listed for a two day trial commencing 25th July 2000. At the trial the defendant was found liable but the compensation was reduced by 25% to take account of contributory negligence by the claimant. The claimant was awarded a total of £78,256.83 plus £1,207.16 interest plus costs.

The proceedings were conducted on behalf of the claimant by an assistant solicitor, admitted November 1998. The bill is divided into two parts.

**Part 1 Costs payable by the defendant to the date of grant of legal aid**

This covers the period from 8th July 1999 to 8th September 1999. In this part the solicitor's time is charged at £140 per hour (including travel and waiting time) and letters out and telephone calls at £14.00 each.

**Part 2 Costs payable by the defendant and L.S.C. from the date of grant of legal aid**

This part covers the period from 9th September 1999 to the present time, the client having the benefit of a legal aid certificate covering these proceedings. In this part, solicitor's time in respect of costs payable by the defendant has been charged as in Part 1 plus costs draftsman's and trainee's time charged at £85 per hour. Solicitor's time in respect of costs payable by the LSC only are charged at the prescribed hourly rates plus enhancement of 50%.

Preparation: £74
Attending counsel in conference or at court: £36.40
Travelling and waiting: £32.70
Routine letters out: £7.40
Routine telephone calls: £4.10

| Item No. | Description of work done | Payable by L.S.C. only | | | Payable by Defendant | | |
|---|---|---|---|---|---|---|---|
| | | V.A.T. | Disburse-ments | Profit Costs | V.A.T. | Disburse-ments | Profit Costs |
| | **Part 1: COSTS TO DATE OF GRANT OF LEGAL AID.** | | | | | | |
| | **Claimant** | | | | | | |
| 1 | 8th July 1999 - First Instructions - 0.75 hours | | | | | | £ 105.0 |
| 2 | Routine Letters out - 3 | | | | | | £ 42.0 |
| | **Witnesses of Fact** | | | | | | |
| 3 | Routine Letters out - 2 | | | | | | £ 28.0 |
| | **The Defendant** | | | | | | |
| 4 | 8th July 1999 - Timed letter sent - 0.5 hours | | | | | | £ 70.0 |
| 5 | VAT on total profit costs (17.5% of £245) | | | | £ 42.88 | | |
| | To Summary | | | | £ 42.88 | £ - | £ 245.0 |
| | **Part 2: COSTS FROM DATE OF GRANT OF LEGAL AID** | | | | | | |
| | 7th October 1999 - Claim issued | | | | | | |
| 6 | Issue fee | | | | — | £ 400.00 | |
| | 21st October 1999 - Particulars of claim served | | | | | | |
| | 25th November 1999 - Time for service of defence extended by agreement to 14th January 2000 | | | | | | |
| | 17th January 2000 - Filing allocation questionnaire | | | | | | |
| 7 | Fee on allocation | | | | — | £ 80.00 | |
| | 20th January 2000 - Case allocated to multi track | | | | | | |
| | 9th February 2000 - Case management conference<br>Engaged 0.75 hours £105.00<br>Travel and waiting 2.00 hours £280.00 | | | | | | |
| 8 | Total solicitor's fee for attending | | | | | | £ 385.0 |
| | 23rd February 2000 - Claimant's list of documents | | | | | | |
| | 12th April 2000 - Payment into court of £25,126.33 | | | | | | |
| | 13th April 2000 - Filing listing questionnaire | | | | | | |
| 9 | Fee on listing | | | | — | £ 400.00 | |
| | 28th June 2000 - Pre-trial review<br>Engaged 1.5 hours £210.00<br>Travel and waiting 2.00 hours £280.00 | | | | | | |
| 10 | Total solicitor's fee for attending | | | | | | £ 490.0 |
| 11 | Counsel's brief fee for attending pre-trial review (Miss GH) | | | | £ 105.00 | £ 600.00 | |
| | To Summary | £ — | £ — | £ — | £ 105.00 | £ 1,480.00 | £ 875.0 |

| Item No. | Description of work done | Payable by L.S.C. only | | | Payable by Defendant | | |
|---|---|---|---|---|---|---|---|
| | | V.A.T. ments | Disburse- Costs | Profit | V.A.T. ments | Disburse- Costs | Profit |
| | 25th July 2000 - Attending first day of trial: adjourned part heard<br>Engaged in court 5.00 hours £700.00<br>Engaged in conference<br>0.75 hours £105.00<br>Travel and waiting 1.5 hours £210.00 | | | | | | |
| 12 | Total solicitor's fee for attending | | | | | | £1,015.00 |
| 13 | Counsel's brief fee for trial (Miss GH) | | | | £ 350.00 | £2,000.00 | |
| 14 | Fee of expert witness (Dr IJ) | | | | — | £ 850.00 | |
| 15 | Expenses of witnesses of fact | | | | — | £ 84.00 | |
| | 26th July 2000 - Attending second day of trial when judgment was given for the claimant in the sum of £78,256.83 plus £1,207.16 interest plus costs<br>Engaged in court 3.00 hours £420.00<br>Engaged in conference<br>1.5 hours £210.00<br>Travel and waiting 1.5 hours £210.00 | | | | | | |
| 16 | Total solicitor's fee for attending | | | | | | £ 840.00 |
| 17 | Counsel's fee for second day (Miss GH) | | | | £ 113.75 | £ 650.00 | |
| | **Claimant ~ (1)** Payable by Defendant<br>Timed attendances in person and by telephone - see Schedule 1 | | | | | | |
| 18 | Total fees for Schedule 1 - 7.50 hours | | | | | | £1,050.00 |
| 19 | Routine letters out and telephone calls - 26 (14 + 12) | | | | | | £ 364.00 |
| | **Claimant ~ (2)** Payable by LSC only<br>11th September 1999 - telephone call<br>Engaged 0.25 hours £18.50<br>Enhancement 50% £9.25 | | | | | | |
| 20 | Total solicitor's fee | | £ 27.75 | | | | |
| | 10th April 2000 - telephone call<br>Engaged 0.1 hours £4.10<br>Enhancement 50% £2.05 | | | | | | |
| 21 | Total solicitor's fee | | £ 6.15 | | | | |
| | **Witnesses of fact**<br>Timed attendances in person, by letter out and by telephone - see Schedule 2 | | | | | | |
| 22 | Total fees for Schedule 2 - 5.2 hours | | | | | | £ 728.00 |
| 23 | Routine letters out (including e mails) and telephone calls - 6 (4 + 2) | | | | | | £ 84.00 |
| 24 | Paid travelling on 9th October 1999 | | | | £ 4.02 | £ 22.96 | |
| | To Summary | £ — | £ — | £ 33.90 | £ 467.77 | £3,606.96 | £4,081.00 |

| Item No. | Description of work done | Payable by L.S.C. only | | | Payable by Defendant | | |
|---|---|---|---|---|---|---|---|
| | | V.A.T. ments | Disburse- Costs | Profit | V.A.T. ments | Disburse- Costs | Profit |
| 25 | **Medical expert (Dr IJ)**<br>11th September 1999 - long letter out 0.33 hours | | | | | | £ 46.2 |
| 26 | 30th January 2000 - long letter out 0.25 hours | | | | | | £ 35.0 |
| 27 | 23rd May 2000 - telephone call 0.2 hrs | | | | | £ 28.00 | |
| 28 | Routine letters out and telephone calls - 10 (6 + 4) | | | | | | £ 140.0 |
| 29 | Dr IJ's fee for report | | | | — | £ 350.00 | |
| 30 | **Solicitors for the defendant**<br>19th February 2000 - telephone call 0.25 hours | | | | | | £ 35.0 |
| 31 | Routine letters out and telephone calls - 24 (18 + 6) | | | | | | £ 336.0 |
| 32 | **Communications with the court**<br>Routine letters out and telephone calls - 9 (8 + 1) | | | | | | £ 126.0 |
| 33 | **Communications with Counsel**<br>Routine letters out (including e mails) and telephone calls - 19 (11 + 8) | | | | | | £ 266.0 |
| 34 | **Legal Aid Board and LSC** ~ Payable by LSC only<br>2nd August 2000 - Report on case<br>Engaged 0.5 hours £37.00<br>Enhancement 50% £18.50<br>Total solicitor's fee | | | £ 55.50 | | | |
| 35 | Routine letters out and telephone calls<br>Letters out - 2 £14.80<br>Telephones call - 4 £16.40<br>Total solicitor's fee | | | £ 31.20 | | | |
| 36 | **Work done on documents**<br>Timed attendances - see Schedule 3<br>Total fees for Schedule 3 - 45.25 hours at £140 + 12 hours at £85 | | | | | | £7,355.0 |
| 37 | **Work done on negotiations**<br>23rd March 2000 - meeting at offices of solicitors for the Defendant<br>Engaged - 1.5 hours £210.00<br>Travel and waiting 1.25 hours £175.00<br>Total solicitor's fee for meeting | | | | | | £ 385.0 |
| 38 | **Other work done ~ (1)** Payable by Defendant<br>Preparing and checking bill<br>Engaged: Solicitor - 1 hour £140.00<br>Engaged: Costs Draftsman - 4 hours £340.00<br>Total on other work done (1) | | | | | | £ 480.00 |
| | To Summary | £ — | £ — | £ 86.70 | £ — | £ 350.00 | £9,232.20 |

| | Description of work done | Payable by L.S.C. only | | | Payable by Defendant | | |
|---|---|---|---|---|---|---|---|
| Item No. | | V.A.T. ments | Disburse- Costs | Profit | V.A.T. ments | Disburse- Costs | Profit |
| | **Other work done** ~ (2) Payable by LSC only<br>Preparing and checking bill<br>Engaged: Solicitor - no claim<br>Engaged: Costs Draftsman - 1 hour £74.00 | | | | | | |
| 39 | Total on other work done (2) | | | £ 74.00 | | | |
| 40 | VAT on total profit costs payable by Defendant (17.5% of £14,176.20) | | | £2,480.84 | | | |
| 41 | VAT on total profit costs payable by LSC only (17.5% of £205.60) | £ 35.98 | | | | | |
| | To summary | £ 35.98 | £ — | £ 74.00 | £2,480.84 | £ — | £ — |
| | **SUMMARY** | | | | | | |
| | **Part 1** - Pre Legal Aid | | | | | | |
| | Page 3 | £ — | £ — | £ — | £ 42.88 | £ — | £ 245.00 |
| | **Part 2** - Costs since grant of legal aid | | | | | | |
| | Page 3 | £ — | £ — | £ — | £ 105.00 | £ 1,480.00 | £ 875.00 |
| | Page 4 | £ — | £ — | £ 33.90 | £ 467.77 | £3,606.96 | £4,081.00 |
| | Page 5 | £ — | £ — | £ 86.70 | £ — | £ 350.00 | £9,232.20 |
| | Page 6 | £ 35.98 | £ — | £ 74.00 | £2,480.84 | £ — | £ — |
| | **Totals** | £ 35.98 | £ — | £ 194.60 | £3,096.49 | £5,436.96 | £14,433.20 |
| | **Grand totals** | | | | | | |
| | Costs payable by Defendant | | | | | | £22,966.65 |
| | Costs payable by LSC only | | | | | | £ 230.58 |
| | Grand total: | | | | | | £23,197.23 |

SCHEDULE OF COSTS PRECEDENTS
PRECEDENT D

IN THE HIGH COURT OF JUSTICE 1999 - B - 9999

QUEEN'S BENCH DIVISION

BRIGHTON DISTRICT REGISTRY

BETWEEN

AB Claimant

~ and ~

CD Defendant

**CLAIMANT'S BILL OF COSTS TO BE ASSESSED PURSUANT TO THE ORDER DATED 26th JULY 2000 AND IN ACCORDANCE WITH REGULATION 107A OF THE CIVIL LEGAL AID (GENERAL) REGULATIONS 1989**

Legal Aid Certificate No. 01. 01. 99. 32552X issued on 9th September 1999.

V.A.T. No. 33 4404 90

In these proceedings the claimant sought compensation for personal injuries and other losses suffered in a road accident which occurred on Friday 1st January 1999 near the junction between Bolingbroke Lane and Regency Road, Brighton, East Sussex. The claimant had been travelling as a front seat passenger in a car driven by the defendant. The claimant suffered severe injuries when, because of the defendant's negligence, the car left the road and collided with a brick wall.

The defendant was later convicted of various offences arising out of the accident including careless driving and driving under the influence of drink or drugs.

In the civil action the defendant alleged that immediately before the car journey began the claimant had known that the defendant was under the influence of alcohol and therefore consented to the risk of injury or was contributorily negligent as to it. It was also alleged that, immediately before the accident occurred, the claimant wrongfully took control of the steering wheel so causing the accident to occur.

The claimant first instructed solicitors, E F & Co, in this matter in July 1999. The claim form was issued in October 1999 and in February 2000 the proceedings were listed for a two day trial commencing 25th July 2000. At the trial the defendant was found liable but the compensation was reduced by 25% to take account of contributory negligence by the claimant. The claimant was awarded a total of £78,256.83 plus £1,207.16 interest plus costs.

The proceedings were conducted on behalf of the claimant by an assistant solicitor, admitted November 1998. The bill is divided into three parts.

**Part 1 Costs payable by the defendant to the date of grant of legal aid**

This covers the period from 8th July 1999 to 8th September 1999. In this part the solicitor's time is charged at £140 per hour (including travel and waiting time) and letters out and telephone calls at £14.00 each.

**Part 2 Costs payable by the defendant from the date of grant of legal aid**

This part covers the period from 9th September 1999 to the present time, the client having the benefit of a legal aid certificate covering these proceedings. In this part, solicitor's time in respect of costs payable by the defendant has been charged as in Part 1 plus costs draftsman's and trainee's time charged at £85 per hour.

**Part 3 Costs payable by the LSC only**

This part covers the same period as Part 2. In this part solicitor's time in respect of costs payable by the LSC only are charged at the prescribed hourly rates plus enhancement of 50%.

Preparation: £74
Attending counsel in conference or at court: £36.40
Travelling and waiting: £32.70
Routine letters out: £7.40
Routine telephone calls: £4.10

| Item No. | Item | | Amount claimed | VAT | Amount allowed | VAT |
|---|---|---|---|---|---|---|
| | **Part 1: COSTS PAYABLE BY THE DEFENDANT** | | | | | |
| | **Claimant** | | | | | |
| 1 | 8th July 1999 - First Instructions - 0.75 hours | | £ 105.00 | £ 18.38 | | |
| 2 | Routine Letters out - 3 | | £ 42.00 | £ 7.35 | | |
| | **Witnesses of Fact** | | | | | |
| 3 | Routine Letters out - 2 | | £ 28.00 | £ 4.90 | | |
| | **The Defendant** | | | | | |
| 4 | 8th July 1999 - Timed letter sent - 0.5 hours | | £ 70.00 | £ 12.25 | | |
| | To Summary | | £ 245.00 | £ 42.88 | | |
| | **Part 2: COSTS PAYABLE BY THE DEFENDANT** | | | | | |
| | 7th October 1999 - Claim issued | | | | | |
| 5 | Issue fee | | £ 400.00 | — | | |
| | 21st October 1999 - Particulars of claim served | | | | | |
| | 25th November 1999 - Time for service of defence extended by agreement to 14th January 2000 | | | | | |
| | 17th January 2000 - Filing allocation questionnaire | | | | | |
| 6 | Fee on allocation | | £ 80.00 | — | | |
| | 20th January 2000 - Case allocated to multi track | | | | | |
| | 9th February 2000 - Case management conference | | | | | |
| | Engaged 0.75 hours | £105.00 | | | | |
| | Travel and waiting 2.00 hours | £280.00 | | | | |
| 7 | Total solicitor's fee for attending | | £ 385.00 | £ 67.38 | | |
| | 23rd February 2000 - Claimant's list of documents | | | | | |
| | 12th April 2000 - Payment into court of £25,126.33 | | | | | |
| | 13th April 2000 - Filing listing questionnaire | | | | | |
| 8 | Fee on listing | | £ 400.00 | — | | |
| | 28th June 2000 - Pre-trial review | | | | | |
| | Engaged 1.5 hours | £210.00 | | | | |
| | Travel and waiting 2.00 hours | £280.00 | | | | |
| 9 | Total solicitor's fee for attending | | £ 490.00 | £ 85.75 | | |
| 10 | Counsel's brief fee for attending pre-trial review (Miss GH) | | £ 600.00 | £ 105.00 | | |

| Item No. | Item | Amount claimed | VAT | Amount allowed | VAT |
|---|---|---|---|---|---|
| | 25th July 2000 - Attending first day of trial: adjourned part heard<br>Engaged in court 5.00 hours £700.00<br>Engaged in conference 0.75 hours £105.00<br>Travel and waiting 1.5 hours £210.00 | | | | |
| 11 | Total solicitor's fee for attending | £1,015.00 | £ 177.63 | | |
| 12 | Counsel's brief fee for trial (Miss GH) | £2,000.00 | £ 350.00 | | |
| 13 | Fee of expert witness (Dr IJ) | £ 850.00 | | | |
| 14 | Expenses of witnesses of fact | £ 84.00 | | | |
| | 26th July 2000 - Attending second day of trial when judgment "was given for the claimant in the sum of £78,256.83 plus" "£1,207.16 interest plus costs"<br>Engaged in court 3.00 hours £420.00<br>Engaged in conference 1.5 hours £210.00<br>Travel and waiting 1.5 hours £210.00 | | | | |
| 15 | Total solicitor's fee for attending | £ 840.00 | £ 147.00 | | |
| 16 | Counsel's fee for second day (Miss GH) | £ 650.00 | £ 113.75 | | |
| | **Claimant** | | | | |
| | Timed attendances in person and by telephone - see Schedule 1 | | | | |
| 17 | Total fees for Schedule 1 - 7.50 hours | £1,050.00 | £ 183.75 | | |
| 18 | Routine letters out and telephone calls - 26 (14 + 12) | £ 364.00 | £ 63.70 | | |
| | **Witnesses of fact** | | | | |
| | "Timed attendances in person, by letter out and by " | | | | |
| | telephone - see Schedule 2 | | | | |
| 19 | Total fees for Schedule 2 - 5.2 hours | £ 728.00 | £ 127.40 | | |
| 20 | Routine letters out (including e mails) and telephone calls - 6 (4 + 2) | £ 84.00 | £ 14.70 | | |
| 21 | Paid travelling on 9th October 1999 | £ 22.96 | £ 4.02 | | |
| | **Medical expert (Dr IJ)** | | | | |
| 22 | 11th September 1999 - long letter out 0.33 hours | £ 46.20 | £ 8.09 | | |
| 23 | 30th January 2000 - long letter out 0.25 hours | £ 35.00 | £ 6.13 | | |
| 24 | 23rd May 2000 - telephone call 0.2 hours | £ 28.00 | £ 4.90 | | |
| 25 | Routine letters out and telephone calls - 10 (6 + 4) | £ 140.00 | £ 24.50 | | |
| 26 | Dr IJ's fee for report | £ 350.00 | — | | |
| | **Solicitors for the defendant** | | | | |
| 27 | 19th February 2000 - telephone call 0.25 hours | £ 35.00 | £ 6.13 | | |
| 28 | Routine letters out and telephone calls - 24 (18 + 6) | £ 336.00 | £ 58.80 | | |
| | **Communications with the court** | | | | |
| 29 | Routine letters out and telephone calls - 9 (8 + 1) | £ 126.00 | £ 22.05 | | |

| Item No. | Item | | Amount claimed | VAT | Amount allowed | VAT |
|---|---|---|---|---|---|---|
| | **Communications with Counsel** | | | | | |
| 30 | Routine letters out (including e mails) and telephone calls - 19 (11 + 8) | | £ 266.00 | £ 46.55 | | |
| | **Work done on documents** | | | | | |
| | Timed attendances - see Schedule 3 | | | | | |
| 31 | Total fees for Schedule 3 - 45.25 hours at £140 + 12 hours at £85 | | £7,355.00 | £1,287.13 | | |
| | **Work done on negotiations** | | | | | |
| | 23rd March 2000 - meeting at offices of solicitors for the Defendant | | | | | |
| | Engaged - 1.5 hours | £210.00 | | | | |
| | Travel and waiting - 1.25 hours | £175.00 | | | | |
| 32 | Total solicitor's fee for meeting | | £ 385.00 | £ 67.38 | | |
| 33 | **Other work done** | | | | | |
| | Preparing and checking bill | | | | | |
| | Engaged: Solicitor - 1 hour | £140.00 | | | | |
| | Engaged: Costs Draftsman 4 hours | £340.00 | | | | |
| | Total on other work done | | £ 480.00 | £ 84.00 | | |
| | To summary | | £19,625.16 | £3,055.70 | | |
| | **Part 3: COSTS PAYABLE BY LSC ONLY** | | | | | |
| | **Claimant** | | | | | |
| | 11th September 1999 - telephone call | | | | | |
| | Engaged 0.25 hours | £18.50 | | | | |
| | Enhancement 50% | £9.25 | | | | |
| 34 | Total solicitor's fee | | £ 27.75 | £ 4.86 | | |
| | 10th April 2000 - telephone call | | | | | |
| | Engaged 0.1 hours | £4.10 | | | | |
| | Enhancement 50% | £2.05 | | | | |
| 35 | Total solicitor's fee | | £ 6.15 | £ 1.08 | | |
| | **Legal Aid Board and LSC** | | | | | |
| | 2nd August 2000 - Report on case | | | | | |
| | Engaged 0.5 hours | £37.00 | | | | |
| | Enhancement 50% | £18.50 | | | | |
| 36 | Total solicitor's fee | | £ 55.50 | £ 9.71 | | |
| | Routine letters out and telephone calls | | | | | |
| | Letters out - 2 | £14.80 | | | | |
| | Telephone calls - 4 | £16.40 | | | | |
| 37 | Total solicitor's fee | | £ 31.20 | £ 5.46 | | |
| | **Other work done** | | | | | |
| | Preparing and checking bill | | | | | |
| | Engaged: Solicitor - no claim | | | | | |
| | Engaged: Costs Draftsman - 1 hours | £74.00 | | | | |
| 38 | Total on other work done | | £ 74.00 | £ 12.95 | | |
| | To summary | | £ 194.60 | £ 34.06 | | |

| Item No. | Item | | Amount claimed | VAT | Amount allowed | VAT |
|---|---|---|---|---|---|---|
| | **SUMMARY** | | | | | |
| | **Costs payable by the Defendant** | | | | | |
| | | Part 1 | £ 245.00 | £ 42.88 | | |
| | | Part 2 | £19,625.16 | £3,055.70 | | |
| | Total costs payable by the Defendant | | £19,870.16 | £3,098.58 | | |
| | **Costs payable by LSC only** | | | | | |
| | Part 3 | | £ 194.60 | £ 34.06 | | |
| | **Grand Totals** | | | | | |
| | Costs payable by the Defendant | | £19,870.16 | £3,098.58 | | |
| | Costs payable by LSC only | | £ 194.60 | £ 34.06 | | |
| | Grand total | | £20,064.76 | £3,132.63 | | |

SCHEDULE OF COSTS PRECEDENTS
PRECEDENT E

**Legal Aid/LSC Schedule of Costs**

IN THE HIGH COURT OF JUSTICE 1999 - B - 9999

QUEEN'S BENCH DIVISION

BRIGHTON DISTRICT REGISTRY

BETWEEN

AB Claimant

~ and ~

CD Defendant

**CLAIMANT'S BILL OF COSTS: LEGAL AID/LSC SCHEDULE**

| Item No. | Description of work done | | V.A.T. | Disburse-ments | Profit Costs |
|---|---|---|---|---|---|
| 6 | Issue fee | | — | £ 400.00 | |
| 7 | Allocation fee | | — | £ 80.00 | |
| 8 | Solicitor's fee for hearing | | | | |
| | Engaged 0.75 hours | £55.50 | | | |
| | Enhancement thereon at 50% | £27.75 | | | |
| | Travel and waiting 2.00 hours | £65.40 | | | |
| | Total solicitor's fee for attending | | | | £ 148.65 |
| 9 | Fee on listing | | — | £ 400.00 | |
| 10 | Solicitor's fee for hearing | | | | |
| | Engaged 1.5 hours | £111.00 | | | |
| | Enhancement thereon at 50% | £55.50 | | | |
| | Travel and waiting 2.00 hours | £65.40 | | | |
| | Total solicitor's fee for attending | | | | £ 231.90 |
| 11 | Counsel's fee | | £ 105.00 | £ 600.00 | |
| 12 | Solicitor's fee for trial | | | | |
| | Engaged in court 5.00 hours | £182.00 | | | |
| | Engaged in conference 0.75 hours | £27.30 | | | |
| | Enhancement thereon at 50% | £104.65 | | | |
| | Travel and waiting 1.50 hours | £49.05 | | | |
| | Total solicitor's fee for attending | | | | £ 363.00 |
| 13 | Counsel's brief fee for trial | | £ 350.00 | £2,000.00 | |
| 14 | Expert's fee for trial | | — | £ 850.00 | |
| 15 | Witnesses' expenses | | — | £ 84.00 | |
| | To summary | | £ 455.00 | £4,414.00 | £ 743.55 |

| Item No. | Description of work done | | V.A.T. | Disburse-ments | Profit Costs |
|---|---|---|---|---|---|
| 16 | Solicitor's fee for trial (second day) | | | | |
| | Engaged in court 3.00 hours | £109.20 | | | |
| | Engaged in conference 1.50 hours | £54.60 | | | |
| | Enhancement thereon at 50% | £81.90 | | | |
| | Travel and waiting 1.50 hours | £49.05 | | | |
| | Total solicitor's fee for attending | | | | £ 294.75 |
| 17 | Counsel's fee for second day of trial | | £ 113.75 | £ 650.00 | |
| 18 | Timed attendances on Claimant (1) | | | | |
| | 7.5 hours | £555.00 | | | |
| | Enhancement thereon at 50% | £277.50 | | | £ 832.50 |
| 19 | Routine communications with Claimant (1) | | | | |
| | Letters out - 14 | £103.60 | | | |
| | Telephone calls - 12 | £49.20 | | | £ 152.80 |
| 22 | Timed attendances on and communications with witnesses of fact | | | | |
| | 5.2 hours | £384.80 | | | |
| | Enhancement thereon at 50% | £192.40 | | | £ 577.20 |
| 23 | Routine communications with witnesses of fact | | | | |
| | Letters out - 4 | £29.60 | | | |
| | Telephone calls - 2 | £8.20 | | | £ 37.80 |
| 24 | Paid travelling | | 4.02 | 22.96 | |
| 25 | Timed attendance on medical expert | | | | |
| | 0.33 hours | £24.42 | | | |
| | Enhancement thereon at 50% | £12.21 | | | £ 36.63 |
| 26 | Timed communications with medical expert | | | | |
| | 0.25 hours | £18.50 | | | |
| | Enhancement thereon at 50% | £9.25 | | | £ 27.75 |
| 27 | Timed communications with medical expert | | | | |
| | 0.2 hours | £14.80 | | | |
| | Enhancement thereon at 50% | £7.40 | | | £ 22.20 |
| 28 | Routine communications with medical expert | | | | |
| | Letters out - 6 | £44.40 | | | |
| | Telephone calls - 4 | £16.40 | | | £ 60.80 |
| 29 | Expert's fee for report | | — | £ 350.00 | |
| 30 | Timed communications with solicitors for Defendant | | | | |
| | 0.25 hours | £18.50 | | | |
| | Enhancement thereon at 50% | £9.25 | | | £ 27.75 |
| 31 | Routine communications with solicitors for Defendant | | | | |
| | Letters out - 18 | £133.20 | | | |
| | Telephone calls - 6 | £24.60 | | | £ 157.80 |
| 32 | Routine communications with the court | | | | |
| | Letters out - 8 | £59.20 | | | |
| | Telephone calls - 1 | £4.10 | | | £ 63.30 |
| | To summary | | £ 117.77 | £1,022.96 | £2,291.28 |

| Item No. | Description of work done | | V.A.T. | Disburse-ments | Profit Costs |
|---|---|---|---|---|---|
| 33 | Routine communications with Counsel | | | | |
| | Letters out - 11 | £81.40 | | | |
| | Telephone calls - 8 | £32.80 | | | £ 114.20 |
| 36 | Work done on documents | | | | |
| | 57.25 hours | £4,236.50 | | | |
| | Enhancement thereon at 50% | £2,118.25 | | | £6,354.75 |
| 37 | Work done on negotiations | | | | |
| | Engaged - 1.5 hours | £111.00 | | | |
| | Enhancement thereon at 50% | £55.50 | | | |
| | Travel and waiting - 1.25 hours | £40.88 | | | £ 207.38 |
| 38 | Other work done (1) | | | | |
| | Preparing and checking bill | | | | £ 370.00 |
| 40 | VAT on total profit costs set out above ( 17.5% of £10,216.86 ) | | £1,787.95 | | |
| | To summary | | £1,787.95 | £ — | £7,046.33 |
| | **SUMMARY** | | | | |
| | | Page 1 | £ 455.00 | £4,414.00 | £ 743.55 |
| | | Page 2 | £ 117.77 | £1,022.96 | £2,291.28 |
| | | Page 3 | £1,787.95 | £ — | £7,046.33 |
| | | Totals: | £2,360.72 | £5,436.96 | £10,081.16 |
| | | Grand total: | | | £17,878.84 |

**(2) CERTIFICATE AS TO INTEREST AND PAYMENTS**

I certify that:

☐ No rulings have been made in this case which affects my/the receiving party's entitlement (if any) to interest on costs.

or

☐ The only rulings made in this case as to interest are as follows:
*[give brief details as to the date of each ruling, the name of the Judge who made it and the text of the ruling]*

and

☐ No payments have been made by any paying party on account of costs included in this bill of costs.

or

☐ The following payments have been made on account of costs included in this bill of costs:
*[give brief details of the amounts, the dates of payment and the name of the person by or on whose behalf they were paid]*

**(3) CERTIFICATE AS TO INTEREST OF ASSISTED PERSON/ LSC FUNDED CLIENT PURSUANT TO REGULATION 119 OF THE CIVIL LEGAL AID (GENERAL) REGULATIONS 1989**

I certify that the assisted person/ LSC funded client has no financial interest in the detailed assessment.

or

I certify that a copy of this bill has been sent to the assisted person/ LSC funded client pursuant to Regulation 119 of the Civil Legal Aid General Regulations 1989 with an explanation of his/her interest in the detailed assessment and the steps which can be taken to safeguard that interest in the assessment. He/she has/has not requested that the costs officer be informed of his/her interest and has/has not requested that notice of the detailed assessment hearing be sent to him/her.

SCHEDULE OF COSTS PRECEDENTS
PRECEDENT F

**Certificates for inclusion in bill of costs**

- Appropriate certificates under headings (1) and (2) are required in all cases. The appropriate certificate under (3) is required in all cases in which the receiving party is an assisted person or a LSC funded client. Certificates (4), (5) and (6) are optional. Certificate (6) may be included in the bill, or, if the dispute as to VAT recoverability arises after service of the bill, may be filed and served as a supplementary document amending the bill under paragraph 39.10 of this Practice Direction.

- All certificates must be signed by the receiving party or by his solicitor. Where the bill claims costs in respect of work done by more than one firm of solicitors, certificate (1), appropriately completed, should be signed on behalf of each firm.

**(1) CERTIFICATE AS TO ACCURACY**

I certify that this bill is both accurate and complete [ and ]

☐ *(where the receiving party was funded by legal aid/LSC)*
[in respect of Part(s) ..... of the bill] all the work claimed was done pursuant to a certificate issued by the Legal Aid Board/ Legal Services Commission granted to [the assisted person] [the LSC funded client].

☐ *(where costs are claimed for work done by an employed solicitor)*
[in respect of Part(s) .... of the bill] the case was conducted by a solicitor who is an employee of the receiving party.

☐ *(other cases where costs are claimed for work done by a solicitor)*
[in respect of Part(s) ..... of the bill] the costs claimed herein do not exceed the costs which the receiving party is required to pay me/my firm.

**(4) CONSENT TO THE SIGNING OF THE CERTIFICATE WITHIN 21 DAYS OF DETAILED ASSESSMENT PURSUANT TO REGULATION 112 AND 121 OF THE CIVIL LEGAL AID (GENERAL) REGULATIONS 1989**

I certify that notice of the fees reduced or disallowed on detailed assessment has been given in writing to counsel on [ date ].

or

I certify that: there having been no reduction or disallowance of counsel's fees it is not necessary to give notice to counsel.

I/we consent to the final costs certificate being issued immediately.

**(5) CERTIFICATE IN RESPECT OF DISBURSEMENTS NOT EXCEEDING £500**

I hereby certify that all disbursements listed in this bill which individually do not exceed £500 (other than those relating to counsel's fees) have been duly discharged.

**(6) CERTIFICATE AS TO RECOVERY OF VAT**

With reference to the pending assessment of the [claimant's/defendant's] costs and disbursements herein which are payable by the [claimant/defendant] we the undersigned [solicitors to] [auditors of] the [claimant/defendant] hereby certify that the [claimant/defendant] on the basis of its last completed VAT return [would/would not be entitled to recover would/be entitled to recover only percent of the] Value Added Tax on such costs and disbursements, as input tax pursuant to Section 14 of the Value Added Tax Act 1983.

SCHEDULE OF COSTS PRECEDENTS
PRECEDENT G

IN THE HIGH COURT OF JUSTICE 2000 B 9999
QUEEN'S BENCH DIVISION

BRIGHTON DISTRICT REGISTRY

BETWEEN

AB
Claimant

- and -

CD
Defendant

## POINTS OF DISPUTE SERVED BY THE DEFENDANT

| Item | Dispute | Claimant's Comments |
|---|---|---|
| General point | Base rates claimed for the assistant solicitor and other fee earners are excessive. Reduce to £100 and £70 respectively plus VAT. Each item in which these rates are claimed should be recalculated at the reduced rates. | |
| (1) | The premium claimed is excessive. Reduce to £95. | |

| Item | Dispute | Claimant's Comments |
|---|---|---|
| (14) | The claim for timed attendances on claimant (schedule 1) is excessive. Reduce to 4 hours ie. £400 at reduced rates. | |
| (29) | The total claim for work done on documents by the assistant solicitor is excessive. A reasonable allowance in respect of documents concerning court and counsel is 8 hours, for documents concerning witnesses and the expert witness, 6.5 hours, for work done on arithmetic, 2.25 hours and for other documents, 5.5 hours. Reduce to 22.25 hours ie. £2,225 at reduced rates (£3,380 in total). | |
| (31) | The time claimed is excessive. Reduce solicitors time to 0.5 hours ie. to £50 at reduced rates and reduce the costs draftsman's time to three hours ie. £210 (£260 in total). | |
| (32) | The success fee claimed is excessive. Reduce to 25% ie. £100 plus VAT of £17.50. | |
| (33) | The total base fees when recalculated on the basis of the above points amount to £7,788, upon which VAT is £1,362.90. | |
| (34) | The success fee claimed is excessive. Reduce to 25% of £7,788 ie £1,947.50 plus VAT of £340.73. | |
| (36) | The success fee claimed is excessive.Reduce to 50% ie £1,625 plus VAT of £284.38. | |

Served on .......................... [date] by ............................................. [name] [solicitors for] the Defendant.

SCHEDULE OF COSTS PRECEDENTS
PRECEDENT H

IN THE HIGH COURT OF JUSTICE 2000 - B - 9999

QUEEN'S BENCH DIVISION

BRIGHTON DISTRICT REGISTRY

BETWEEN

AB Claimant

and

CD Defendant

**ESTIMATE OF CLAIMANT'S COSTS DATED 12th APRIL 2001**

The claimant instructed E F & Co under a conditional fee agreement dated 8th July 2000 in respect of which the following hourly rates are recoverable as base costs

Partner - £180 per hour plus VAT
Assistant Solicitor - £140 per hour plus VAT
Other fee earners - £85 per hour plus VAT

| Item No. | Description of work done | V.A.T. | Disburse-ments | Profit Costs |
|---|---|---|---|---|
| | **PART 1: BASE COSTS ALREADY INCURRED** | | | |
| | 8th July 2000 - EF & Co instructed | | | |
| | 7th October 2000 - Claim issued | | | |
| 1 | Issue fee | — | £ 400.00 | |
| | 21st October 2000 - Particulars of claim served | | | |
| | 25th November 2000 - Time for service of defence extended by agreement to 14th January 2001 | | | |
| 2 | Fee on allocation | — | £ 80.00 | |
| | 20th January 2001 - case allocated to multi-track | | | |
| | 9th February 2001 - Case management conference at which costs were awarded to the claimant and the base costs were summarily assessed at £400 (paid on 24th February 2001) | | | — |
| | 23rd February 2001 - Claimant's list of documents | | | |
| | **ATTENDANCES, COMMUNICATIONS AND WORK DONE** | | | |
| | **Claimant** | | | |
| 3 | 0.75 hours at £180 | | | £ 135.00 |
| 4 | 4.4 hours at £140 | | | £ 616.00 |
| | To Summary | £ — | £ 480.00 | £ 751.00 |

| Item No. | Description of work done | V.A.T. | Disburse-ments | Profit Costs |
|---|---|---|---|---|
| | **Witnesses of Fact** | | | |
| 5 | 3.8 hours at £140 | | | £ 532.00 |
| 6 | Paid travelling on 9th October 2000 | £ 4.02 | £ 22.96 | |
| | **Medical expert (Dr. IJ)** | | | |
| 7 | 1.5 hours at £140 | | | £ 210.00 |
| 8 | Dr. IJ"s fee for report | | £ 350.00 | |
| | **Defendant and his solicitor** | | | |
| 9 | 2.5 hours at £140 | | | £ 350.00 |
| | **Court (communications only)** | | | |
| 10 | 0.4 hours at £140 | | | £ 56.00 |
| | **Documents** | | | |
| 11 | 0.75 hours at £180 and 22.25 hours at £140 | | | £3,250.00 |
| | **Negotiations** | | | |
| 12 | 2.75 hours at £140 | | | £ 385.00 |
| 13 | VAT on solicitor's base fees | £ 968.45 | | |
| | To Summary | £ 972.47 | £ 372.96 | £4,783.00 |
| | **PART2: BASE COSTS TO BE INCURRED** | | | |
| 14 | Fee on listing | — | £ 400.00 | |
| | Attendance at pre-trial review | | | |
| 15 | 5 hours at £140 | | | £ 700.00 |
| 16 | Counsel's base fee for pre-trial review | | £ 750.00 | |
| | Attendance at trial | | | |
| 17 | 20 hours at £140 | | | £2,800.00 |
| 18 | Counsel's base fee for trial including refresher | | £3,000.00 | |
| 19 | Fee of expert witness (Dr. IJ) | — | £1,000.00 | |
| 20 | Expenses of witnesses of fact | — | £ 150.00 | |
| | **ATTENDANCES, COMMUNICATIONS AND WORK TO BE DONE** | | | |
| | **Claimant** | | | |
| 21 | 1 hour at £180 | | | £ 180.00 |
| 22 | 8 hours at £140 | | | £1,120.00 |
| | **Witnesses of fact** | | | |
| 23 | 5 hours at £140 | | | £ 700.00 |
| | **Medical expert (Dr. IJ)** | | | |
| 24 | 1 hour at £140 | | | £ 140.00 |
| | **Defendant and his solicitor** | | | |
| 25 | 2 hours at £140 | | | £ 280.00 |
| | To Summary | £ — | £5,300.00 | £5,920.00 |

| Item No. | Description of work done | V.A.T. | Disburse-ments | Profit Costs |
|---|---|---|---|---|
| | **Court (communications only)** | | | |
| 26 | 1 hour at £140 | | | £ 140.00 |
| | **Counsel (communications only)** | | | |
| 27 | 3 hours at £140 | | | £ 420.00 |
| | **Documents** | | | |
| 28 | 1 hour at £180, 25 hours at £140 and 15 hours at £85 | | | £4,995.00 |
| | **Negotiations** | | | |
| 29 | 5 hours at £140 | | | £ 700.00 |
| | **Other work** | | | |
| 30 | 5 hours at £140 | | | £ 700.00 |
| 31 | VAT on solicitor's base fees | £2,253.13 | | |
| | To Summary | £2,253.13 | £ — | £6,955.00 |
| | **SUMMARY** | | | |
| | **Part 1** | | | |
| | Page 1 | £ — | £ 480.00 | £ 751.00 |
| | Page 2 | £ 972.47 | £ 372.96 | £4,783.00 |
| | Total base costs already incurred | £ 972.47 | £ 852.96 | £5,534.00 |
| | **Part 2** | | | |
| | Page 2 | £ — | £5,300.00 | £5,920.00 |
| | Page 3 | £2,253.13 | £ — | £6,955.00 |
| | Total base costs to be incurred | £2,253.13 | £5,300.00 | £12,875.00 |
| | Total of base costs | £3,225.60 | £6,152.96 | £18,409.00 |
| | Grand total | | | £27,787.56 |

SCHEDULE OF COSTS PRECEDENTS
PRECEDENT J

IN THE HIGH COURT OF JUSTICE

| Claim No. | |
|---|---|

SUPREME COURT COSTS OFFICE

IN THE MATTER OF [name of solicitor or solicitors' firm]

Claimant

SEAL

Defendant(s)

**CLAIM FORM (CPR Part 8)**

Details of claim (see also overleaf)

The following orders are applied for:

( ) An order in standard form for the delivery of a bill of costs in [all cases and matters] [the following causes and matters .................................................................................................................................................. ] in which the Defendant has acted for the Claimant(s).

( ) An order in standard form for the detailed assessment of the bill(s) dated ........................................ ............................ [and] [bearing the invoice numbers ..................................................................... delivered by the [claimant/Defendant] to the [Defendant/Claimant/person named ............................ ]

( ) An order dealing with the costs of this application

Defendant's name and address

| | £ |
|---|---|
| Court fee | |
| Solicitor's costs | |
| Issue date | |

The court office at the Supreme Court Costs Office, Cliffords Inn, Fetter Lane, London EC4A 1DQ is open between 10.00 am and 4.30 pm, Monday to Friday.

When corresponding with the court, please address forms or letters to the Court Manager and quote the claim number.

| Claim No. | |
|---|---|

Details of claim (continued)

Statement of Truth
*(I believe) (The Claimant believes) that the facts stated in these particulars of claim are true.
*I am duly authorised by the Claimant to sign this statement.

Full name ...........................................................................................................
Name of Claimant's solicitor's firm

Signed ...................................................... position or office held ........................................
*(Claimant) (Litigation friend) (Claimant's solicitor) (if signing on behalf of firm or company)

*delete as appropriate

Claimant's or claimant's solicitor's address to which documents should be sent if different from overleaf. If you are prepared to accept service by DX, fax or e-mail, please add details.

SCHEDULE OF COSTS PRECEDENTS: PRECEDENT K

DATED the [DATE]

IN THE HIGH COURT OF JUSTICE [Case No]

[DIVISION]

[JUDGE TYPE] [JUDGE NAME]

BETWEEN:

[CLAIMANT]

Claimant

– and –

[DEFENDANT]

Defendant

UPON THE APPLICATION OF THE [PARTY]

AND UPON HEARING [ATTEND]

AND UPON READING the documents on the Court File

IT IS ORDERED THAT

1 The [PARTY 1] must within [NUMBER OF DAYS] deliver to the [PARTY 2], or to his solicitor, a bill of costs in all causes and matters in which he has been concerned for the [PARTY 2]

2 The [PARTY 1] must give credit in that bill for all money received by him from or on account of the [PARTY 2]

## SCHEDULE OF COSTS PRECEDENTS: PRECEDENT L

## ORDER ON CLIENT'S APPLICATION FOR DETAILED ASSESSMENT OF SOLICITOR'S BILL

Upon hearing . . upon reading . .

IT IS ORDERED

(1) A detailed assessment must be made of the bill dated [ ] delivered to the claimant by the defendant.

(2) On makikng the detailed assessment, the court must also assess the costs of these proceedings and certify what is due to or from either party in respect of the bill and the costs of these proceedings.

(3) Until these proceedings are concluded the defendant must not commence or continue any proceedings against the claimant in respect of the bill mentioned above.

(4) Upon payment by the claimant of any sum certified as due to the defendant in these proceedings the defendant must deliver to the claimant all the documentation in the defendant's possession or control which belong to the claimant.

SCHEDULE OF COSTS PRECEDENTS: PRECEDENT M

ORDER ON SOLICITOR'S APPLICATION FOR ASSESSMENT UNDER THE SOLICITOR'S ACT 1974 PART III

Upon hearing . . upon reading . .
IT IS ORDERED(1) A detailed assessment must be made of the bill dated [ ] delivered to the defendant by the claimant.

(2) If the defendant attends the detailed assessment the court making that assessment must also assess the costs of these proceedings and certify what is due to or from either party in respect of the bill and the costs of these proceedings.

(3) Until these proceedings are concluded the claimant must not commence or continue any proceedings against the defendant in respect of the bill mentioned above.

(4) Upon payment by the defendant of any sum certified as due to the claimant in these procedings the claimant must deliver to the defendant all the documentation in the defendant's possession or control which belong to the defendant.

SCHEDULE OF COSTS PRECEDENTS
PRECEDENT P

**Solicitors Act: Breakdown of Costs**

IN THE HIGH COURT OF JUSTICE Claim Number

QUEEN'S BENCH DIVISION

SUPREME COURT COSTS OFFICE

BETWEEN

EF Claimant

~ and ~

GH & Co Defendants

**BREAKDOWN OF DEFENDANT'S BILL OF COSTS DATED 26TH FEBRUARY 1999 TO BE ASSESSED PURSUANT TO THE ORDER DATED 27TH APRIL 1999**

The claimant instructed the defendants in connection with a summons for careless or inconsiderate driving which had been served upon him. By letter dated 21st October 1998 the defendants wrote to the claimant setting out their terms of business including the hourly rates of the fee earners who would act on his instructions. On 23rd October 1998 the claimant dated and signed a copy of that letter and returned it to the defendants so indicating his acceptance of the terms set out.

The proceedings were of the highest importance to the claimant who feared losing his licence and who wished to defend any civil proceedings that might be taken against him as a result of the prosecution. The defendants entered into correspondence with the CPS and eventually obtained their witness statements and invited them to consent to an adjournment because of the absence overseas of an important witness for the claimant (Mr LM). Eventually the defendants successfully applied to the court for an adjournment, and also applied for and obtained a witness summons. At the trial the claimant was found guilty and was fined £300 and 4 points were endorsed on his driving licence.

Proceedings were conducted by an assistant solicitor admitted in 1990 whose time is charged at an agreed rate of £150 per hour with routine letters out and telephone calls at an agreed rate of £15 each. At the trial a trainee attended with counsel. The trainee's time is charged at an agreed rate of £75 per hour.

**Cash account for client: EF**

| **Received** | | **Paid** | |
|---|---|---|---|
| From client on account generally: 22nd October 1998 | 1,500.00 | Refund to client: 26th February 1999 | 385.00 |
| From client on account generally: 12th February 1999 | **1,000.00** | Balancing Item | **2,115.00** |
| | **2,500.00** | | **2,500.00** |
| Balance due to client EF: | **£2,115.00** | | |

| | Item | | V.A.T. | Disburse-ments | Profit Costs |
|---|---|---|---|---|---|
| | **Attendances on Court and Counsel** | | | | |
| | 5th November 1998 - application made for an adjournment for the convenience of a witness | | | | |
| | 13th November 1998 - contested hearing of the application | | | | |
| | Engaged 10 minutes | £ 25.00 | | | |
| | Travel and waiting 30 minutes | £ 75.00 | | | |
| 1 | Total solicitor's fee for hearing | | £ 17.50 | | £ 100.00 |
| | 17th November 1998 - conference with counsel | | | | |
| | Engaged 45 minutes | £ 112.50 | | | |
| | Travel and waiting 1 hour | £ 150.00 | | | |
| 2 | Total solicitor's fee for conference | | £ 45.94 | | £ 262.50 |
| 3 | Counsel's fee for conference (paid: Miss JK) | | £ 13.13 | £ 75.00 | |
| | 15th February 1999 - Brief to counsel - 4 pages A4 | | | | |
| | 23rd February 1999 - attending the trial | | | | |
| | Trainee engaged in court 1 hour | £ 75.00 | | | |
| | Engaged in conference 30 minutes | £ 37.50 | | | |
| | Travel and waiting (apportioned) 45 minutes | £ 56.25 | | | |
| 4 | Total trainee solicitor's fee for trial | | £ 29.53 | | £ 168.75 |
| 5 | Counsel's brief fee (paid: Miss JK) | | £ 17.50 | £ 100.00 | |
| | **Claimant** | | | | |
| 6 | 21st October 1998 - first instructions 1 hour | | £ 26.25 | | £ 150.00 |
| 7 | 16th November 1998 - finalising proof of evidence 45 minutes | | £ 19.69 | | £ 112.50 |
| 8 | Routine letters out and telephone calls - 12 (9 + 3) | | £ 31.50 | | £ 180.00 |
| | **Witness (Mr LM)** | | | | |
| | Personal attendance by trainee solicitor | | | | |
| | Engaged 45 minutes | £ 56.25 | | | |
| | Travel and waiting 1 hour | £ 75.00 | | | |
| 9 | Total trainee solicitor's fee for attendance | | £ 22.97 | | £ 131.25 |
| 10 | Routine letters out - 6 | | £ 15.75 | | £ 90.00 |
| | **Other persons** | | | | |
| 11 | Routine letters out and telephone calls to the CPS - 8 (6 + 2) | | £ 21.00 | | £ 120.00 |
| | **Communications with the court** | | | | |
| 12 | Routine letters out - 6 | | £ 15.75 | | £ 90.00 |
| 13 | **Communications with Counsel** | | | | |
| | Routine letters out and telephone calls - 8 (4 + 4) | | £ 21.00 | | £ 120.00 |
| | **Work done on documents** | | | | |
| 14 | Instructions to counsel - 30 minutes | | £ 13.13 | | £ 75.00 |
| 15 | Attendance note of conference - 15 minutes | | £ 6.56 | | £ 37.50 |
| 16 | Brief to counsel - 30 minutes | | £ 13.13 | | £ 75.00 |
| 17 | Attendance note of trial (trainee) - 45 minutes | | £ 9.84 | | £ 56.25 |
| | | | £ 340.17 | £ 175.00 | £1,768.75 |
| | **Summary** | | | | |
| | **Total costs claimed in breakdown £1,943.75 + £340.17 VAT.** (Total costs billed £1899.00 + £315.00 VAT) | | | | |

# Notice of Funding of Case or Claim

| In the | |
|---|---|
| **Claim No.** | |
| **Claimant** (include Ref.) | |
| **Defendant** (include Ref.) | |

Notice of funding by means of a conditional fee agreement, insurance policy or undertaking given by a prescribed body should be given to the court and all other parties to the case:

- on commencement of proceedings
- on filing an acknowledgment of service, defence or other first document; and
- at any later time that such an arrangement is entered into, changed or terminated

**Take notice that** in respect of [all claims herein][the following claims ............
the case of ............ *(specify name of party)*

[is now][was] being funded by:
*(Please tick those boxes which apply)*

☐ a conditional fee agreement dated ........ which provides for a success fee;
☐ an insurance policy issued on *(date)* ........ by *(name of insurers)* ........ ;
☐ an undertaking given on *(date)* ........ by *(name of prescribed body)* ........ in the following terms ............

The funding of the case has now changed:

☐ the above funding has now ceased
☐ the conditional fee agreement has been terminated
☐ a conditional agreement dated ........ which provides for a success fee has been entered into
☐ the insurance policy dated ........ has been cancelled
☐ an insurance policy has been issued by *(name of insurer)* ............
on *(date)* ........
☐ the undertaking given on *(date)* ........ has been terminated
☐ an undertaking has been given on *(date)* ........ by *(name of prescribed body)* ............
in the following terms ............

**Signed** ............ **Date** ............
Solicitor for the (claimant) (defendant) (Part 20 defendant)
(respondent)(appellant)

**The court office at**

is open between 10 am and 4 pm Monday to Friday. When corresponding with the court, please address forms or letters to the Court Manager and quote the claim numbe

**N251** Notice of funding of case or claim (7.00) *The Court Service Publications Un*

# Notice of commencement of assessment of bill of costs

| In the | |
|---|---|
| Claim No. | |
| Claimant (include Ref.) | |
| Defendant (include Ref.) | |

To the claimant(defendant)

Following an ........................................ (*insert name of document eg. order, judgment*) dated ................ (copy attached) I have prepared my Bill of Costs for assessment. The Bill totals *£ .......... If you choose to dispute this bill and your objections are not upheld at the assessment hearing, the full amount payable (including the assessment fee) will be £ ............ (together with interest (*see note below*)). I shall also seek the costs of the assessment hearing

Your points of dispute must include

- details of the items in the bill of costs which are disputed
- concise details of the nature and grounds of the dispute for each item and, if you seek a reduction in those items, suggest, where practicable, a reduced figure

You must serve your points of dispute by .............................. (*insert date 21 days from the date of service of this notice*) on me at:- *(give full name and address for service including any DX number or reference)*

You must also serve copies of your points of dispute on all other parties to the assessment identified below *(you do not need to serve your points of dispute on the court).*

I certify that I have also served the following person(s) with a copy of this notice and my Bill of Costs:- *(give details of persons served)*

If I have not received your points of dispute by the above date, I will ask the court to issue a default costs certificate for the full amount of my bill *(see above*)* plus fixed costs and court fee in the total amount of £ ..................

**Signed** ........................................ **Date** ..................

(Claimant)(Defendant)('s solicitor)

**Note:** Interest may be added to all High Court judgments and certain county court judgments of £5,000 or more under the Judgments Act 1838 and the County Courts Act 1984.

The court office at

is open between 10 am and 4 pm Monday to Friday. When corresponding with the court, please address forms or letters to the Court Manager and quote the claim number.

N252 Notice of commencement of assessment of bill of costs (12.99) *The Court Service Publications Unit*

# Notice of Amount allowed on Provisional Assessment

| In the | |
|---|---|
| Claim No. | |
| Claimant (including ref) | |
| Defendant (including ref) | |
| Date | |

To [Claimant][Defendant]['s Solicitor]

**Take notice** that the [claimant's][defendant's][receiver's] bill of costs in this action has been provisionally assessed and is returned with this notice

If you wish to be heard on the assessment, you must, within 14 days of the receipt of this notice inform the court in writing and return the bill of costs to the court. A date for assessment will then be fixed.

If you accept the provisional assessment as final, please complete and return the bill together with the balance of the assessment fee.

**Note:** In Legal aid only/LSC only cases

1) Within 7 days of receipt of the notice the solicitor must notify counsel in writing where the fees claimed on counsel's behalf have been provisonally reduced or disallowed.
2) The solicitor should not accept the provisonal assessment as final without first enquiring whether any counsel whose fees have been provisionally reduced or disallowed has also accepted it.
3) Attention is drawn to the need to endorse on the bill a certificate in the form of precedent F(4) before returning the bill to the court.

The court office at

is open between 10 am and 4 pm Monday to Friday. Address all communications to the Court Manager quoting the claim number.

N253 Notice of Amount allowed on Provisional Assessment (7.00)

# Request for a Default Costs Certificate

| In the | |
|---|---|
| **Claim No.** | |
| **Claimant** (include Ref.) | |
| **Defendant** (include Ref.) | |

I certify that the attached Notice of Commencement was served on the paying party ..................................................

(*and give details of any other party served with the notice*)

on ............................................................ (*insert date*)

I also certify that I have not received any points of dispute and that the time for receiving them has now elapsed.

I now request the court to issue a certificate for the amount of the bill of costs plus such fixed costs and court fees as are appropriate in this case.

**Signed** ............................................................ **Date** ..................................

(Claimant)(Defendant)('s Solicitor)

The court office at

s open between 10 am and 4 pm Monday to Friday. When corresponding with the court, please address forms or letters to the Court Manager and quote the claim number.

N254 - w3 Request for a Default Costs Certificate (4.99) *Printed on behalf of The Court Service*

# Default Costs Certificate

| In the | |
|---|---|
| County | |
| **Claim No.** | |
| **Claimant** (inlcuding ref) | |
| **Defendant** (inlcuding ref) | |
| **Date** | |

To [Claimant][Defendant]['s Solicitor]

As you have not raised any points of dispute on the [defendant's][claimant's] bill of costs, the costs of the claim have been allowed and the total sum of £ is now payable.

You must pay this amount to the [defendant][claimant] [within 14 days from the date of this order] [on or before [ ]]

The date from which any entitlement to interest under this certficate commences is [date]

## Take Notice

**To the defendant (claimant)**

**If you do not pay in accordance with this order your goods may be removed and sold or other enforcement proceedings may be taken against you. If your circumstances change and you cannot pay, ask at the court office about what you can do**

Further interest may be added if judgment has been given for £5,000 or more or is in respect of a debt which attracts contractual or statutory interest for late payment.

This judgment has been registered on the Register of County Court Judgr This may make it difficult for you to get credit. **If you pay in full withi month** you can ask the court to cancel the entry on the Register. You will n give proof of payment. You can (for a fee) also obtain a Certificate of Cancel from the court. If you pay the debt in full after one month you can ask the c mark the entry on the Register as satisfied and (for a fee) obtain a Certific Satisfaction to prove that the debt has been paid.

## Address for Payment

## How to Pay

- PAYMENT(S) MUST BE MADE to the person named at the address for payment quoting their reference and the court case number.
- **DO NOT bring or send payments to the court. THEY WILL NOT BE ACCEPT**
- You should allow <u>at least</u> 4 days for your payment to reach the claimant (defendant) or his representative.
- Make sure that you keep records and can account for all payments made. Proof may be required if there is any disagreement. It is not safe to send cas unless you use registered post.
- A leaflet giving further advice about payment can be obtained from the cou
- If you need more information you should contact the claimant (defenda or his representative.

The court office at

is open between 10 am and 4 pm Monday to Friday. Address all communications to the Court Manager quoting the claim number

**N255CC** Default costs certificate

**N255HC**

## Default Costs Certificate

| **Default Costs Certificate** | **In the High Court of Justice** | |
|---|---|---|
| | | **Division** **District Registry** |
| To [Claimant] [Defendant] ['s solicitor] | **Claim No.** | |
| | **Claimant** (including ref.) | |
| | **Defendant** (including ref.) | |
| | **Date** | |

As you have not raised any points of dispute on the [defendant's] [claimant's] bill of costs, the costs of the claim have been allowed and the total sum of £ is now payable. The VAT included in the total sum is £ . You must pay this amount to the [defendant] [claimant] [within 14 days from the date of this order] [on or before [ ]].

The date from which any entitlement to interest under this certificate commences is [*date*].

**Take Notice**

**To the defendant (claimant)**

**If you do not pay in accordance with this order your goods may be removed and sold or other enforcement proceedings may be taken against you. If your circumstances change and you cannot pay, ask at the court office about what you can do**

**Address for payment**

**How to Pay**

- **PAYMENT(S) MUST BE MADE to the person named at the address for payment, quoting their reference and the court case number**
- **DO NOT bring or send payments to the court. THEY WILL NOT BE ACCEPTED.**
- **You should allow at least 4 days for your payment to reach the claimant (defendant) or his representative**
- **Make sure that you keep records and can account for all payments made. Proof may be required if there is any disagreement. It is not safe to send cash unless you use registered post.**
- **A leaflet giving further advice about payment can be obtained from the court.**
- **If you need more information you should contact the claimant (defendant) or his representative.**

**The court office at**

**is open between 10 am and 4 pm Monday to Friday. Address all communications to the Court Manager quoting the claim number.**

## N256

## Final Costs Certificate

| **Final Costs Certificate** | **In the** |
|---|---|
| | **County Court** |
| To [Claimant][Defendant]['s solicitor] | **Claim No.** |
| | **Claimant** (including ref.) |
| | **Defendant** (including ref.) |
| | **Date** |

Upon the [claimant][defendant] filing a completed bill of costs in this claim

District Judge][ ] has assessed the total cost as £ [including £ for the costs of the detailed assessment. The VAT included in the total is £ ]

[And £ ] already having been paid under the interim costs certificate issued on [ ]]

You must pay [the balance of] £ to the [claimant][defendant] [within 14 days from the date of this order] [on or before [ ]]

The date from which any entitlement to interest under this certificate commences is [*date*].

### Take Notice

**To the defendant (claimant)**

**If you do not pay in accordance with this order your goods may be removed and sold or other enforcement proceedings may be taken against you. If your circumstances change and you cannot pay, ask at the court office about what you can do**

Further interest may be added if judgment has been given for £5,000 or more or is in respect of a debt which attracts contractual or statutory interest for late payment.

### Address for Payment

This judgment has been registered on the Register of County Court Judgments. This may make it difficult for you to get credit. **If you pay in full within one month** you can ask the court to cancel the entry on the Register. You will need to give proof of payment. You can (for a fee) also obtain a Certificate of Cancellation from the court. If you pay the debt in full after one month you can ask the court to mark the entry on the Register as satisfied and (for a fee) obtain a Certificate of Satisfaction to prove that the debt has been paid.

### How to Pay

- **PAYMENT(S) MUST BE MADE to the person named at the address for payment, quoting their reference and the court case number**
- **DO NOT bring or send payments to the court. THEY WILL NOT BE ACCEPTED.**
- You should allow at least 4 days for your payment to reach the claimant (defendant) or his representative
- Make sure that you keep records and can account for all payments made. Proof may be required if there is any disagreement. It is not safe to send cash unless you use registered post.
- A leaflet giving further advice about payment can be obtained from the court.
- If you need more information you should contact the claimant (defendant) or his representative.

The court office at

is open between 10 am and 4 pm Monday to Friday. Address all communications to the Court Manager quoting the claim number.

**N256(HC)**

**Final Costs Certificate**

**Final Costs Certificate**

| **In the High Court of Justice** <br> **Division** <br> **District Registry** | |
|---|---|
| **Claim No.** | |
| **Claimant** (including ref.) | |
| **Defendant** (including ref.) | |
| **Date** | |

To [Claimant] [Defendant] ['s solicitor]

Upon the [claimant] [defendant] filing a completed bill of costs in this claim

Master[ ] has assessed the total cost as £ [including £ for the costs of the detailed assessment. The VAT included in the total is £ ]

[And £ ] already having been paid under the interim costs certificate issued on [ ]]

You must pay [the balance of] £ to the [claimant] [defendant] [within 14 days from the date of this order] [on or before [ ]]

The date from which any entitlement to interest under this certificate commences is [*date*].

**Take Notice**

**To the defendant (claimant)**

**If you do not pay in accordance with this order your goods may be removed and sold or other enforcement proceedings may be taken against you. If your circumstances change and you cannot pay, ask at the court office about what you can do**

**Address for payment**

**How to Pay**

- **PAYMENT(S) MUST BE MADE to the person named at the address for payment, quoting their reference and the court case number**
- **DO NOT bring or send payments to the court. THEY WILL NOT BE ACCEPTED.**
- You should allow at least 4 days for your payment to reach the claimant (defendant) or his representative
- Make sure that you keep records and can account for all payments made. Proof may be required if there is any disagreement. It is not safe to send cash unless you use registered post.
- A leaflet giving further advice about payment can be obtained from the court.
- If you need more information you should contact the claimant (defendant) or his representative.

The court office at

is open between 10 am and 4 pm Monday to Friday. Address all communications to the Court Manager quoting the claim number.

**N257**

## Interim Costs Certificate

| **Interim costs certificate** | **In the** | |
|---|---|---|
| | **Claim No.** | |
| To [Claimant] [Defendant] ['s solicitor] | **Claimant** (including ref.) | |
| | **Defendant** (including ref.) | |
| | **Date** | |

Upon application by the [claimant] [defendant] for [a detailed assessment hearing] [the issue of an interim costs certificate by agreement].

[Master] [District Judge] [Costs Officer] [ ] has ordered that you must pay

£ to the [claimant] [defendant] [within 14 days from the date of this order]

[on or before [ ]] [into court to await the issue of a final costs certificate].

**Take Notice**

**To the defendant (claimant)**

**If you do not pay in accordance with this order your goods may be removed and sold or other enforcement proceedings may be taken against you. If your circumstances change and you cannot pay, ask at the court office about what you can do**

**Address for payment**

**How to Pay**

- **PAYMENT(S) MUST BE MADE to the person named at the address for payment, quoting their reference and the court case number**
- **DO NOT bring or send payments to the court. THEY WILL NOT BE ACCEPTED.**
- You should allow at least 4 days for your payment to reach the claimant (defendant) or his representative
- Make sure that you keep records and can account for all payments made. Proof may be required if there is any disagreement. It is not safe to send cash unless you use registered post.
- A leaflet giving further advice about payment can be obtained from the court.
- If you need more information you should contact the claimant (defendant) or his representative.

The court office at

is open between 10 am and 4 pm Monday to Friday. Address all communications to the Court Manager quoting the claim number.

# Request for Detailed Assessment Hearing (general form)

| In the | |
|---|---|
| Claim No. | |
| Claimant (include Ref.) | |
| Defendant (include Ref.) | |

I certify that the Notice of Commencement was served on the paying party

(*and give details of any other party served with the notice*)

on (*insert date*)

I now ask the court to arrange an assessment hearing

I enclose copies of (*tick as appropriate*)

- ☐ the document giving the right to detailed assessment;
- ☐ a copy of the Notice of Commencement;
- ☐ the bill of costs;
- ☐ the paying party's points of dispute annotated as necessary in order to show which items have been agreed and their value and to show which items remain in dispute and their value;
- ☐ points in reply (if any)
- ☐ a statement giving the name and address for service of any person I intend to serve with this notice;
- ☐ the relevant details of any additional liability claimed;
- ☐ a copy of all the orders made by the court relating to the costs of the proceedings which are to be assessed;
- ☐ any fee notes of counsel and receipts or accounts for other disbursements relating to items in dispute;
- ☐ [where solicitors' costs are disputed] the client care letter delivered to the receiving party or the solicitor's retainer.

I believe the hearing with take (*give estimate of time court should allow*).

I enclose my fee of £

**Signed** . . . . . . . . . . . . . . . . . . . . . . . . **Date** . . . . . . . . . .

(Claimant)(Defendant)('s Solicitor)

The court office at

is open between 10 am and 4 pm Monday to Friday. When corresponding with the court, please address forms or letters to the Court Manager and quote the claim number.

**N258** Request for Detailed Assessment Hearing (general form) (7.00) *Printed on behalf of The Court Service*

# Request for detailed assessment (Legal aid/LSC only)

| In the | |
|---|---|
| Claim No. | |
| Claimant (include Ref.) | |
| Defendant (include Ref.) | |

I now ask the court to provisionally assess the bill* (arrange an assessment hearing as the assisted person/LSC funded client wishes to be heard)

I enclose copies of *(tick as appropriate)*

☐ the document giving the right to detailed assessment;

☐ the bill of costs;

☐ a statement giving the name and address for service of any person I intend to serve with this notice;

☐ a copy of all the orders made by the court relating to the costs of the proceedings which are to be assessed;

☐ any fee notes of counsel and receipts or accounts for other disbursements relating to items in dispute;

☐ all civil legal aid certificates and LSC certificates and amendments to them; notice of discharge or revocation and specific legal aid authorities;

☐ the relevant papers in support of the bill (Supreme Court Costs Office/PRFD assessments only)

*I certify that the assisted person/LSC funded client wishes to attend the assessment hearing and I believe the hearing will take .......
***(give estimate of time court should allow).***

I enclose my fee of £ . . . . . . . .

***(delete if not applicable)***

**Signed** ........................................................ **Date** ............................

(Claimant)(Defendant)('s Solicitor)

The court office at

is open between 10 am and 4 pm Monday to Friday. When corresponding with the court, please address forms or letters to the Court Manager and quote the claim number.

N258A Request for detailed assessment (legal aid/LSC only) (7.00) *The Court Service Publications Unit*

# Request for detailed assessment (Costs payable out of a fund other than the Community Legal Service Fund)

| In the | |
|---|---|
| **Claim No.** | |
| **Claimant** (include Ref.) | |
| **Defendant** (include Ref.) | |

I now ask the court to provisionally assess the bill or arrange an assessment hearing.

I enclose copies of (*tick as appropriate*)

- ☐ The document giving the right to detailed assessement;
- ☐ the bill of costs;
- ☐ a statement giving the name and address for service of any person having a financial interest in the outcome of the assessment;
- ☐ a copy of all the orders made by the court relating to the costs of the proceedings which are to be assessed;
- ☐ any fee notes of counsel and receipts or accounts for other disbursements relating to items claimed;
- ☐ the relevant details of any additional liability claimed;
- ☐ the relevant papers in support of the bill (Supreme Court Costs Office/ PRFD assessments only)

I enclose my fee of £ . . . . . .

**Signed** ........................................................ **Date** ..........................
(Claimant)(Defendant)(Receiver)('s solicitor)

The court office at

is open between 10 am and 4 pm Monday to Friday. When corresponding with the court, please address forms or letters to the Court Manager and quote the claim number.

N258B Request for detailed assessment (cost payable out of a fund other than the Community Legal Service Fund) (7.00) *The Court Service Publications Unit*

# Request for detailed assessment hearing pursuant to an order under Part III of the Solicitors Act 1974

| In the | |
|---|---|
| Claim No. | |
| Claimant (include Ref.) | |
| Defendant (include Ref.) | |

I certify that the [party] . . . . . . . . . . . . . . . . . . has served a breakdown of costs in this case and the [party] . . . . . . . . . . . . . . . . . . has served points of dispute thereon.

I now ask the court to arrange an assessment hearing.

I enclose copies of (*tick as appropriate*)

- ☐ the order made under Part III of the Solicitors Act 1974 in this case;
- ☐ the bill(s) of costs to be assessed;
- ☐ the breakdown(s);
- ☐ any fee notes of counsel and receipts or accounts for other disbursements served with the breakdown of costs;
- ☐ a statement giving names, addresses and references of the persons to whom the court should give notice of the hearing;
- ☐ the [party's] points of dispute plus copies to be sent to the other parties to these proceedings details of whom are given above;
- ☐ the points in reply (if any)

I believe the hearing will take . . . . . . . . (*give estimate of time court should allow*).

I enclose my fee of £ . . . . . . .

**Signed** ........................................................ **Date** ..........................

(Claimant)(Defendant)('s solicitor)

The court office at

is open between 10 am and 4 pm Monday to Friday. When corresponding with the court, please address forms or letters to the Court Manager and quote the claim number.

N258C Request for detailed assessment hearing pursuant to an order under Part III of the Solicitors Act 1974 (7.00) *The Court Service Publications Unit*

# Statement of Costs (summary assessment)

**In the**

**Court**

**Case Reference**

**Judge/Master**

**Case Title**

**[Party]'s Statement of Costs for the hearing on** *(date)* **(interim application/fast track trial)**

Description of fee earners*
(a) *(name) (grade) (hourly rate claimed)*
(b) *(name) (grade) (hourly rate claimed)*

Attendances on *(party)*
(a) *(number)* hours at £ £
(b) *(number)* hours at £ £

Attendances on opponents
(a) *(number)* hours at £ £
(b) *(number)* hours at £ £

Attendance on others
(a) *(number)* hours at £ £
(b) *(number)* hours at £ £

Site inspections etc
(a) *(number)* hours at £ £
(b) *(number)* hours at £ £

Work done on negotiations
(a) *(number)* hours at £ £
(b) *(number)* hours at £ £

Other work, not covered above
(a) *(number)* hours at £ £
(b) *(number)* hours at £ £

Work done on documents
(a) *(number)* hours at £ £
(b) *(number)* hours at £ £

Attendance at hearing
(a) *(number)* hours at £ £
(b) *(number)* hours at £ £
(a) *(number)* hours travel and waiting at £ £
(b) *(number)* hours travel and waiting at £ £

**Sub Total £**

**N260** Statement of Costs (summary assessment) (7.00) *Printed on behalf of The Court Service*

**Brought forward £**

Counsel's fees *(name) (year of call)*

Fee for [advice/conference/documents] £

Fee for hearing £

Other expenses

[court fees] £

Others £

*(give brief description)*

**Total** £

Amount of VAT claimed

on solicitors and counsel's fees £

on other expenses £

**Grand Total** **£**

The costs estimated above do not exceed the costs which the *(party)* is liable to pay in respect of the work which this estimate covers.

Dated

Signed

Name of firm of solicitors
[partner] for the *(party)*

* 3 grades of fee earner are suggested: (1) Solicitors with over 4 years post qualification experience (2) Other solicitors and legal executives and fee earners of equivalent experience (3) Trainee solicitors and fee earners of equivalent experience. 'Legal Executive' means a Fellow of the Institute of Legal Executives. Those who are not Fellows of the Institute are not entitled to call themselves legal executives and in principle are therefore not entitled to the same hourly rate as a legal executive. In respect of each fee earner communications should be treated as attendances and routine communications should be claimed at one tenth of the hourly rate.

**N260** Statement of Costs (summary assessment) (7.00)

*Printed on behalf of The Court Service*

# APPENDIX I

**elete I-002 and substitute:**

Part II

Costs on Judgment without Trial for Possession of Land

1

(1) Where the claim is for the possession of land, and the claimant obtains judgment-

(a) under CPR Part 12 (default judgment); or
(b) under CPR Part 24 (summary judgment)

r possession of the land and costs, then, subject to sub-paragraph (2), there shall allowed the costs prescribed by paragraph 2 of this Part of this Appendix.

(2) Where the claimant is also entitled under the judgment to damages to be assessed, or where the plaintiff claims any remedy of the nature specified in Order 45, rule 3(2), this Part of this Appendix shall not apply.

he costs to be allowed under this Part of this Appendix shall be £143.75, together ith any court fee, and additional costs where appropriate set out the Table below.

**elete 3 and 4 in paragraph I–004.***

# APPENDIX J

**mend paragraphs J–011, J–012 and J–015 as follows:**

7. In RSC Order 106— **J–011**

(a) in rule 12—

(i) in paragraph (1) for "notice of appeal", substitute "appellant's notice";
(ii) for paragraph (3), substitute—
"(3) The appellant's notice must be filed at the court within 14 days after the date on which a statement of the tribunal's findings was filed pursuant to section 48(1) of the Act."; and
(iii) omit paragraph (4);

(b) in rule 13(1) for "notice of appeal", substitute "appellant's notice"; and
(c) in rule 16 for "notice of appeal", substitute "appellant's notice".

**Delete M-001 and substitute:**

## Claims for the Recovery of Property

**Directions**

1. The Tables in this Part of this Appendix show the amount to be enter on the claim form or application in respect of solicitors' charges—

   (c) in a claim for the recovery of property, including land, with or witho a claim for a sum of money (other than a claim to which CPR Part 4 applies), for the purpose of Part II of this Appendix or of fixing t amount which the plaintiff may receive in respect of solicitors' charg without assessment whether by the detailed or summary procedure the event of the defendant giving up possession and paying the amou claimed, if any, and costs.

2. In addition to the amount entered in accordance with the relevant tab the appropriate court fees shall be entered on the application.
3. In the tables the expression "claim" means—

   (a) the sum of money claimed; or
   (b) in relation to a claim for the recovery of land (with or without a clai for a sum of money), a sum exceeding £600 but not exceeding £2,00
   (c) in relation to a claim for the recovery of property other than mon or land, the value of the property claimed or in the case of goo supplied under a hire purchase agreement, the unpaid balance of t total price.

4. The tables do not apply where the application or the claim form is to b served out of England and Wales or where service by an alternative meth is ordered.

**M–004** **Delete (d)(ii) in column 1 of the Table in paragraph M-004 and substitute:**

(iii) possession of land, where one of the grounds for possession arrears of rent (whether or not the order for possession is su pended on terms) and the defendant has neither delivered defence, admission or counterclaim, nor otherwise denied liabi ity; and

**Insert after the Table in paragraph M-004:**

Note: Where proceedings are issued before March 25, 2002, d(ii) applies as if had not been amended as above (The Civil Procedure (Amendment No. 5) Rul 2001, No. 4015 (L.32), R 43(1)).

**M–005** **Delete items 7, 8 and 11 of the Table in paragraph M-005**

**Delete item 10 of the Table in paragraph M-005 and substitute:**

10. Where an order for possession is made under Section II of CPR Part 5 (Possession claims) without the attendance of the claimant, for preparin and filing the application,
the documents attached to the application and the request for possessic
£79.50

# APPENDIX O

## THE PRINCIPAL REGISTRY OF THE FAMILY DIVISION

**Costs** **President's Direction**
**Civil Procedure Rules 1998** **24 July 2000**

O-002

The President's Direction dated the 22nd April 1999 applied the (Civil Procedure) Practice Direction about Costs Supplementing Parts 43 to 48 of the Civil Procedure Rules ("the costs direction") to family proceedings (within the Family Proceedings Rules 1991) and to proceedings in the Family Division. A further edition of the costs direction (effective from the 3rd July 2000) has been published and it is hereby directed that the further edition (and all subsequent editions as and when they are published and come into effect) shall extend to family proceedings and to proceedings in the Family Division in the same way as did the costs direction and to the extent applicable to such proceedings.

The further edition of the costs direction includes provisions applicable to proceedings following changes in the manner in which legal services are funded pursuant to the Access to Justice Act 1999. It should be noted that although the cost of the premium in respect of legal costs insurance (section 29) or the cost of funding by a prescribed membersip organisation (section 30) may be recoverable, family proceedings (within section 58A(2) of the Courts and Legal Services Act 1990) cannot be the subject of an enforceable conditional fee agreement.

Issued with the approval of the Lord Chancellor

Elizabeth Butler-Sloss
President

# APPENDIX P

**Delete paragraphs P-001 to P-019 and substitute:**

## The Insolvency Rules 1986
## (S.I. 1986 No. 9125)

The Lord Chancellor, in the exercise of his powers under sections 411 and 412 of the Insolvency Act 1986, with the concurrence of the Secretary of State, and after consulting the committee existing for that purpose under section 413 of that Act, hereby makes the following Rules:—

## INTRODUCTORY PROVISIONS

**0.1. Citation and commencement**

These Rules may be cited as the Insolvency Rules 1986 and shall come into forc on 29th December 1986.

**[ 0.2.— Construction and interpretation**

(1) In these Rules—

"the Act" means the Insolvency Act 1986 (any reference to a numbere section being to a section of that Act);

"the Companies Act" means the Companies Act 1985[1];

"CPR" means the Civil Procedure Rules 1998.[2] and "CPR" followed by Part or rule by number means the Part or rule with that number in thos Rules;

"RSC" followed by an Order by number means the Order with th number set out in Schedule 1 to the CPR; and

"the Rules" means the Insolvency Rules 1986.

(2) References in the Rules to ex parte hearings shall be construed as referenc to hearing without notice being served on any other party; references applications made ex parte as references to applications made withou notice being served on any other party and other references which incluc the expression "ex parte" shall be similarly construed.

(3) Subject to paragraphs (1) and (2), Part 13 of the Rules has effect for the interpretation and application.][3]

**0.3.— Extent**

(1) Parts 1, 2 and 4 of the Rules, and Parts 7 to 13 as they relate to compan insolvency, apply in relation to companies which the courts in England an Wales have jurisdiction to wind up.

(2) [Rule 3.1 applies to all receivers to whom Part III of the Act applies an the remainder of ][1]Part 3 of the Rules applies to administrative receive appointed otherwise than under section 51 (Scottish receivership).

(3) Parts 5 and 6 of the Rules, and Parts 7 to 13 as they relate to individu insolvency, extend to England and Wales only.

## CHAPTER 6

*Costs and Detailed Assessment*

**[ 7.33. Application of the CPR**

(1) Subject to provision to inconsistent effect made as follows in this Chapte CPR Part 43 (scope of costs rules and definitions), Part 44 (general rul about costs), Part 45 (fixed costs), Part 47 (procedure for detailed asses ment of costs and default provisions) and Part 48 (costs — special case shall apply to insolvency proceedings with any necessary modifications.][1]

[1] 1985, c. 5
[2] S.I. 1998 No. 3132 (L. 17); amended by S.I. 1999 No.1008 (L. 8).
[3] Substituted by S.I. 1999 No. 1022 Sch. ,1 Para. 1.
[1] Words inserted by S..I 1987 No. 1919 Sch. 1(1)(1), Para. 2.
[1] Substituted by S.I. 1999 No.1022 Sch. 1, Para. 3.

**7.34.— Requirement to assess costs by the detailed procedure**

(1) Subject as follows, where the costs, charges or expenses of any person are payable out of the insolvent estate, the amount of those costs, charges or expenses shall be decided by detailed assessment unless agreed between the responsible insolvency practitioner and the person entitled to payment, and in the absence of such agreement the responsible insolvency practitioner may serve notice in writing requiring that person to commence detailed assessment proceedings in accordance with CPR Part 47 (procedure for detailed assessment of costs and default provisions) in the court to which the insolvency proceedings are allocated or, where in relation to a company there is no such court, that in relation to any court having jurisdiction to wind up the company.

(2) If a liquidation or creditors' committee established in insolvency proceedings (except administrative receivership) resolves that the amount of any such costs, charges or expenses should be decided by detailed assessment, the insolvency practitioner shall require detailed assessment in accordance with CPR Part 47.

(3) Where the amount of the costs, charges or expenses of any person employed by an insolvency practitioner in insolvency proceedings are required to be decided by detailed assessment or fixed by order of the court this does not preclude the insolvency practitioner from making payments on account to such person on the basis of an undertaking by that person to repay immediately any money which may, when detailed assessment is made, prove to have been overpaid, with interest at the rate specified in section 17 of the Judgments Act 1838[1] on the date payment was made and for the period from the date of payment to that of repayment.

(4) In any proceedings before the court, including proceedings on a petition, the court may order costs to be decided by detailed assessment.

(5) Unless otherwise directed or authorised, the costs of a trustee in bankruptcy or a liquidator are to be allowed on the standard basis for which provision is made in CPR rule 44.4 (basis of assessment) and rule 44.5 (factors to be taken into account in deciding the amount of costs).

(6) This Rule applies additionally (with any necessary modifications) to winding-up and bankruptcy proceedings commenced before the coming into force of the Rules.][2]

**7.35.— Procedure where detailed assessment required**

(1) Before making a detailed assessment of the costs of any person employed in insolvency proceedings by a responsible insolvency practitioner, the costs officer shall require a certificate of employment, which shall be endorsed on the bill and signed by the insolvency practitioner.

(2) The certificate shall include–

(a) the name and address of the person employed,
(b) details of the functions to be carried out under the employment, and
(c) a note of any special terms of remuneration which have been agreed.

(3) Every person whose costs in insolvency proceedings are required to be decided by detailed assessment shall, on being required in writing to do so by the insolvency practitioner, commence detailed assessment proceedings

[1] 1838 c. 110 (1 & 2 Vict.).
[2] Substituted by S.I. 1999/1022 Sch. 1, Para. 3.

in accordance with CPR Part 47 (procedure for detailed assessment of cost and default provisions).

(4) If that person does not commence detailed assessment proceedings withi 3 months of the requirement under paragraph (3), or within such furthe time as the court, on application, may permit, the insolvency practitione may deal with the insolvent estate without regard to any claim by tha person, whose claim is forfeited by such failure to commence proceedings

(5) Where in any such case such a claim lies additionally against an insolvenc practitioner in his personal capacity, that claim is also forfeited by suc failure to commence proceedings.

(6) Where costs have been incurred in insolvency proceedings in the Hig Court and those proceedings are subsequently transferred to a count court, all costs of those proceedings directed by the court or otherwis required to be assessed may nevertheless, on the application of the perso who incurred the costs, be ordered to be decided by detailed assessment i the High Court.][1]

**[ 7.36.— Costs of sheriff**

(1) Where a sheriff–

(a) is required under section 184(2) or 346(2) to deliver up goods o money, or

(b) has under section 184(3) or 346(3) deducted costs from the proceed of an execution or money paid to him,

the responsible insolvency practitioner may require in writing that the amount c the sheriff's bill of costs be decided by detailed assessment.

(2) Where such a requirement is made, Rule 7.35(4) applies.

(3) Where, in the case of a deduction under paragraph (1)(b), any amoun deducted is disallowed at the conclusion of the detailed assessment prc ceedings, the sheriff shall forthwith pay a sum equal to that disallowed t the insolvency practitioner for the benefit of the insolvent estate.][1]

**[ 7.37.— Petitions presented by insolvents**

(1) In any case where a petition is presented by a company or individual ("th insolvent") against himself, any solicitor acting for the insolvent shall i his bill of costs give credit for any sum or security received from the insolv ent as a deposit on account of the costs and expenses to be incurred i respect of the filing and prosecution of the petition; and the deposit sha be noted by the costs officer on the final costs certificate.

(2) Paragraph (3) applies where a petition is presented by a person other tha the insolvent to whom the petition relates and before it is heard the insolv ent presents a petition for the same order, and that order is made.

(3) Unless the court considers that the insolvent estate has benefited by th insolvent's conduct, or that there are otherwise special circumstances justi fying the allowance of costs, no costs shall be allowed to the insolvent o his solicitor out of the insolvent estate.][1]

**[ 7.38. Costs paid otherwise than out of the insolvent estate**

Where the amount of costs is decided by detailed assessment under an order of th court directing that those costs are to be paid otherwise than out of the insolven

[1] Substituted by S.I. 1999 No. 1022 Sch. 1, Para. 3.
[1] Substituted by S.I. 1999 No. 1022 Sch. 1, Para. 3.
[1] Substituted by SI 1999/1022 Sch. 1, Para. 3

state, the costs officer shall note on the final costs certificate by whom, or the manner in which, the costs are to be paid.][1]

**7.39. Award of costs against official receiver or responsible insolvency practitioner**

Without prejudice to any provision of the Act or Rules by virtue of which the official receiver is not in any event to be liable for costs and expenses, where the official receiver or a responsible insolvency practitioner is made a party to any proceedings on the application of another party to the proceedings, he shall not be personally liable for costs unless the court otherwise directs.][1]

**[7.40. Applications for costs**

(1) This Rule applies where a party to, or person affected by, any proceedings in an insolvency–

(a) applies to the court for an order allowing his costs, or part of them, incidental to the proceedings, and

(b) that application is not made at the time of the proceedings.

(2) The person concerned shall serve a sealed copy of his application on the responsible insolvency practitioner, and, in winding up by the court or bankruptcy, on the official receiver.

(3) The insolvency practitioner and, where appropriate, the official receiver may appear on the application.

(4) No costs of or incidental to the application shall be allowed to the applicant unless the court is satisfied that the application could not have been made at the time of the proceedings.][1]

**[7.41. Costs and expenses of witnesses**

(1) Except as directed by the court, no allowance as a witness in any examination or other proceedings before the court shall be made to the bankrupt or an officer of the insolvent company to which the proceedings relate.

(2) A person presenting any petition in insolvency proceedings shall not be regarded as a witness on the hearing of the petition, but the costs officer may allow his expenses of travelling and subsistence.][1]

**[7.42. Final costs certificate**

(1) A final costs certificate of the costs officer is final and conclusive as to all matters which have not been objected to in the manner provided for under the rules of the court.

(2) Where it is proved to the satisfaction of a costs officer that a final costs certificate has been lost or destroyed, he may issue a duplicate.][1]

[1] Substituted by S.I. 1999 No. 1022 Sch. 1, Para. 3.
[1] Substituted by S.I. 1999 No. 1022 Sch. 1, Para. 3.
[1] Substituted by S.I. 1999 No. 1022 Sch. 1, Para. 3.
[1] Substituted by S.I. 1999 No. 1022 Sch. 1, Para. 3.
[1] Substituted by S.I. 1999 No. 1022 Sch. 1, Para. 3.

# APPENDIX Q

**Delete Appendix Q substitute:**

2000 No. 823

LEGAL SERVICES

The Conditional Fee Agreements Order 2000

Made 20th March 2000
Coming into force 1st April 2000

Q–001 The Lord Chancellor, in exercise of the powers conferred upon him by section 58(4)(a) and (c) of the Courts and Legal Services Act 1990(a), and all other powers enabling him in that behalf, having consulted in accordance with section 58A(5)(b) of that Act, makes the following Order, a draft of which has been laid before and approved by resolution of each House of Parliament:

**Citation, commencement and interpretation**

Q–002 1.—(1) This Order may be cited as the Conditional Fee Agreements Order 2000 and shall come into force on 1st April 2000.
(2) In this Order "the Act" means the Courts and Legal Services Act 1990.

**Revocation of 1998 Order**
**Appendix R**
**Appendix R**

Q–003 2. The Conditional Fee Agreements Order 1998(c) is revoked.

**Agreements providing for success fees**

Q–004 3. All proceedings which, under section 58 of the Act, can be the subject of an enforceable conditional fee agreement, except proceedings under section 82 of the Environmental Protection Act 1990(d), are proceedings specified for the purposes of section 58(4)(a) of the Act.

**Amount of for success fees**

Q–005 4. In relation to all proceedings specified in article 3, the percentage specified for the purposes of section 58(4)(c) of the Act shall be 100%.

(a) 1990 c. 41. Section 58 was substituted by section 27(1) of the Access to Justice Act 1999 (c. 22).
(b) Section 58A was added by section 27(1) of the Access to Justice Act 1999 (c. 22).
(c) S.I. 1998/1860.
(d) 1990 c. 43.

# APPENDIX R

**Delete Appendix R substitute:**

2000 No. 692

LEGAL SERVICES, ENGLAND AND WALES

The Conditional Fee Agreements Regulations 2000

| | |
|---|---|
| Made | 9th March 2000 |
| Laid before Parliament | 10th March 2000 |
| Coming into force | 1st April 2000 |

R–001 The Lord Chancellor, in exercise of the powers conferred on him by sections 58(3)(c), 58A(3) and 119 of the Courts and Legal Services Act 1990(a) and all other powers enabling him hereby makes the following Regulations:

**Citation, commencement and interpretation**

R–002 1.—(1) These Regulations may be cited as the Conditional Fee Agreements Regulations 2000.

(2) These Regulations come into force on 1st April 2000.

(3) In these Regulations—

"client" includes, except where the context otherwise requires, a person who—

(a) has instructed the legal representative to provide the advocacy or litigation services to which the conditional fee agreement relates, or

(b) is liable to pay the legal representative's fees in respect of those services; and

"legal representative" means the person providing the advocacy or litigation services to which the conditional fee agreement relates.

**Requirements for contents of conditional fee agreements: general**

R–003 2.—(1) A conditional fee agreement must specify—

(a) the particular proceedings or parts of them to which it relates (including whether it relates to any appeal, counterclaim or proceedings to enforce a judgement or order),

(b) the circumstances in which the legal representative's fees and expenses, or part of them, are payable,

(c) what payment, if any, is due—

(i) if those circumstances only partly occur,

(ii) irrespective of whether those circumstances occur, and

(a) 1990 c. 41; sections 58 and 58A are substituted by section 27 of the Access to Justice Act 1999 (c. 22); section 119 is an interpretation provision and is cited because of the meaning given to the word "prescribed".

(iii) on the termination of the agreement for any reason, and

(d) the amounts which are payable in all the circumstances and cases specified or the method to be used to calculate them and, in particular, whether the amounts are limited by reference to the damages which may be recovered on behalf of the client.

(2) A conditional fee agreement to which regulation 4 applies must contain a statement that the requirements of that regulation which apply in the case of that agreement have been complied with.

**Requirements for contents of conditional fee agreements providing for success fees**

R–004 3.—(1) A conditional fee agreement which provides for a success fee—

(a) must briefly specify the reasons for setting the percentage increase at the level stated in the agreement, and

(b) must specify how much of the percentage increase, if any, relates to the cost to the legal representative of the postponement of the payment of his fees and expenses.

(2) If the agreement relates to court proceedings, it must provide that where the percentage increase becomes payable as a result of those proceedings, then—

(a) if—

(i) any fees subject to the increase are assessed, and

(ii) the legal representative or the client is required by the court to disclose to the court or any other person the reasons for setting the percentage increase at the level stated in the agreement,

he may do so,

(b) if—

(i) any such fees are assessed, and

(ii) any amount in respect of the percentage increase is disallowed on the assessment on the ground that the level at which the increase was set was unreasonable in view of facts which were or should have been known to the legal representative at the time it was set,

that amount ceases to be payable under the agreement, unless the court is satisfied that it should continue to be so payable, and

(c) if—

(i) sub-paragraph (b) does not apply, and

(ii) the legal representative agrees with any person liable as a result of the proceedings to pay fees subject to the percentage increase that a lower amount than the amount payable in accordance with the conditional fee agreement is to be paid instead,

the amount payable under the conditional fee agreement in respect of those fees shall be reduced accordingly, unless the court is satisfied that the full amount should continue to be payable under it.

(3) In this regulation "percentage increase" means the percentage by which the amount of the fees which would be payable if the agreement were not a conditional fee agreement is to be increased under the agreement.

**Information to be given before conditional fee agreements made**

R–005 4.—(1) Before a conditional fee agreement is made the legal representative must—

(a) inform the client about the following matters, and

(b) if the client requires any further explanation, advice or other information about any of those matters, provide such further explanation, advice or other information about them as the client may reasonably require.

(2) Those matters are—

(a) the circumstances in which the client may be liable to pay the costs of the legal representative in accordance with the agreement,
(b) the circumstances in which the client may seek assessment of the fees and expenses of the legal representative and the procedure for doing so,
(c) whether the legal representative considers that the client's risk of incurring liability for costs in respect of the proceedings to which agreement relates is insured against under an existing contract of insurance,
(d) whether other methods of financing those costs are available, and, if so, how they apply to the client and the proceedings in question,
(e) whether the legal representative considers that any particular method or methods of financing any or all of those costs is appropriate and, if he considers that a contract of insurance is appropriate or recommends a particular such contract—

(i) his reasons for doing so, and
(ii) whether he has an interest in doing so.

(3) Before a conditional fee agreement is made the legal representative must explain its effect to the client.
(4) In the case of an agreement where—

(a) the legal representative is a body to which section 30 of the Access to Justice Act 1999(a) (recovery where body undertakes to meet costs liabilities) applies, and
(b) there are no circumstances in which the client may be liable to pay any costs in respect of the proceedings,

paragraph (1) does not apply.
(5) Information required to be given under paragraph (1) about the matters in paragraph (2)(a) to (d) must be given orally (whether or not it is also given in writing), but information required to be so given about the matters in paragraph (2)(e) and the explanation required by paragraph (3) must be given both orally and in writing.
(6) This regulation does not apply in the case of an agreement between a legal representative and an additional legal representative.

**Form of agreement**

R–006

5.—(1) A conditional fee agreement must be signed by the client and the legal representative.
(2) This regulation does not apply in the case of an agreement between a legal representative and an additional legal representative.

**Amendment of agreement**

R–007

6. Where an agreement is amended to cover further proceedings or parts of them—

(a) regulations 2, 3 and 5 apply to the amended agreement as if it were a fresh agreement made at the time of the amendment, and
(b) the obligations under regulation 4 apply in relation to the amendments in so far as they affect the matters mentioned in that regulation.

**Revocation of 1995 Regulations**

R–008 7. The Conditional Fee Agreements Regulations 1995(b) are revoked.

Dated 9th March 2000

........................................................................................................................

2000 No. 693

The Access to Justice (Membership Organisations) Regulations 2000

| | |
|---|---|
| Made | 9th March 200 |
| Laid before Parliament | 10th March 200 |
| Coming into force | 1st April 200 |

R–009 The Lord Chancellor, in exercise of the powers conferred on him by section 30(1 and (3) to (5) of the Access to Justice Act 1999(a) and all other powers enablin him hereby makes the following Regulations:

**Citation, commencement and interpretation**

R–010 1.—(1) These Regulations may be cited as the Access to Justice (Membershi Organisations) Regulations 2000.

(2) These Regulations come into force on 1st April 2000.

**Bodies of a prescribed description**

R–011 2. The bodies which are prescribed for the purpose of section 30 of the Access to Justice Act 1999 (recovery where body undertakes to meet costs liabilities) are those bodies which are for the time being approved by the Lord Chancellor for that purpose.

**Requirements for arrangements to meet costs liabilities**

R–012 3.—(1) Section 30(1) of the Access to Justice Act 1999 applies to arrangements which satisfy the following conditions.

(2) The arrangements must be in writing.

(3) The arrangements must contain a statement specifying—

(a) the circumstances in which the member or other party may be liable to pay costs of the proceedings,

(b) whether such a liability arises—

(i) if those circumstances only partly occur,

(ii) irrespective of whether those circumstances occur, and

(iii) on the termination of the arrangements for any reason,

(c) the basis on which the amount of the liability is calculated, and

(d) the procedure for seeking assessment of costs.

(4) A copy of the part of the arrangements containing the statement must be given to the member or other party to the proceedings whose liabilities the body is undertaking to meet as soon as possible after the undertaking is given.

(a) 1999 c. 22.

**Recovery of additional amount for insurance costs**

4.—(1) Where an additional amount is included in costs by virtue of section 30(2) of the Access to Justice Act 1999 (costs payable to a member of a body or other person party to the proceedings to include an additional amount in respect of provision made by the body against the risk of having to meet the member's or other person's liabilities to pay other parties' costs), that additional amount must not exceed the following sum. **R–013**

(2) That sum is the likely cost to the member of the body or, as the case may be, the other person who is a party to the proceedings in which the costs order is made of the premium of an insurance policy against the risk of incurring a liability to pay the costs of other parties to the proceedings.

Dated 9th March 2000

---

**After paragraph R–013 insert:**

STATUTORY INSTRUMENT 2000 NO. 2988 **R–014**

The Collective Conditional Fee Agreements Regulations 2000

LEGAL SERVICES, ENGLAND AND WALES

The Collective Conditional Fee Agreements Regulations 2000

| | |
|---|---|
| Made | 7th November 2000 |
| Laid before Parliament | 8th November 2000 |
| Coming into force | 30th November 2000 |

The Lord Chancellor, in exercise of the powers conferred upon him by sections 58(3)(c), 58A(3) and 119 of the Courts and Legal Services Act 1990[*1*] hereby makes the following Regulations:

**Citation, commencement and interpretation**

**1.** - (1) These regulations may be cited as the Collective Conditional Fee Agreements Regulations 2000, and shall come into force on November 30 2000.
(2) In these Regulations, except where the context requires otherwise—

"client" means a person who will receive advocacy or litigation services to which the agreement relates;
"collective conditional fee agreement" has the meaning given in regulation 3;
"conditional fee agreement" has the same meaning as in section 58 of the Courts and Legal Services Act 1990;
"funder" means the party to a collective conditional fee agreement who, under that agreement, is liable to pay the legal representative's fees;
"legal representative" means the person providing the advocacy or litigation services to which the agreement relates.

**Transitional provisions**

**2.** These Regulations shall apply to agreements entered into on or after 30th November 2000, and agreements entered into before that date shall be treated as if these Regulations had not come into force.

**Definition of "collective conditional fee agreement"**

3.—(1) Subject to paragraph (2) of this regulation, a collective conditional fee agreement is an agreement which—

(a) disregarding section 58(3)(c) of the Courts and Legal Services Act 1990, would be a conditional fee agreement; and
(b) does not refer to specific proceedings, but provides for fees to be payable on a common basis in relation to a class of proceedings, or, if it refers to more than one class of proceedings, on a common basis in relation to each class.

(2) An agreement may be a collective conditional fee agreement whether or not—

(a) the funder is a client; or
(b) any clients are named in the agreement.

**Requirements for contents of collective conditional fee agreements: general**

4.—(1) A collective conditional fee agreement must specify the circumstances in which the legal representative's fees and expenses, or part of them, are payable.
(2) A collective conditional fee agreement must provide that, when accepting instructions in relation to any specific proceedings the legal representative must—
(a) inform the client as to the circumstances in which the client may be liable to pay the costs of the legal representative; and
(b) if the client requires any further explanation, advice or other information about the matter referred to in sub-paragraph (a), provide such further explanation, advice or other information about it as the client may reasonably require.

(3) Paragraph (2) does not apply in the case of an agreement between a legal representative and an additional legal representative.
(4) A collective conditional fee agreement must provide that, after accepting instructions in relation to any specific proceedings, the legal representative must confirm his acceptance of instructions in writing to the client.

**Requirements for contents of collective conditional fee agreements providing for success fees**

5.—(1) Where a collective conditional fee agreement provides for a success fee the agreement must provide that, when accepting instructions in relation to any specific proceedings the legal representative must prepare and retain a written statement containing—
(a) his assessment of the probability of the circumstances arising in which the percentage increase will become payable in relation to those proceedings ("the risk assessment");
(b) his assessment of the amount of the percentage increase in relation to those proceedings, having regard to the risk assessment; and
(c) the reasons, by reference to the risk assessment, for setting the percentage increase at that level.

(2) If the agreement relates to court proceedings it must provide that where the success fee becomes payable as a result of those proceedings, then

(a) if—
  (i) any fees subject to the increase are assessed, and
  (ii) the legal representative or the client is required by the court to disclose to the court or any other person the reasons for setting the percentage increase at the level assessed by the legal representative,
  he may do so,
(b) if

(i) any such fees are assessed by the court, and

(ii) any amount in respect of the percentage increase is disallowed on the assessment on the ground that the level at which the increase was set was unreasonable in view of facts which were or should have been known to the legal representative at the time it was set

that amount ceases to be payable under the agreement, unless the court is satisfied that it should continue to be so payable, and

(c) if—

(i) sub-paragraph (b) does not apply, and

(ii) the legal representative agrees with any person liable as a result of the proceedings to pay fees subject to the percentage increase that a lower amount than the amount payable in accordance with the conditional fee agreement is to be paid instead,

the amount payable under the collective conditional fee agreement in respect of those fees shall be reduced accordingly, unless the court is satisfied that the full amount should continue to be payable under it.

3) In this regulation "percentage increase" means the percentage by which the mount of the fees which would have been payable if the agreement were not a onditional fee agreement is to be increased under the agreement.

**orm and amendment of collective conditional fee agreement**

.—(1) Subject to paragraph (2), a collective conditional fee agreement must be igned by the funder, and by the legal representative.

2) Paragraph (1) does not apply in the case of an agreement between a legal repres- ntative and an additional legal representative.

3) Where a collective conditional fee agreement is amended, regulations 4 and 5 pply to the amended agreement as if it were a fresh agreement made at the time of the amendment.

**Amendment to the Conditional Fee Agreements Regulations 2000**

7. After regulation 7 of the Conditional Fee Agreements Regulations 2000[2] there hall be inserted the following new regulation:—

**"Exclusion of collective conditional fee agreements**

8. These Regulations shall not apply to collective conditional fee agreements within the meaning of regulation 3 of the Collective Conditional Fee Agreements Regula- tions 2000.".

*Irvine of Lairg,*
C.

Dated 7th November 2000

# APPENDIX T

## Access to Justice Act 1999

PART II

OTHER FUNDING OF LEGAL SERVICES

*Conditional fee and litigation funding agreements*

T–001 27.—(1) For section 58 of the Courts and Legal Services Act 1990 substitute—

58.—(1) A conditional fee agreement which satisfies all of the conditions applicabl to it by virtue of this section shall not be unenforceable by reason only o its being a conditional fee agreement; but (subject to subsection (5)) an other conditional fee agreement shall be unenforceable.

(2) For the purposes of this section and section 58A—

(a) a conditional fee agreement is an agreement with a person providin advocacy or litigation services which provides for his fees an expenses, or any part of them, to be payable only in specified circum stances; and

(b) a conditional fee agreement provides for a success fee if it provides fo the amount of any fees to which it applies to be increased, in specifie circumstances, above the amount which would be payable if it wer not payable only in specified circumstances.

(3) The following conditions are applicable to every conditional fee agree ment—

(a) it must be in writing;

(b) it must not relate to proceedings which cannot be the subject of a enforceable conditional fee agreement; and

(c) it must comply with such requirements (if any) as may be prescribed by the Lord Chancellor.

(4) The following further conditions are applicable to a conditional fee agree- ment which provides for a success fee—

(a) it must relate to proceedings of a description specified by order made by the Lord Chancellor;

(b) it must state the percentage by which the amount of the fees which would be payable if it were not a conditional fee agreement is to be increased; and

(c) that percentage must not exceed the percentage specified in relation to the description of proceedings to which the agreement relates by order made by the Lord Chancellor.

(5) If a conditional fee agreement is an agreement to which section 57 of the Solicitors Act 1974 (non-contentious business agreements between solicitor and client) applies, subsection (1) shall not make it unenforceable.

8A.—

(1) The proceedings which cannot be the subject of an enforceable conditional fee agreement are—

(a) criminal proceedings, apart from proceedings under section 82 of the Environmental Protection Act 1990; and

(b) family proceedings,

(2) In subsection (1) "family proceedings" means proceedings under any one or more of the following—

(a) the Matrimonial Causes Act 1973;
(b) the Adoption Act 1976;
(c) the Domestic Proceedings and Magistrates' Courts Act 1978;
(d) Part III of the Matrimonial and Family Proceedings Act 1984;
(e) Parts I, II and IV of the Children Act 1989;
(f) Part IV of the Family Law Act 1996; and
(g) the inherent jurisdiction of the High Court in relation to children.
Appendix T
Appendix T

(3) The requirements which the Lord Chancellor may prescribe under section 58(3)(c)—

(a) include requirements for the person providing advocacy or litigation services to have provided prescribed information before the agreement is made; and

(b) may be different for different descriptions of conditional fee agreements (and, in particular, may be different for those which provide for a success fee and those which do not).

(4) In section 58 and this section (and in the definitions of "advocacy services" and "litigation services" as they apply for their purposes) "proceedings" includes any sort of proceedings for resolving disputes (and not just proceedings in a court), whether commenced or contemplated.

(5) Before making an order under section 58(4), the Lord Chancellor shall consult—

(a) the designated judges;
(b) the General Council of the Bar;
(c) the Law Society; and
(d) such other bodies as he considers appropriate.

(6) A costs order made in any proceedings may, subject in the case of court proceedings to rules of court, include provision requiring the payment of any fees payable under a conditional fee agreement which provides for a success fee.

(7) Rules of court may make provision with respect to the assessment of any costs which include fees payable under a conditional fee agreement (including one which provides for a success fee)."

(2) In section 120(4) of the Courts and Legal Services Act 1990 (orders and regulations subject to affirmative procedure), for "58," substitute "58(4),".

**28.** In the Courts and Legal Services Act 1990, after section 58A (inserted by section 27 above) insert— T–002

58B.—

(1) A litigation funding agreement which satisfies all of the conditions applicable to it by virtue of this section shall not be unenforceable by reason only of its being a litigation funding agreement.

(2) For the purposes of this section a litigation funding agreement is an agree ment under which—

(a) a person ("the funder") agrees to fund (in whole or in part) the provi sion of advocacy or litigation services (by someone other than th funder) to another person ("the litigant"); and

(b) the litigant agrees to pay a sum to the funder in specified circum stances.

(3) The following conditions are applicable to a litigation funding agreement—

(a) the funder must be a person, or person of a description, prescribed b the Lord Chancellor;

(b) the agreement must be in writing;

(c) the agreement must not relate to proceedings which by virtue of sec tion 58A(1) and (2) cannot be the subject of an enforceable condi tional fee agreement or to proceedings of any such description as ma be prescribed by the Lord Chancellor;

(d) the agreement must comply with such requirements (if any) as may b so prescribed;

(e) the sum to be paid by the litigant must consist of any costs payabl to him in respect of the proceedings to which the agreement relate together with an amount calculated by reference to the funder' anticipated expenditure in funding the provision of the services and

(f) that amount must not exceed such percentage of that anticipate expenditure as may be prescribed by the Lord Chancellor in relatio to proceedings of the description to which the agreement relates.

(4) Regulations under subsection (3)(a) may require a person to be approve by the Lord Chancellor or by a prescribed person.

(5) The requirements which the Lord Chancellor may prescribe under subsec tion (3)(d)—

(a) include requirements for the funder to have provided prescribe information to the litigant before the agreement is made; and

(b) may be different for different descriptions of litigation funding agree ments.

(6) In this section (and in the definitions of "advocacy services" and "litigation services" as they apply for its purposes) "proceedings" includes any sort of proceedings for resolving disputes (and not just proceedings in a court), whether commenced or contemplated.

(7) Before making regulations under this section, the Lord Chancellor shall consult—

(a) the designated judges;

(b) the General Council of the Bar;

(c) the Law Society; and

(d) such other bodies as he considers appropriate.

(8) A costs order made in any proceedings may, subject in the case of court proceedings to rules of court, include provision requiring the payment of any amount payable under a litigation funding agreement.

(9) Rules of court may make provision with respect to the assessment of any costs which include fees payable under a litigation funding agreement."

*Costs*

9. Where in any proceedings a costs order is made in favour of any party who as taken out an insurance policy against the risk of incurring a liability in ose proceedings, the costs payable to him may, subject in the case of court roceedings to rules of court, include costs in respect of the premium of the olicy. T–003

0.—(1) This section applies where a body of a prescribed description undertakes meet (in accordance with arrangements satisfying prescribed conditions) liabilit- s which members of the body or other persons who are parties to proceedings ay incur to pay the costs of other parties to the proceedings. T–004

(2) If in any of the proceedings a costs order is made in favour of any of the members or other persons, the costs payable to him may, subject to subsection (3) and (in the case of court proceedings) to rules of court, include an additional amount in respect of any provision made by or on behalf of the body in connection with the proceedings against the risk of having to meet such liabilities.

(3) But the additional amount shall not exceed a sum determined in a prescribed manner; and there may, in particular, be prescribed as a manner of determination one which takes into account the likely cost to the member or other person of the premium of an insurance policy against the risk of incurring a liability to pay the costs of other parties to the proceedings.

(4) In this section "prescribed" means prescribed by regulations made by the Lord Chancellor by statutory instrument; and a statutory instrument containing such regulations shall be subject to annulment in pursuance of a resolution of either House of Parliament.

(5) Regulations under subsection (1) may, in particular, prescribe as a description of body one which is for the time being approved by the Lord Chancellor or by a prescribed person.

1. In section 51 of the Supreme Court Act 1981 (costs), in subsection (2) (rules egulating matters relating to costs), insert at the end "or for securing that the mount awarded to a party in respect of the costs to be paid by him to such representatives is not limited to what would have been payable by him to them if he had ot been awarded costs." T–005

**After Appendix T insert:**

# APPENDIX U

# CHANCERY DIVISION

**Practice Statement—RSC Order 85—Applications to the court in relation to the administration of a trust—prospective costs orders**

This Practice Statement is about the costs of applications by trustees, or beneficiaries, or other persons concerned, in relation to the administration of a trust including questions of construction, questions relating to the exercise of powers conferred by the trust, or questions as to the validity of the trust.

Where trustees have power to agree to pay the costs of some other party to such an application, and exercise properly such a power, Rule 48.3 applies. In such case, an order is not required and the trustees are entitled to recover out of tl trust fund any costs which they pay pursuant to the agreement made in the exerci of such power.

Where the trustees do not have, or decide not to exercise, a power to make suc an agreement, the trustees or the party concerned may apply to the court at ar stage of proceedings for an order that the costs of any party to the applicatio referred to in paragraph 1 above (including the costs of the trustees) shall be pa out of the fund (a "prospective costs order").

The court, on an application for a prospective costs order, may

(a) in the case of the trustees' costs, authorise the trustees to raise and me such costs out of the fund;
(b) in the case of the costs of any other party, authorise or direct the truste to pay such costs (or any part of them, or the costs incurred up to a particu lar time) out of the trust fund to be assessed, if not agreed by the trustee on the indemnity basis or, if the court directs, on the standard basis, an to make payments from time to time on account of such costs. A mod form of order is set out at the end of this Practice Direction.

The court will always consider whether it is possible to deal with the applicatio for a prospective costs order on paper without a hearing and in an ordinary cas would expect to be able to do so. The trustees must consider whether a hearing i needed for any reason. If they consider that it is they should say so and explai why in their evidence. If any party to the application referred to in paragraph above (or any other person interested in the trust fund) considers that a hearing i necessary (for instance because he wishes to oppose the making of a prospectiv costs order) this should be stated, and the reasons explained, in his evidence, if any or otherwise in a letter to the court.

If the court would be minded to refuse the application on a consideration of th papers alone, the parties will be notified and given the opportunity, within a state time, to ask for a hearing.

The evidence in support of an application for a prospective costs order shoul be given by witness statement. The trustees and the applicant (if different) mus ensure full disclosure of the relevant matters to show that the case is one whicl falls within the category of case where a prospective costs order can properly b made.

The model form of order is designed for use in the more straightforward cases where a question needs to be determined which has arisen in the administration o the trust, whether the claimants are the trustees or a beneficiary. The form may b adapted for use in less straightforward cases, in particular where the proceeding are hostile, but special factors may also have to be reflected in the terms of th order in such a case.

Issued by direction of the Vice-Chancellor
Date: May 1, 2001

Model form of prospective costs order

UPON THE APPLICATION, etc
AND UPON HEARING, etc
AND UPON READING, etc

AND UPON the Solicitors for the ............ Defendant undertaking to make the repayments mentioned in paragraph 2 below in the circumstances there mentioned

T IS [BY CONSENT] ORDERED THAT:

he Claimants as trustees of ............................ ("the [Settlement/Scheme]") do

(a) pay from the assets of the [Settlement/Scheme] the costs of and incidental to these proceedings incurred by the ............ Defendant such costs to be subject to a detailed assessment on the indemnity basis if not agreed and (for the avoidance of doubt) to
  (i) include costs incurred by the ............ Defendant from and after [date] in anticipation of being appointed to represent any class of persons presently or formerly beneficially interested under the trusts of the [Settlement/Scheme] irrespective of whether [he/she] is in fact so appointed; and
  (ii) exclude (in the absence of any further order) costs incurred in prosecuting any Part 20 claim or any appeal
(b) indemnify the ............ Defendant in respect of any costs which he may be ordered to pay to any other party to these proceedings in connection therewith

'ntil the outcome of the detailed assessment (or the agreement regarding costs) ontemplated in paragraph 1 above, the Claimants as trustees do pay from the ssets of the [Settlement/Scheme] to the Solicitors for the ............ Defendant ıonthly (or at such other intervals as may be agreed) such sums on account of the osts referred to in paragraph 1(a) of this Order as the Solicitors for the ............ )efendant shall certify

  (i) to have been reasonably and properly incurred and not to exceed such amount as is likely in their opinion to be allowed on a detailed assessment on the indemnity basis; and
  (ii) to have accrued on account of the present proceedings in the period prior to the date of such certificate and not to have been previously provided for under this Order

'ROVIDED ALWAYS that the Solicitors for the ........... Defendant shall repay uch sums (if any) as, having been paid to them on account, are disallowed on a etailed assessment or are otherwise agreed to be repaid and any such sums shall e repaid together with interest at 1% above the base rate for the time being of Barclays] Bank plc from and including the date of payment to those Solicitors up o and including the date of repayment, such interest to accrue daily

Any party may apply to vary or discharge paragraphs 1 and 2 of this Order but nly in respect of costs to be incurred after the date of such application

Note: this form of order assumes that the trustees are the Claimants. If, in an ppropriate case, the Claimant is a beneficiary and the trustees are Defendants, eferences to the parties need to be adapted accordingly.

**After Appendix U insert:**

# APPENDIX V

Statutory Instrument 2001 No. 1296

The Justices and Justices' Clerks (Costs) Regulations 2001

# JUSTICES OF THE PEACE, ENGLAND AND WALES

# SUPREME COURT OF ENGLAND AND WALES

The Justices and Justices' Clerks (Costs) Regulations 2001

| | |
|---|---|
| Made | 30th March 200 |
| Coming into force | 1st April 200 |

The Lord Chancellor, in exercise of the powers conferred upon him by sectio 53A(4) of the Justices of the Peace Act 1997, makes the following Regulations, draft of which has, in accordance with section 53A(5) of that Act, been laid befor and approved by resolution of each House of Parliament:

**Citation and commencement**

**1.** These Regulations may be cited as the Justices and Justices' Clerks (Costs) Regu lations 2001 and shall come into force on the second day after the day on whic the Regulations are made.

**Interpretation**

2. In these Regulations -

"claim" means a claim for costs made by the receiving party;
"costs judge" means a taxing master of the Supreme Court;
"order" means an order of the court made under section 53A(3) of the Justices c the Peace Act 1997 that the Lord Chancellor make a payment in respect of th costs of a person in the proceedings;
"proceedings" means proceedings in respect of any act or omission of a justice c the peace or a justices' clerk in the execution (or purported execution) of his duty—

(i) as a single justice; or
(ii) as a justices' clerk exercising, by virtue of any statutory provision, any o the functions of a single justice;

"receiving party" means the person in whose favour the order is made.

**The payment of costs by the Lord Chancellor**

**3.** No order shall be made under section 53A(3) of the Justices of the Peace Ac 1997 in favour of—

(a) a public authority; or
(b) a person acting—
(i) on behalf of a public authority, or
(ii) in his capacity as an official appointed by a public authority.

**etermination of costs**

Where the court makes an order, the amount of costs payable by the Lord Chan-llor shall be determined in accordance with these Regulations.

**ourt order and determination of costs by the court**

—(1) Except as provided for in paragraph (2), when making the order the court all—

(a) determine such an amount as it considers sufficient reasonably to compensate the receiving party for any costs properly incurred by him in the proceedings, and
(b) specify that amount in the order.

) The amount of costs shall be determined by a costs judge in accordance with gulations 6 and 7 where—

(a) the hearing has lasted more than one day or there is insufficient time for the court to determine the costs on the day of the hearing, or
(b) the court considers that there is other good reason for the costs judge to determine the amount of costs.

) The court shall serve the order on the receiving party and on the Lord Chan-llor together with, where paragraph (2) applies, notification that costs will be etermined by a costs judge.

**etermination of costs by a costs judge**

.—(1) Where the amount of costs is to be determined by a costs judge, the receiv-g party shall, no later than three months from (but excluding) the date on which e order was made, file his claim and a copy of the order in the Supreme Court osts Office and serve a copy of the claim on the Lord Chancellor.
2) On the application of the receiving party to the Supreme Court Costs Office, the osts judge may, in exceptional circumstances, extend the period of three months.
3) A claim shall—

(a) summarise the items of work done by a legal representative or the receiving party as a litigant in person, as appropriate;
(b) state, where appropriate, the dates on which items of work were done, the time taken and the sums claimed; and
(c) specify any disbursements claimed, including counsel's fees, the circumstances in which they were incurred and the amounts claimed in respect of them,

nd shall be accompanied by receipts or other evidence of the receiving party's ayment of the costs claimed, and any receipts or other documents in support of ny disbursements claimed.
4) If the receiving party wishes to draw any special circumstances to the attention f the costs judge, he shall specify those circumstances in his claim.
5) If the Lord Chancellor wishes to make any written representations in respect of he claim he shall, no later than one month from (but excluding) the date on which he Lord Chancellor received the claim from the receiving party, file any written epresentations at the Supreme Court Costs Office and serve a copy of them on the eceiving party.
6) The costs judge may make directions in respect of—

(a) the claim;
(b) any written representations;
(c) the filing and serving of any further particulars or documents; and
(d) ensuring that the determination of costs is dealt with justly.

(7) Where the costs judge considers it appropriate, the claim shall be listed for a hea ing before him, and the Supreme Court Costs Office shall serve on the receiving par and on the Lord Chancellor notification of the place, date and time of the hearing.

7.(1) The costs judge shall consider the claim and shall allow such costs respect of

(a) such work as appears to him to have been actually and reasonab done; and
(b) such disbursements as appear to him to have been actually and reaso ably incurred,

as he considers sufficient reasonably to compensate the receiving party for a expenses properly incurred by him in the proceedings.
(2) In determining costs under paragraph (1) the costs judge shall take into accou all the relevant circumstances of the case including the nature, importance, con plexity or difficulty of the work and the time involved.
(3) When determining costs for the purposes of this regulation, there shall b allowed a reasonable amount in respect of all costs reasonably incurred and an doubts which the costs judge may have as to whether the costs were reasonab incurred or were reasonable in amount shall be resolved against the receiving part
(4) When the costs judge has determined the amount of costs payable to the recei ing party, the Supreme Court Costs Office shall notify the receiving party and th Lord Chancellor of the amount of costs payable.

Signed by authority of the Lord Chancellor

*Willy Bach*
Parliamentary Secretary Lord Chancellor's Department

Dated March 30, 2001

# SUPREME COURT OF ENGLAND AND WALES
# SUPREME COURT OF NORTHERN IRELAND

## GENERAL COMMISSIONERS OF INCOME TAX

The General Commissioners of Income Tax (Costs) Regulations 2001

*Made* — *March 30, 200*
*Coming into force* — *1st April 200*

The Lord Chancellor, in exercise of the powers conferred upon him by sectio 2A(4) of the Taxes Management Act 1970, makes the following Regulations, draft of which has, in accordance with section 2A(5) of that Act, been laid befor and approved by resolution of each House of Parliament:

**tation and commencement**

These Regulations may be cited as the General Commissioners of Income Tax osts) Regulations 2001 and shall come into force on the second day after the day which the Regulations are made.

**terpretation**

In these Regulations—

laim" means a claim for costs made by the receiving party;
osts judge" means in England and Wales a taxing master of the Supreme Court, d in Northern Ireland the Master (Taxing Office);
rder" means an order of the court made under section 2A(3) of the Taxes Man- ement Act 1970 that the Lord Chancellor make a payment in respect of the costs a person in the proceedings;
roceedings" means proceedings in respect of any act or omission of a General ommissioner in the execution (or purported execution) of his duty as a General ommissioner;
eceiving party" means the person in whose favour the order is made;
upreme Court Costs Office" shall be construed, in relation to Northern Ireland, the Taxing Office of the Supreme Court of Northern Ireland.

**he payment of costs by the Lord Chancellor**

No order shall be made under section 2A(3) of the Taxes Management Act 1970 favour of—

(a) a public authority; or
(b) a person acting—
  (i) on behalf of a public authority, or
  (ii) in his capacity as an official appointed by a public authority.

**etermination of costs**

Where the court makes an order, the amount of costs payable by the Lord Chan- llor shall be determined in accordance with these Regulations.

**ourt order and determination of costs by the court**

. - (1) Except as provided for in paragraph (2), when making the order the court all—

(a) determine such an amount as it considers sufficient reasonably to compensate the receiving party for any costs properly incurred by him in the proceedings, and
(b) specify that amount in the order.

?) The amount of costs shall be determined by a costs judge in accordance with gulations 6 and 7 where

(a) the hearing has lasted more than one day or there is insufficient time for the court to determine the costs on the day of the hearing, or
(b) the court considers that there is other good reason for the costs judge to determine the amount of costs.

3) The court shall serve the order on the receiving party and on the Lord Chan- ellor together with, where paragraph (2) applies, notification that costs will be etermined by a costs judge.

**Determination of costs by a costs judge**

6.—(1) Where the amount of costs is to be determined by a costs judge, the receiving party shall, no later than three months from (but excluding) the date on which the order was made, file his claim and a copy of the order in the Supreme Court Costs Office and serve a copy of the claim on the Lord Chancellor.
(2) On the application of the receiving party to the Supreme Court Costs Office, the costs judge may, in exceptional circumstances, extend the period of three months.
(3) A claim shall—

- (a) summarise the items of work done by a legal representative or the receiving party as a litigant in person, as appropriate;
- (b) state, where appropriate, the dates on which items of work were done, the time taken and the sums claimed; and
- (c) specify any disbursements claimed, including counsel's fees, the circumstances in which they were incurred and the amounts claimed in respect of them,

and shall be accompanied by receipts or other evidence of the receiving party's payment of the costs claimed, and any receipts or other documents in support of any disbursements claimed.
(4) If the receiving party wishes to draw any special circumstances to the attention of the costs judge, he shall specify those circumstances in his claim.
(5) If the Lord Chancellor wishes to make any written representations in respect of the claim he shall, no later than one month from (but excluding) the date on which the Lord Chancellor received the claim from the receiving party, file any written representations at the Supreme Court Costs Office and serve a copy of them on the receiving party.
(6) The costs judge may make directions in respect of -

- (a) the claim;
- (b) any written representations;
- (c) the filing and serving of any further particulars or documents; and
- (d) ensuring that the determination of costs is dealt with justly.

(7) Where the costs judge considers it appropriate, the claim shall be listed for a hearing before him, and the Supreme Court Costs Office shall serve on the receiving party and on the Lord Chancellor notification of the place, date and time of the hearing.

7.—(1) The costs judge shall consider the claim and shall allow such costs in respect of—

- (a) such work as appears to him to have been actually and reasonably done; and
- (b) such disbursements as appear to him to have been actually and reasonably incurred,

as he considers sufficient reasonably to compensate the receiving party for any expenses properly incurred by him in the proceedings.
(2) In determining costs under paragraph (1) the costs judge shall take into account all the relevant circumstances of the case including the nature, importance, complexity or difficulty of the work and the time involved.
(3) When determining costs for the purposes of this regulation, there shall be allowed a reasonable amount in respect of all costs reasonably incurred and any doubts which the costs judge may have as to whether the costs were reasonably incurred or were reasonable in amount shall be resolved against the receiving party.
(4) When the costs judge has determined the amount of costs payable to the receiving party, the Supreme Court Costs Office shall notify the receiving party and the Lord Chancellor of the amount of costs payable.

gned by authority of the Lord Chancellor

*'illy Bach*
arliamentary Secretary, Lord Chancellor's Department

ated March 30, 2001